Senpai is Annoying

Annoying

1

Story & Art by
SHIROMANTA

START

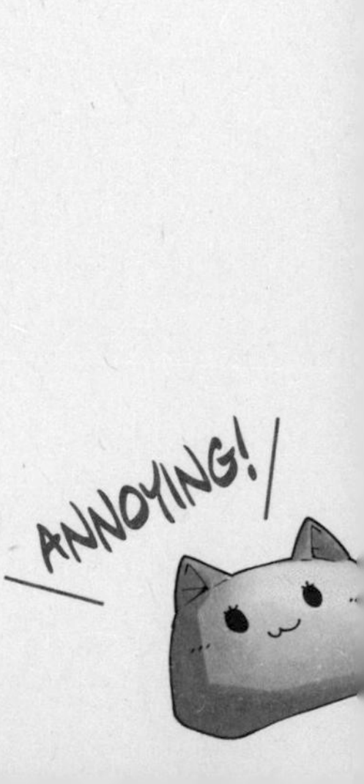
ANNOYING!

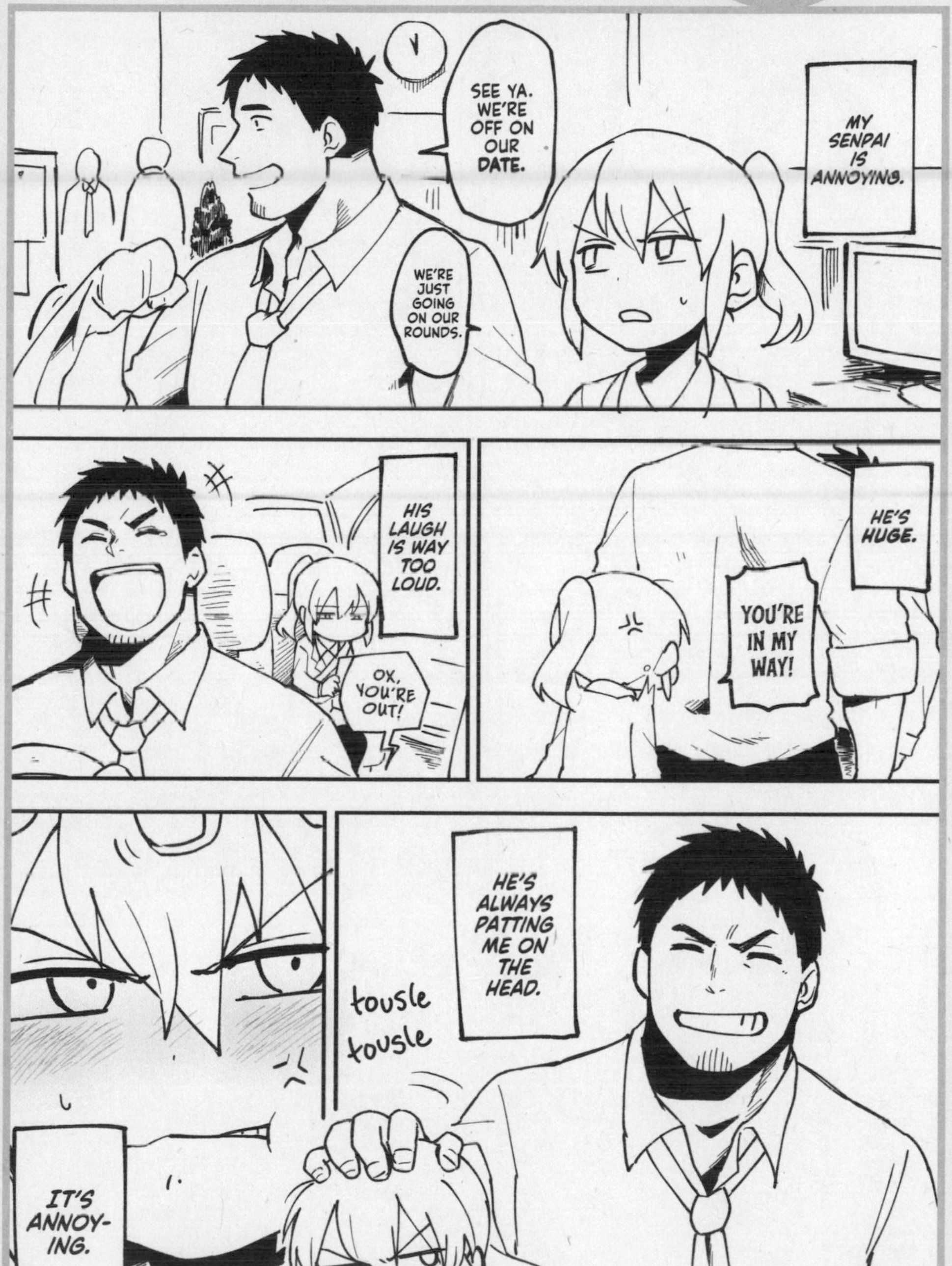
MY SENPAI IS ANNOYING.
SEE YA. WE'RE OFF ON OUR DATE.
WE'RE JUST GOING ON OUR ROUNDS.
HE'S HUGE.
YOU'RE IN MY WAY!
HIS LAUGH IS WAY TOO LOUD.
OX, YOU'RE OUT!
HE'S ALWAYS PATTING ME ON THE HEAD.
tousle tousle
IT'S ANNOY-ING.

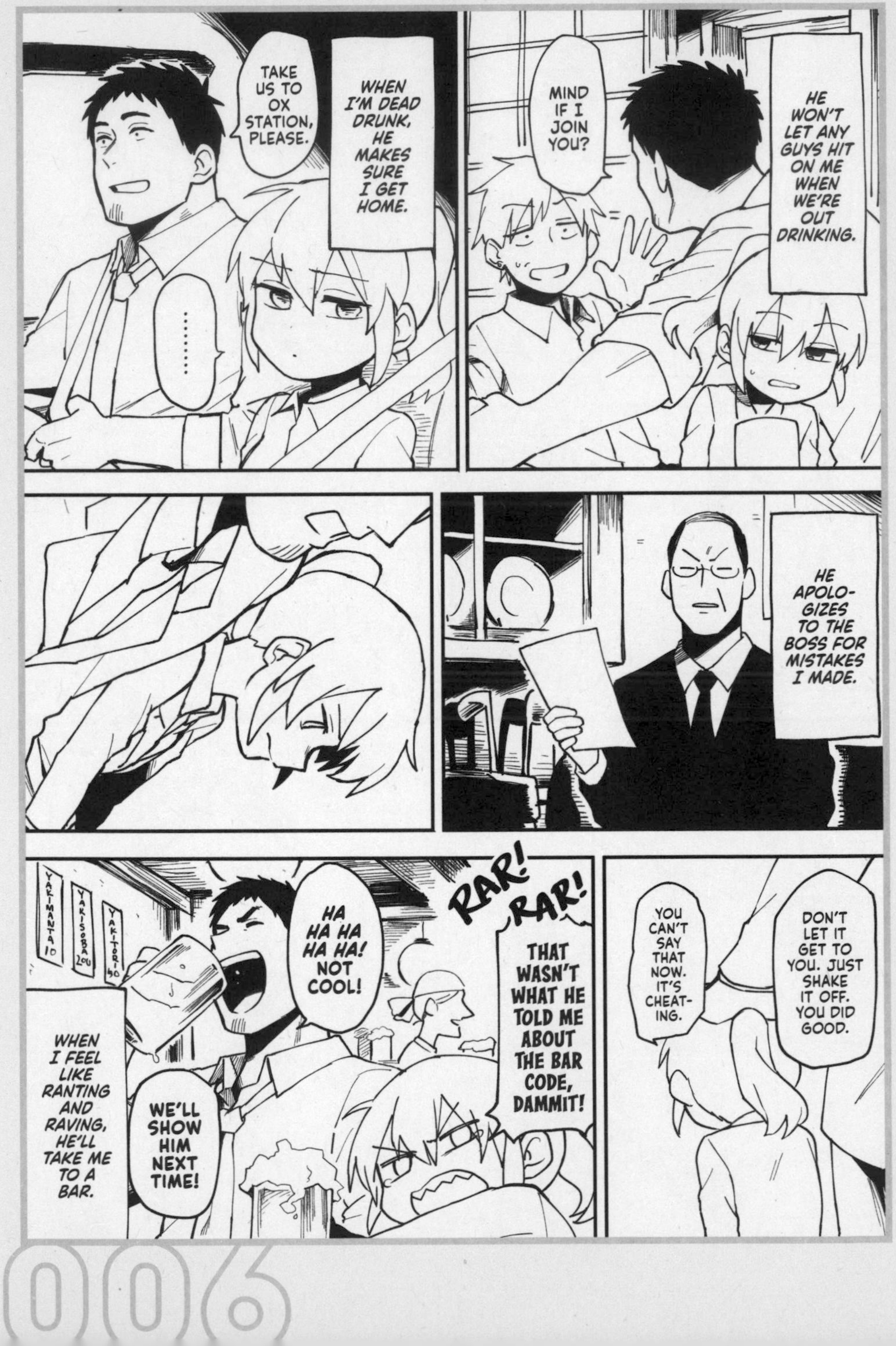
HE WON'T LET ANY GUYS HIT ON ME WHEN WE'RE OUT DRINKING.
MIND IF I JOIN YOU?
WHEN I'M DEAD DRUNK, HE MAKES SURE I GET HOME.
TAKE US TO OX STATION, PLEASE.
......
HE APOLOGIZES TO THE BOSS FOR MISTAKES I MADE.
DON'T LET IT GET TO YOU. JUST SHAKE IT OFF. YOU DID GOOD.
YOU CAN'T SAY THAT NOW. IT'S CHEATING.
RAR! RAR!
THAT WASN'T WHAT HE TOLD ME ABOUT THE BAR CODE, DAMMIT!
HA HA HA HA HA! NOT COOL!
WHEN I FEEL LIKE RANTING AND RAVING, HE'LL TAKE ME TO A BAR.
WE'LL SHOW HIM NEXT TIME!

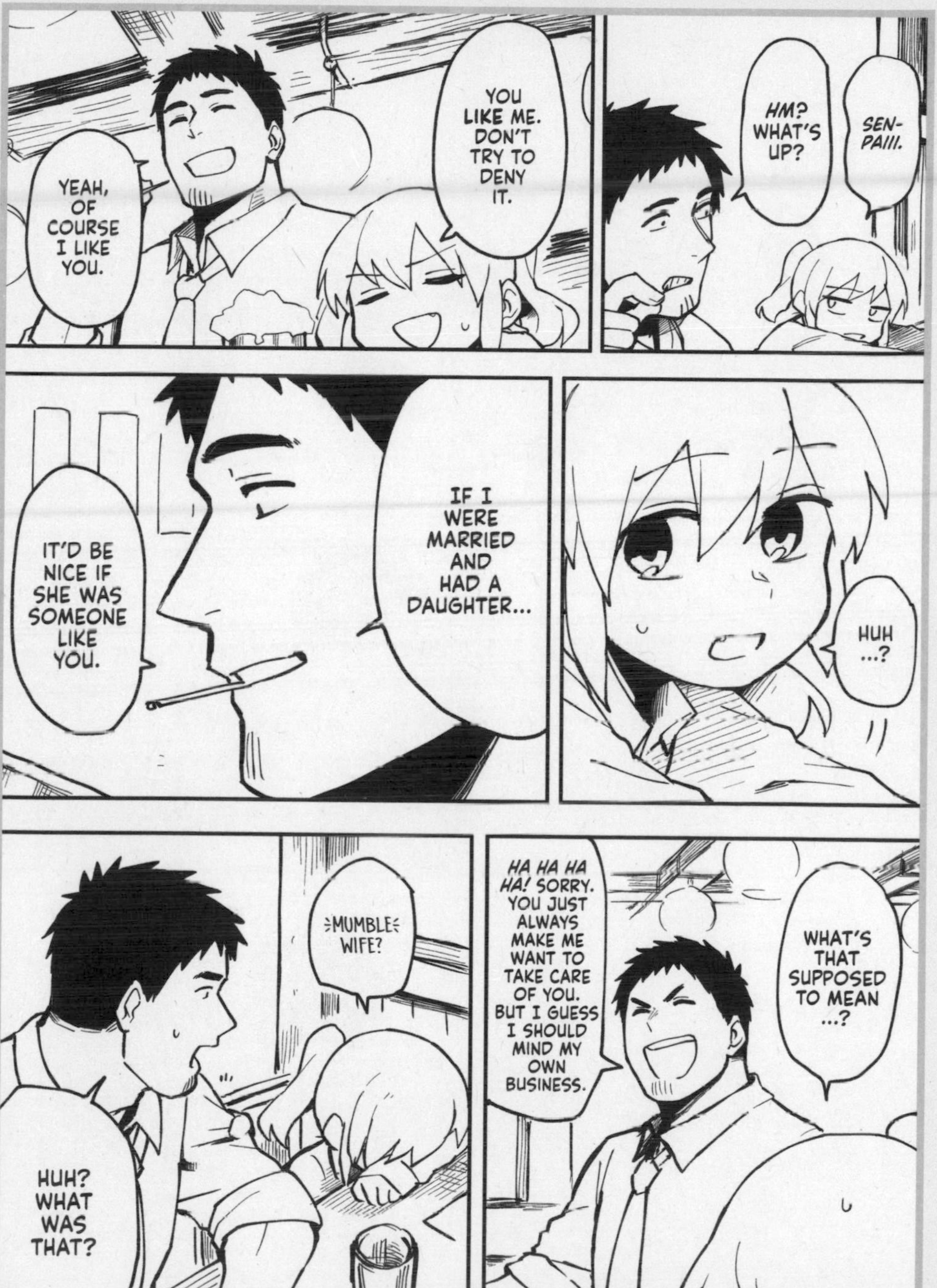
SEN-PAIII.
HM? WHAT'S UP?
YOU LIKE ME. DON'T TRY TO DENY IT.
YEAH, OF COURSE I LIKE YOU.
HUH ...?
IF I WERE MARRIED AND HAD A DAUGHTER...
IT'D BE NICE IF SHE WAS SOMEONE LIKE YOU.
WHAT'S THAT SUPPOSED TO MEAN ...?
HA HA HA HA! SORRY. YOU JUST ALWAYS MAKE ME WANT TO TAKE CARE OF YOU. BUT I GUESS I SHOULD MIND MY OWN BUSINESS.
MUMBLE WIFE?
HUH? WHAT WAS THAT?

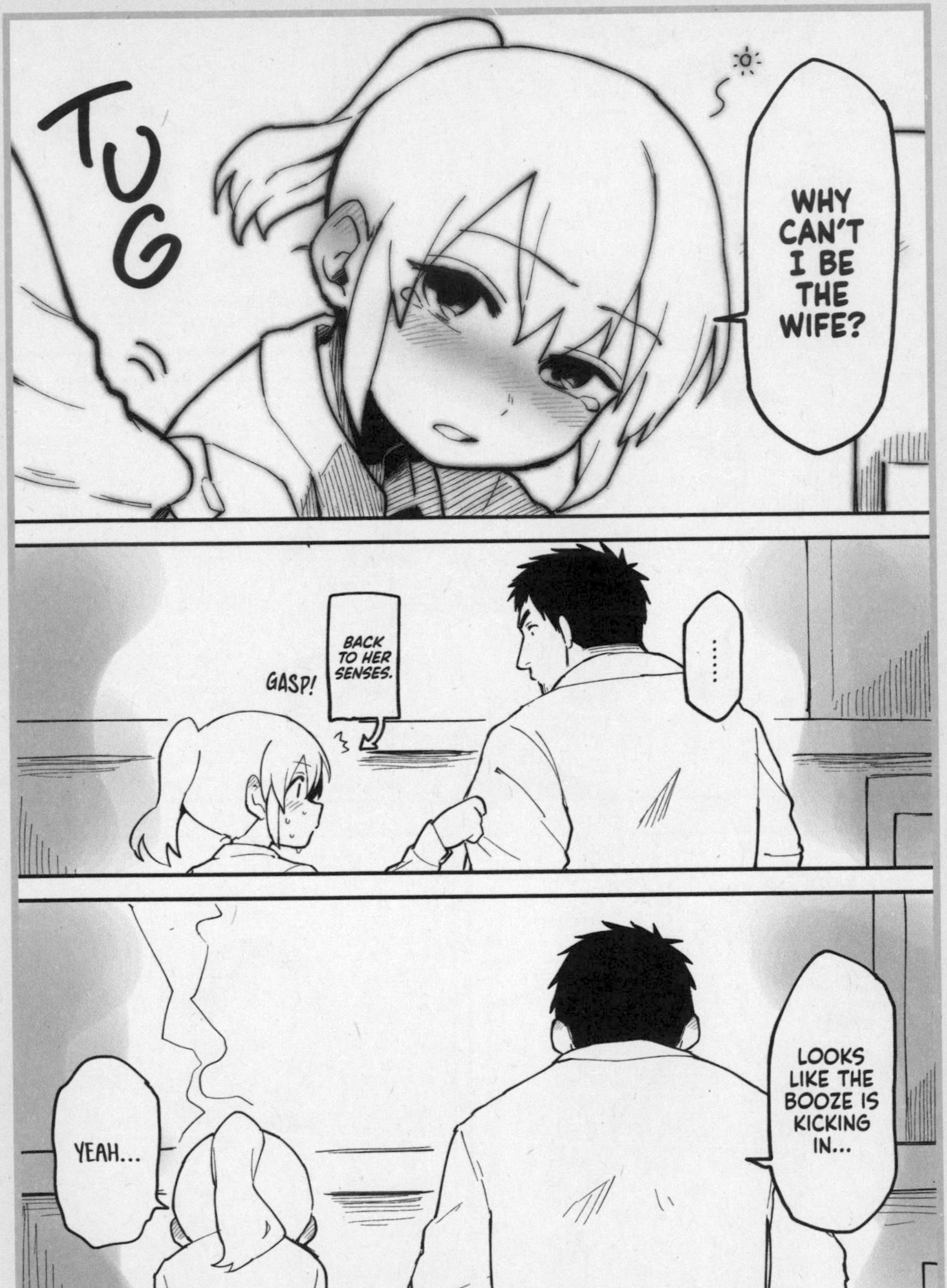
WHY CAN'T I BE THE WIFE?
TUG
......
BACK TO HER SENSES.
GASP!
LOOKS LIKE THE BOOZE IS KICKING IN...
YEAH...

008

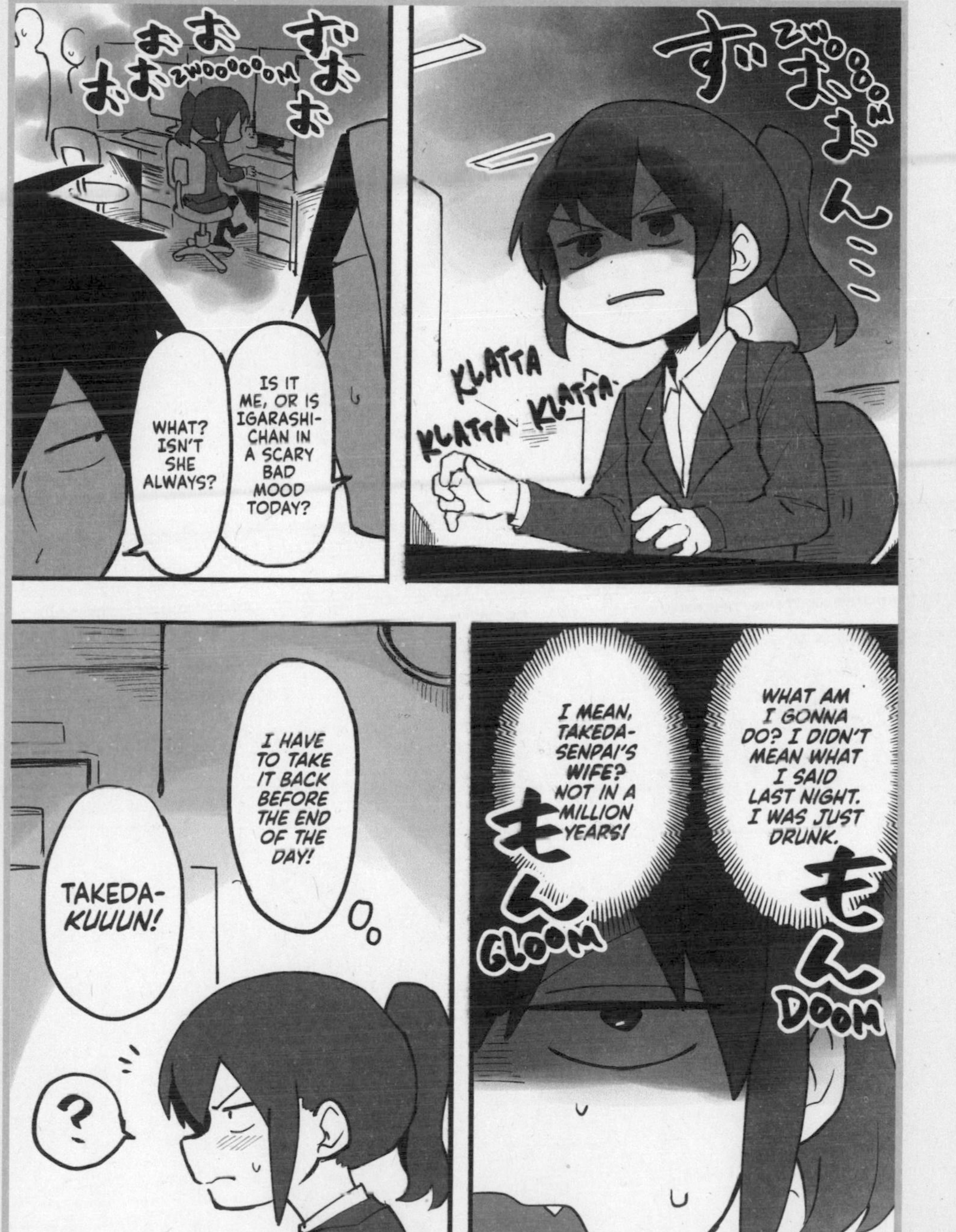
ずおおん
ZWOOOOOM
KLATTA
KLATTA
KLATTA
ZWOOOOOOM
IS IT ME, OR IS IGARASHI-CHAN IN A SCARY BAD MOOD TODAY?
WHAT? ISN'T SHE ALWAYS?
WHAT AM I GONNA DO? I DIDN'T MEAN WHAT I SAID LAST NIGHT. I WAS JUST DRUNK.
もん
DOOM
I MEAN, TAKEDA-SENPAI'S WIFE? NOT IN A MILLION YEARS!
もん
GLOOM
I HAVE TO TAKE IT BACK BEFORE THE END OF THE DAY!
TAKEDA-KUUUN!
?

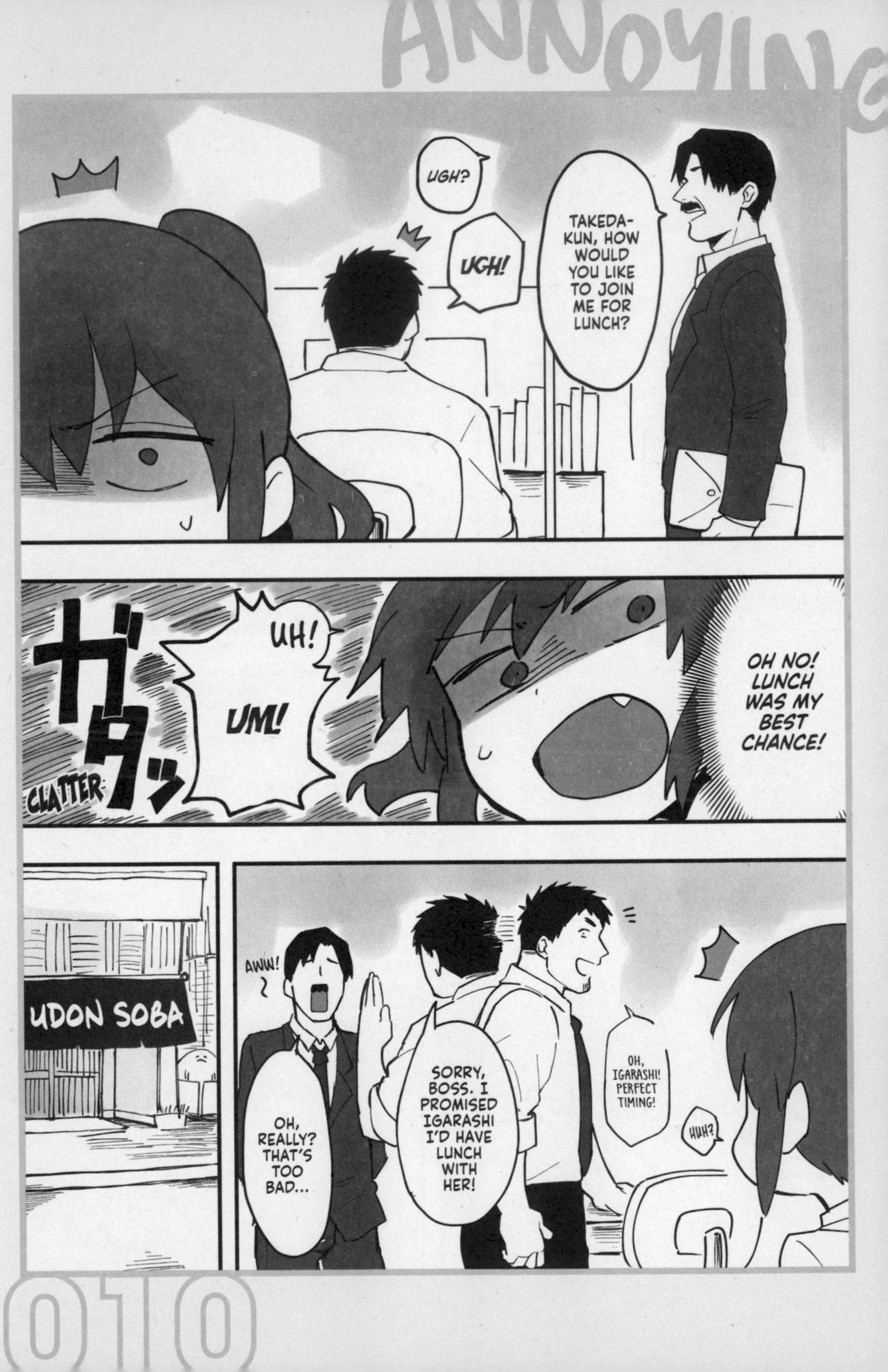
TAKEDA-KUN, HOW WOULD YOU LIKE TO JOIN ME FOR LUNCH?
UGH!
UGH?
OH NO! LUNCH WAS MY BEST CHANCE!
UH!
UM!
ガタッ
CLATTER
OH, IGARASHI! PERFECT TIMING!
HUH?
SORRY, BOSS. I PROMISED IGARASHI I'D HAVE LUNCH WITH HER!
OH, REALLY? THAT'S TOO BAD...
AWW!
UDON SOBA

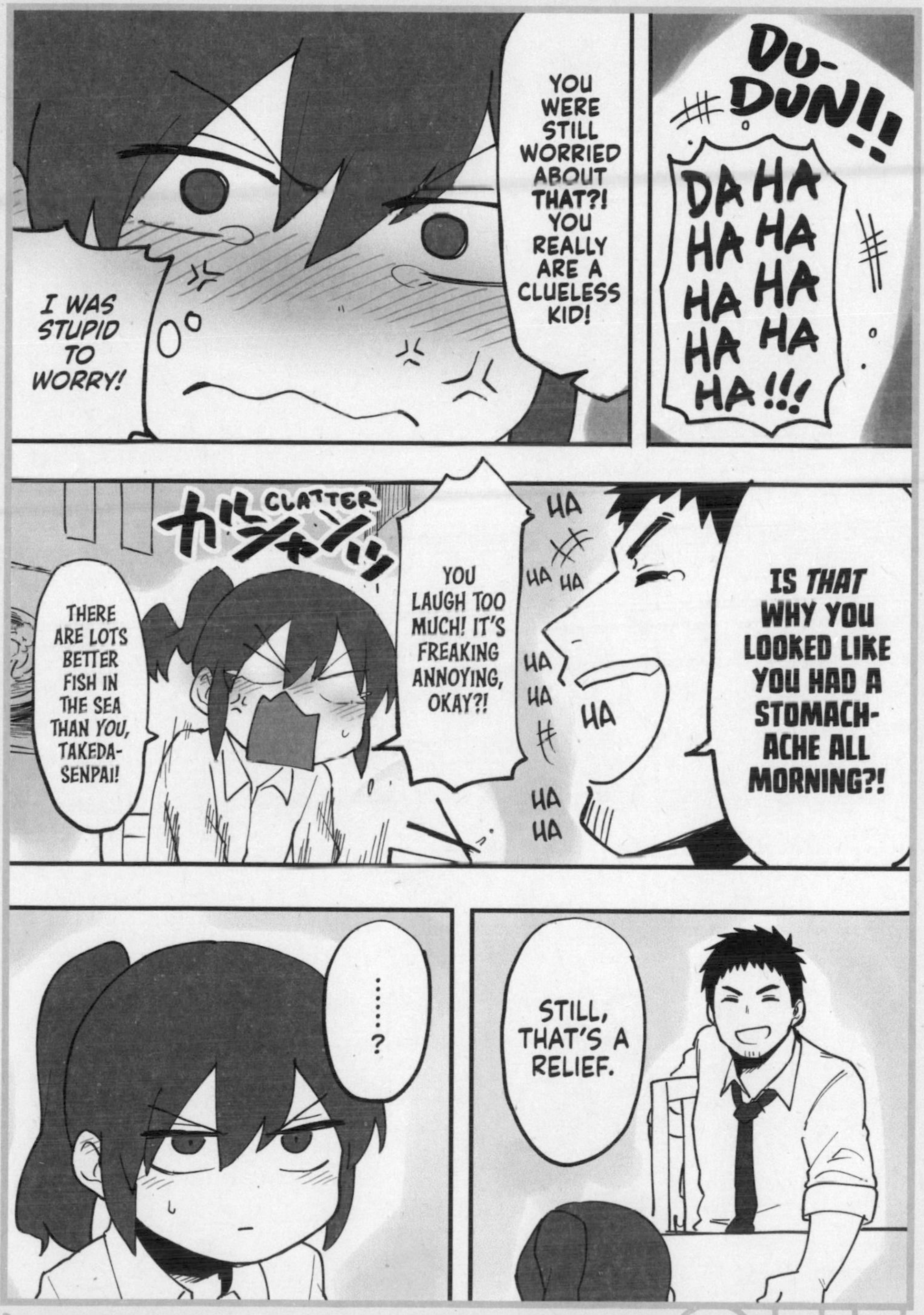
DU-DUN!!
DAHAHAHAHAHAHAHAHAHA!!!
YOU WERE STILL WORRIED ABOUT THAT?! YOU REALLY ARE A CLUELESS KID!
I WAS STUPID TO WORRY!
IS *THAT* WHY YOU LOOKED LIKE YOU HAD A STOMACHACHE ALL MORNING?!
HA HA HA HA HA HA HA HA HA
YOU LAUGH TOO MUCH! IT'S FREAKING ANNOYING, OKAY?!
CLATTER
THERE ARE LOTS BETTER FISH IN THE SEA THAN *YOU*, TAKEDA-SENPAI!
STILL, THAT'S A RELIEF.
......?

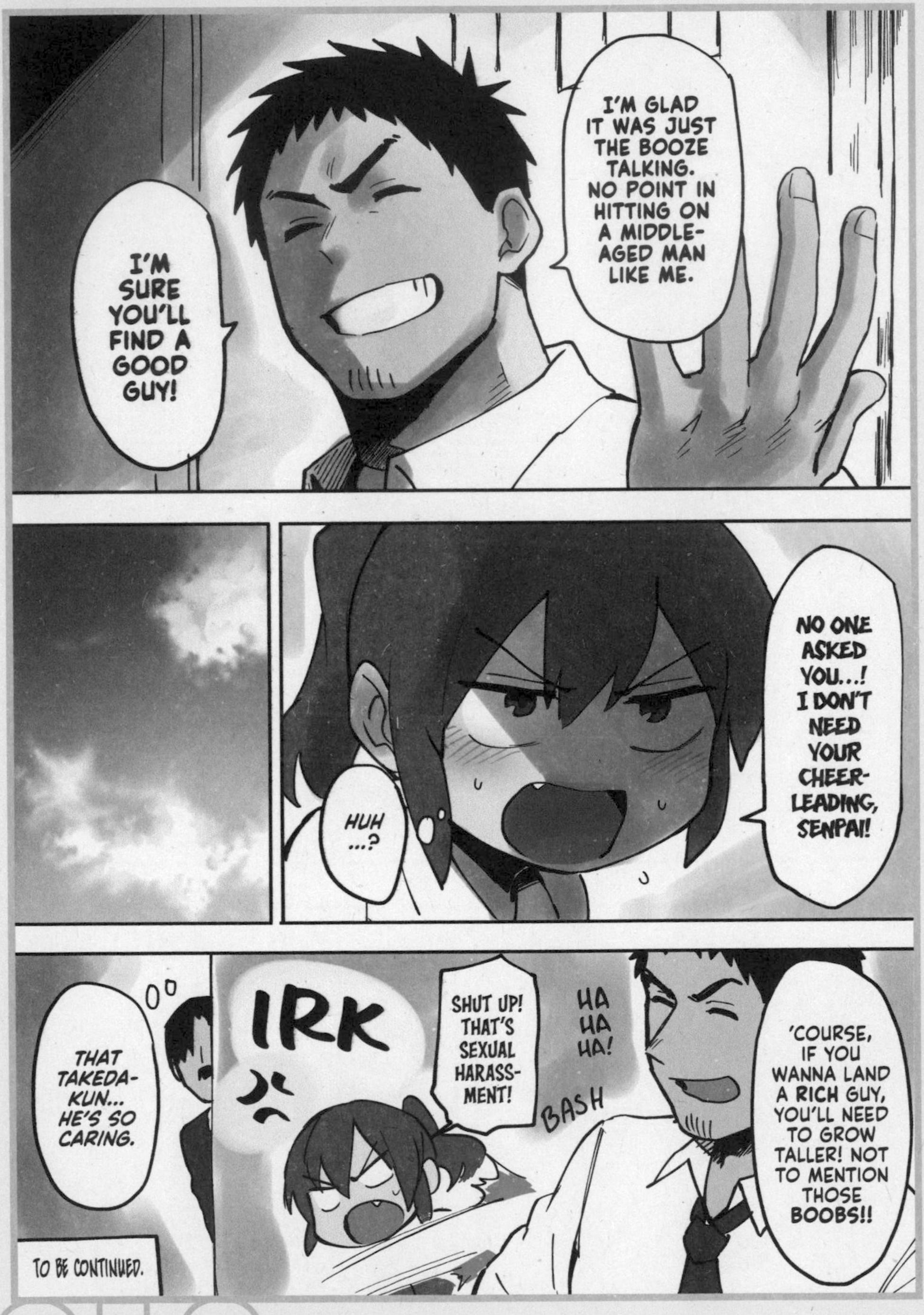

I'M GLAD IT WAS JUST THE BOOZE TALKING. NO POINT IN HITTING ON A MIDDLE-AGED MAN LIKE ME.
I'M SURE YOU'LL FIND A GOOD GUY!
NO ONE ASKED YOU...! I DON'T NEED YOUR CHEER-LEADING, SENPAI!
HUH ...?
'COURSE, IF YOU WANNA LAND A RICH GUY, YOU'LL NEED TO GROW TALLER! NOT TO MENTION THOSE BOOBS!!
HA HA HA!
SHUT UP! THAT'S SEXUAL HARASS-MENT!
IRK
BASH
THAT TAKEDA-KUN... HE'S SO CARING.
TO BE CONTINUED.

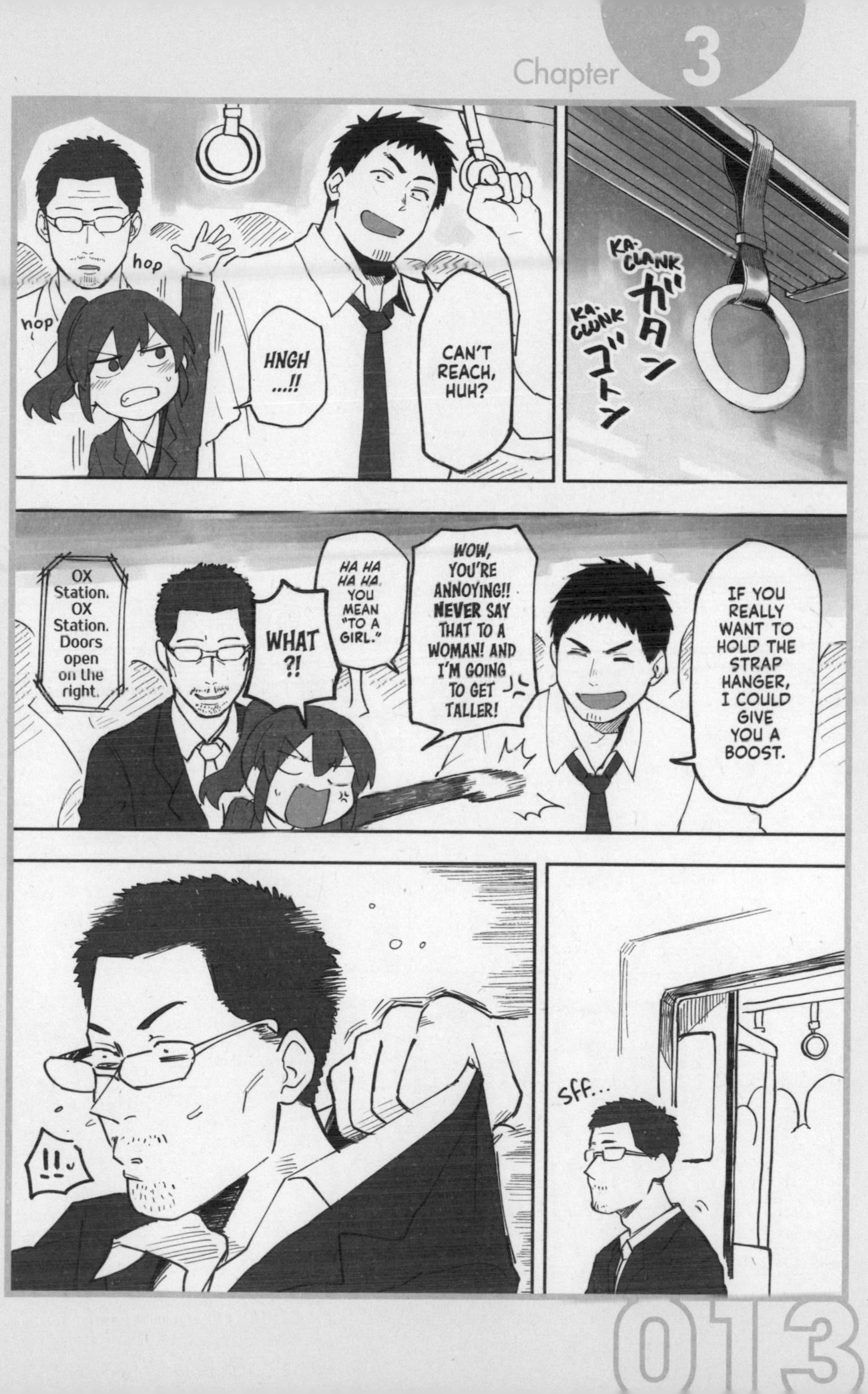
KA-CLANK ガタン
KA-CLUNK ゴトン
CAN'T REACH, HUH?
HNGH ...!!
hop
hop
IF YOU REALLY WANT TO HOLD THE STRAP HANGER, I COULD GIVE YOU A BOOST.
WOW, YOU'RE ANNOYING!! NEVER SAY THAT TO A WOMAN! AND I'M GOING TO GET TALLER!
HA HA HA HA. YOU MEAN "TO A GIRL."
WHAT ?!
OX Station. OX Station. Doors open on the right.
sff...
!!

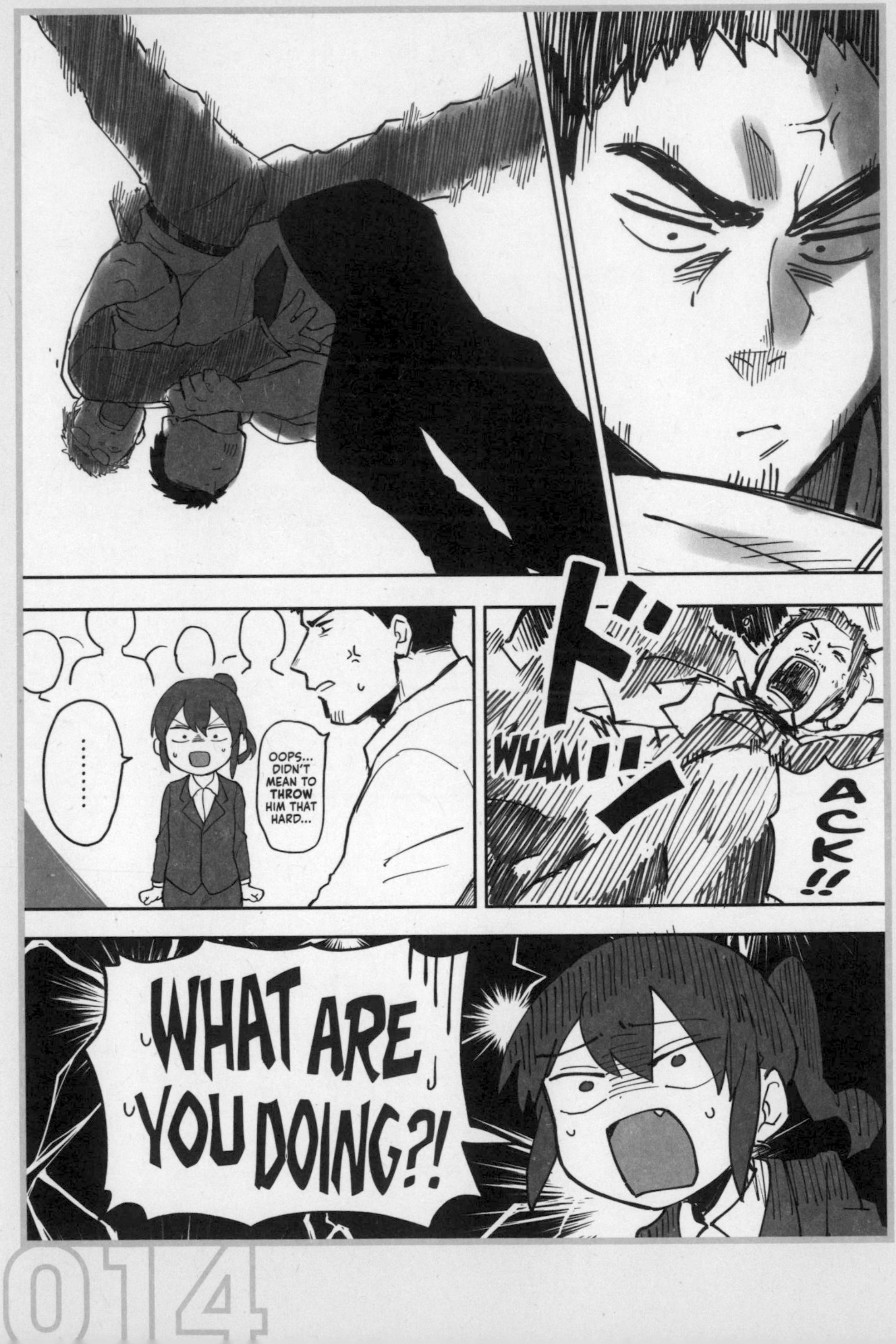
ドー
WHAM!!
ACK!!
OOPS... DIDN'T MEAN TO THROW HIM THAT HARD...
....
WHAT ARE YOU DOING?!

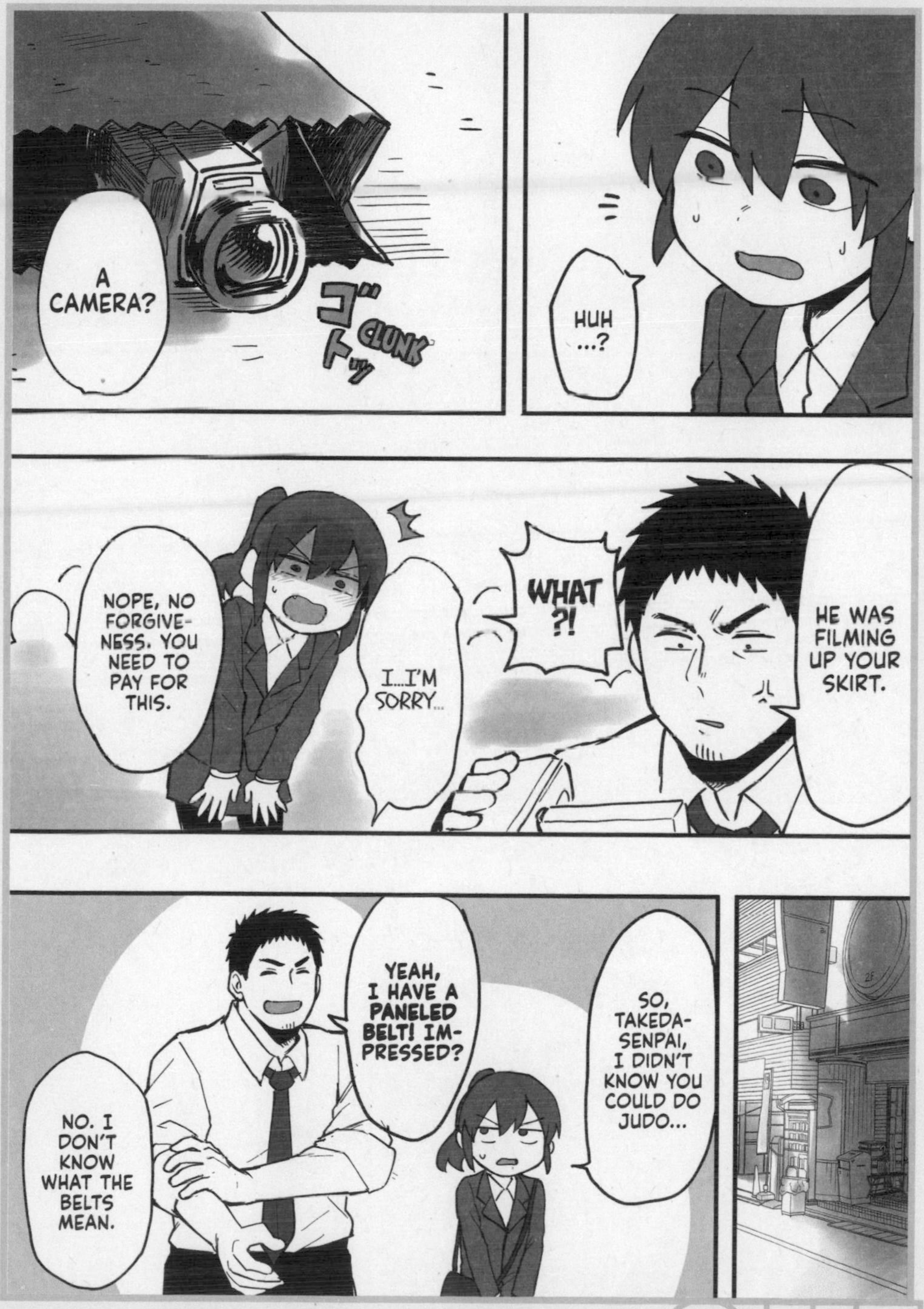
HUH ...?
A CAMERA?
ゴトッ
CLUNK
HE WAS FILMING UP YOUR SKIRT.
WHAT ?!
I...I'M SORRY...
NOPE, NO FORGIVE-NESS. YOU NEED TO PAY FOR THIS.
SO, TAKEDA-SENPAI, I DIDN'T KNOW YOU COULD DO JUDO...
YEAH, I HAVE A PANELED BELT! IM-PRESSED?
NO. I DON'T KNOW WHAT THE BELTS MEAN.

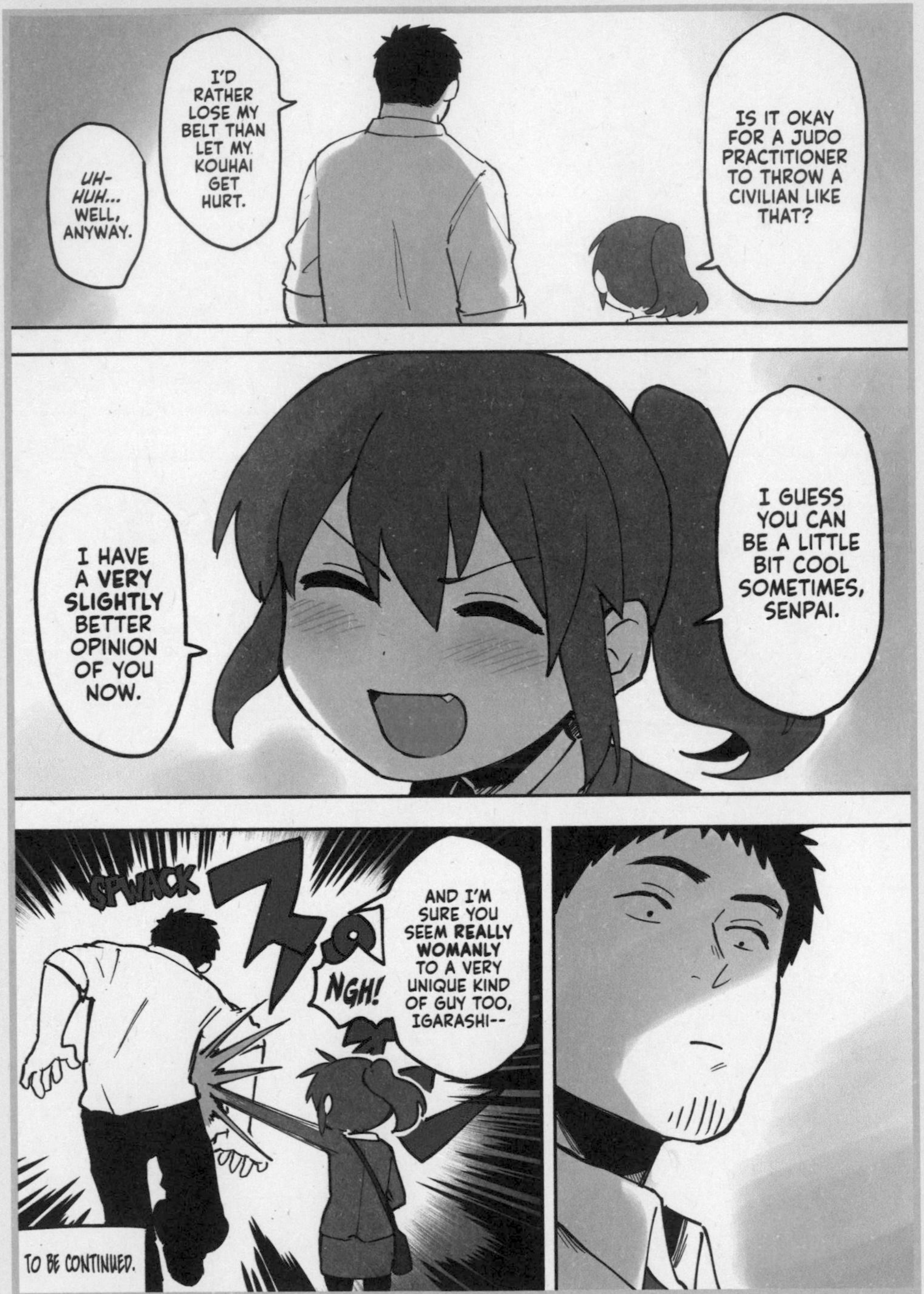
IS IT OKAY FOR A JUDO PRACTITIONER TO THROW A CIVILIAN LIKE THAT?
I'D RATHER LOSE MY BELT THAN LET MY KOUHAI GET HURT.
UH-HUH... WELL, ANYWAY.
I GUESS YOU CAN BE A LITTLE BIT COOL SOMETIMES, SENPAI.
I HAVE A **VERY SLIGHTLY** BETTER OPINION OF YOU NOW.
AND I'M SURE YOU SEEM **REALLY WOMANLY** TO A VERY UNIQUE KIND OF GUY TOO, IGARASHI--
NGH!
SPWACK
TO BE CONTINUED.

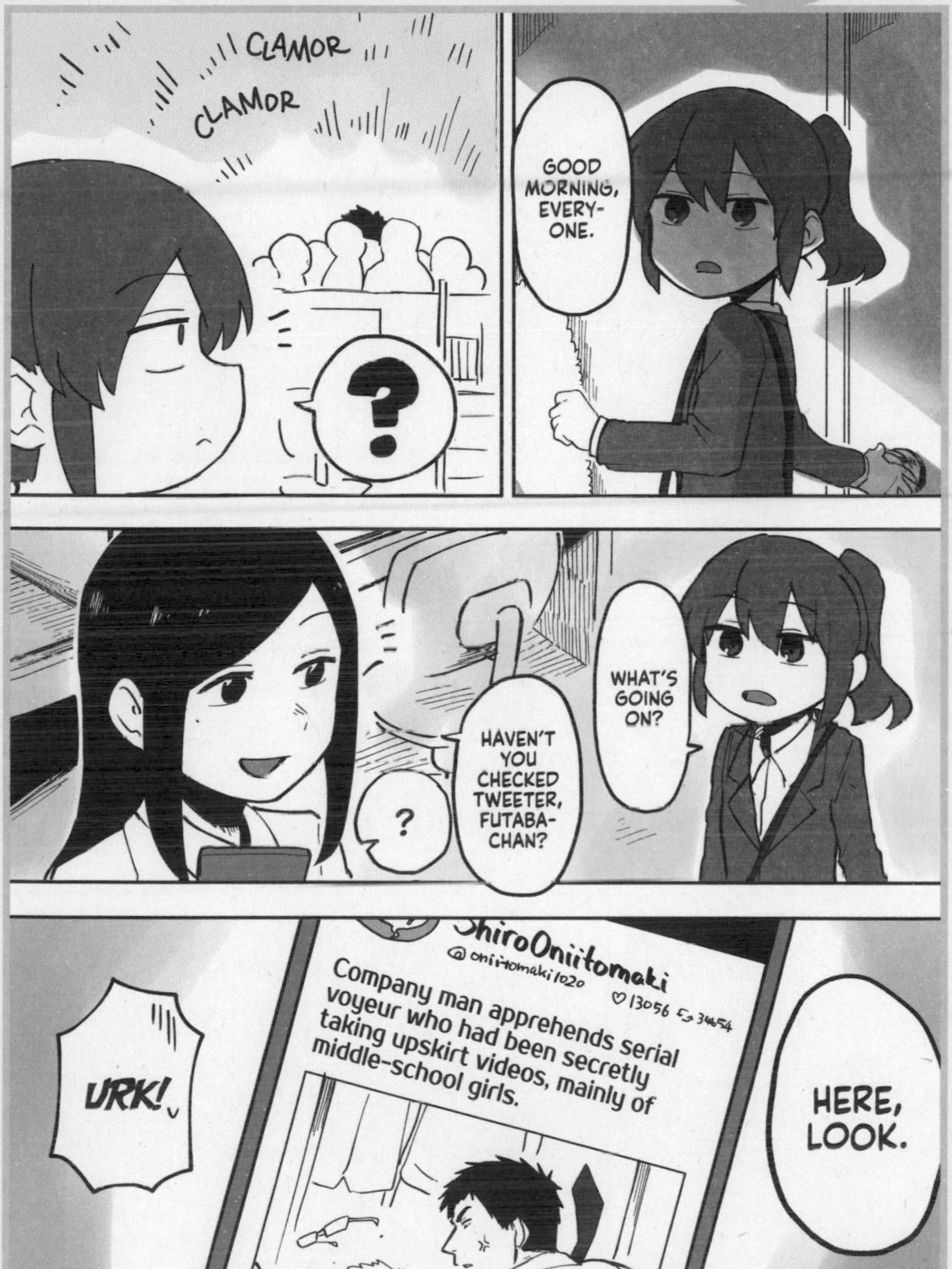
GOOD MORNING, EVERY-ONE.
CLAMOR
CLAMOR
?
WHAT'S GOING ON?
HAVEN'T YOU CHECKED TWEETER, FUTABA-CHAN?
?
HERE, LOOK.
ShiroOniitomaki
@oniitomaki1020
Company man apprehends serial voyeur who had been secretly taking upskirt videos, mainly of middle-school girls.
♡13056
34654
URK!

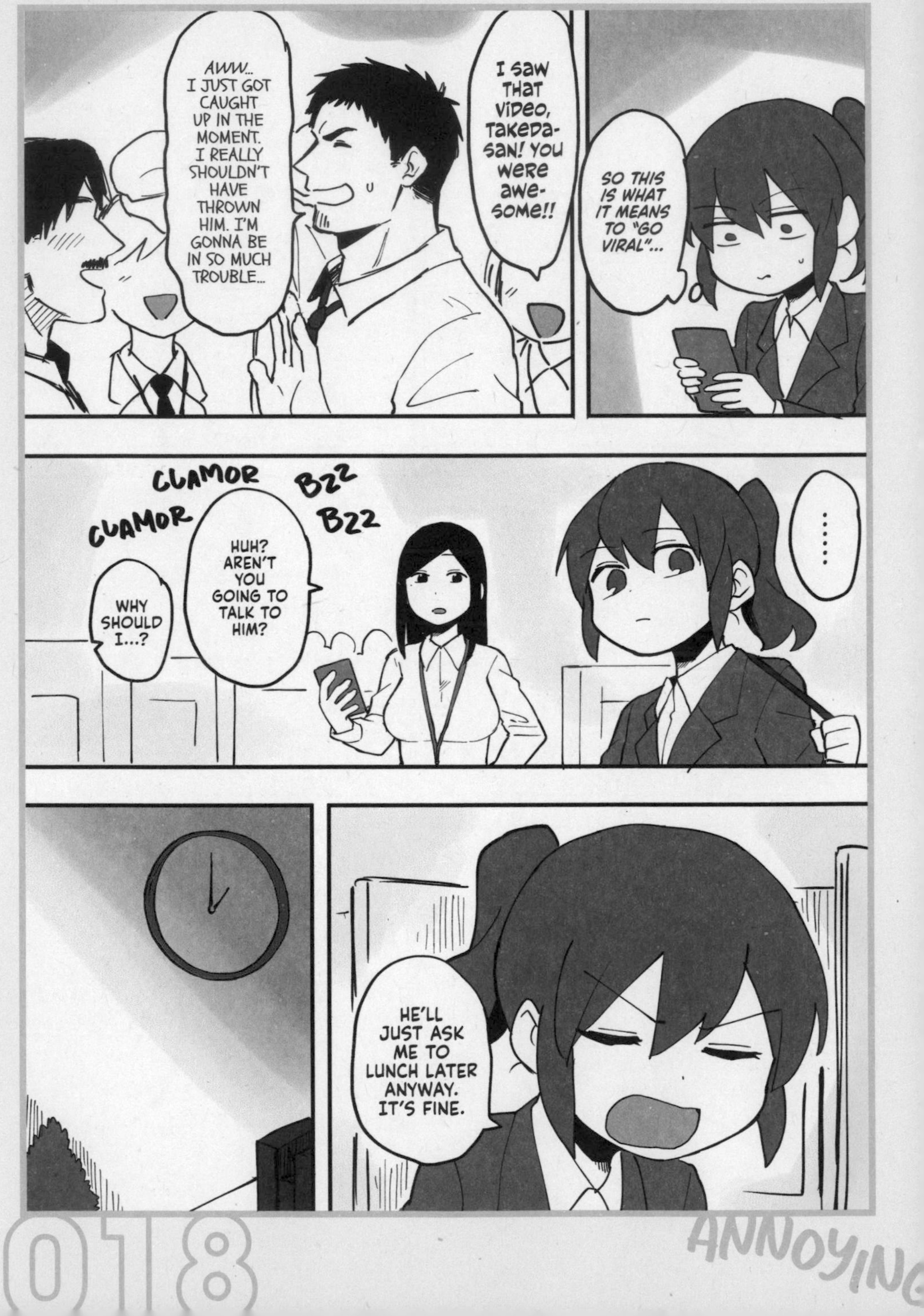
SO THIS IS WHAT IT MEANS TO "GO VIRAL"...
I SAW THAT VIDEO, TAKEDA-SAN! YOU WERE AWESOME!!
AWW... I JUST GOT CAUGHT UP IN THE MOMENT. I REALLY SHOULDN'T HAVE THROWN HIM. I'M GONNA BE IN SO MUCH TROUBLE...
......
BZZ BZZ
CLAMOR CLAMOR
HUH? AREN'T YOU GOING TO TALK TO HIM?
WHY SHOULD I...?
HE'LL JUST ASK ME TO LUNCH LATER ANYWAY. IT'S FINE.

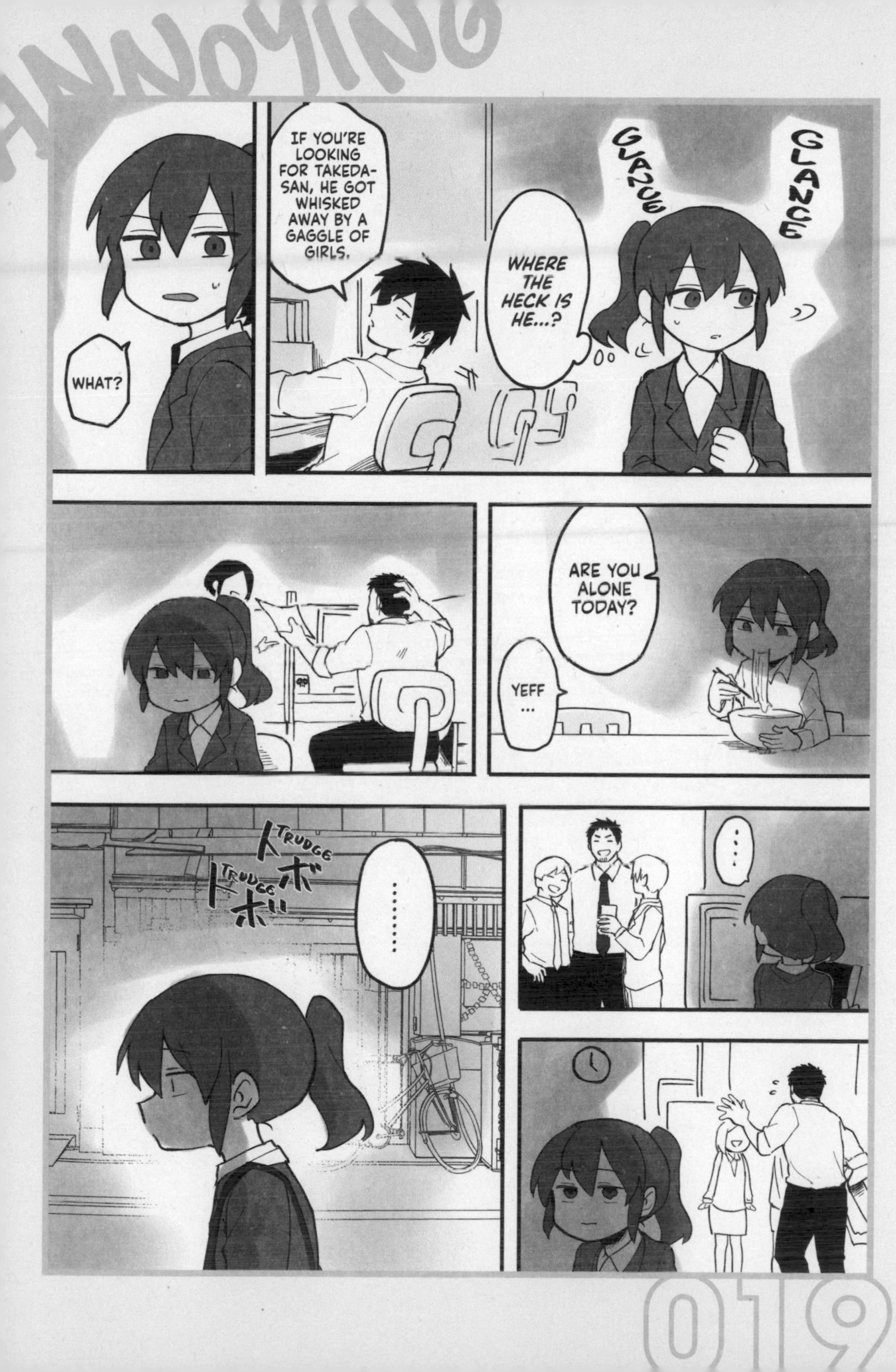
GLANCE
GLANCE
WHERE THE HECK IS HE...?
IF YOU'RE LOOKING FOR TAKEDA-SAN, HE GOT WHISKED AWAY BY A GAGGLE OF GIRLS.
WHAT?
ARE YOU ALONE TODAY?
YEFF ...
....
TRUDGE
TRUDGE
....

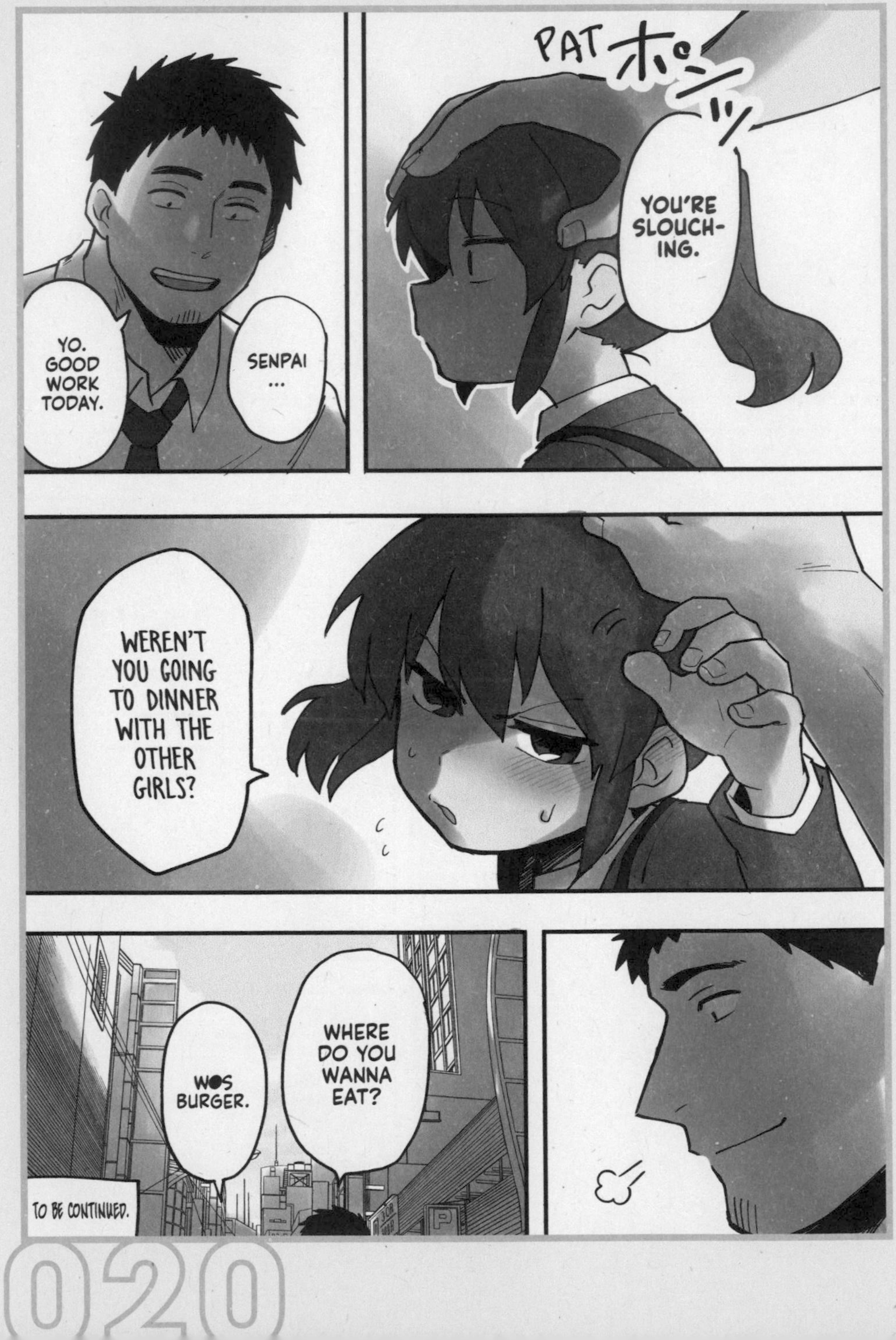
PAT ポンッ
YOU'RE SLOUCHING.
SENPAI ...
YO. GOOD WORK TODAY.
WEREN'T YOU GOING TO DINNER WITH THE OTHER GIRLS?
WHERE DO YOU WANNA EAT?
W●S BURGER.
TO BE CONTINUED.

Chapter 5

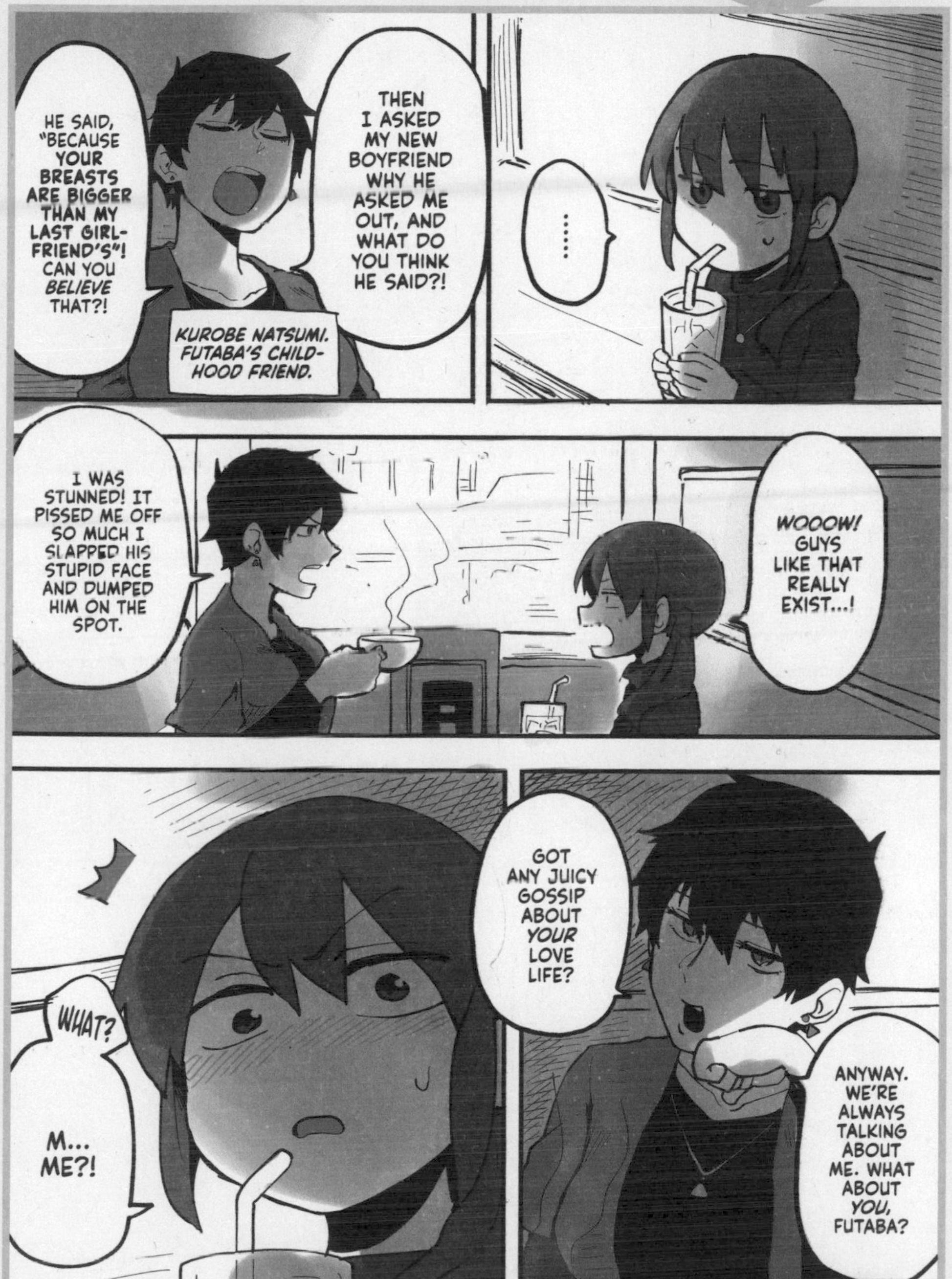
……
THEN I ASKED MY NEW BOYFRIEND WHY HE ASKED ME OUT, AND WHAT DO YOU THINK HE SAID?!
HE SAID, "BECAUSE YOUR BREASTS ARE BIGGER THAN MY LAST GIRL-FRIEND'S"! CAN YOU *BELIEVE* THAT?!
KUROBE NATSUMI. FUTABA'S CHILD-HOOD FRIEND.
WOOOW! GUYS LIKE THAT REALLY EXIST...!
I WAS STUNNED! IT PISSED ME OFF SO MUCH I SLAPPED HIS STUPID FACE AND DUMPED HIM ON THE SPOT.
ANYWAY. WE'RE ALWAYS TALKING ABOUT ME. WHAT ABOUT *YOU,* FUTABA?
GOT ANY JUICY GOSSIP ABOUT *YOUR* LOVE LIFE?
WHAT?
M... ME?!

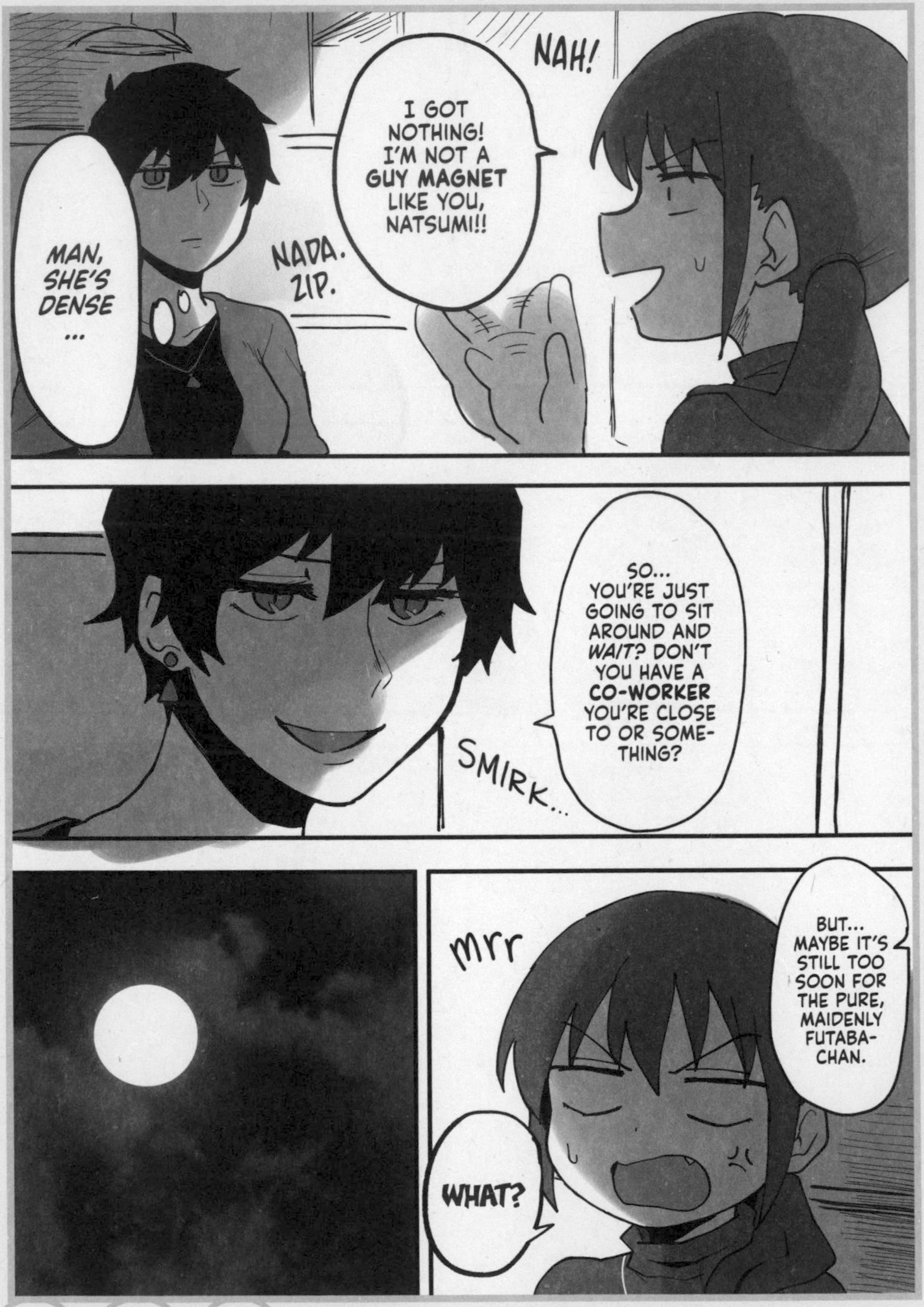
NAH!
I GOT NOTHING! I'M NOT A GUY MAGNET LIKE YOU, NATSUMI!!
NADA. ZIP.
MAN, SHE'S DENSE ...
SO... YOU'RE JUST GOING TO SIT AROUND AND WAIT? DON'T YOU HAVE A CO-WORKER YOU'RE CLOSE TO OR SOME-THING?
SMIRK...
BUT... MAYBE IT'S STILL TOO SOON FOR THE PURE, MAIDENLY FUTABA-CHAN.
mrr
WHAT?

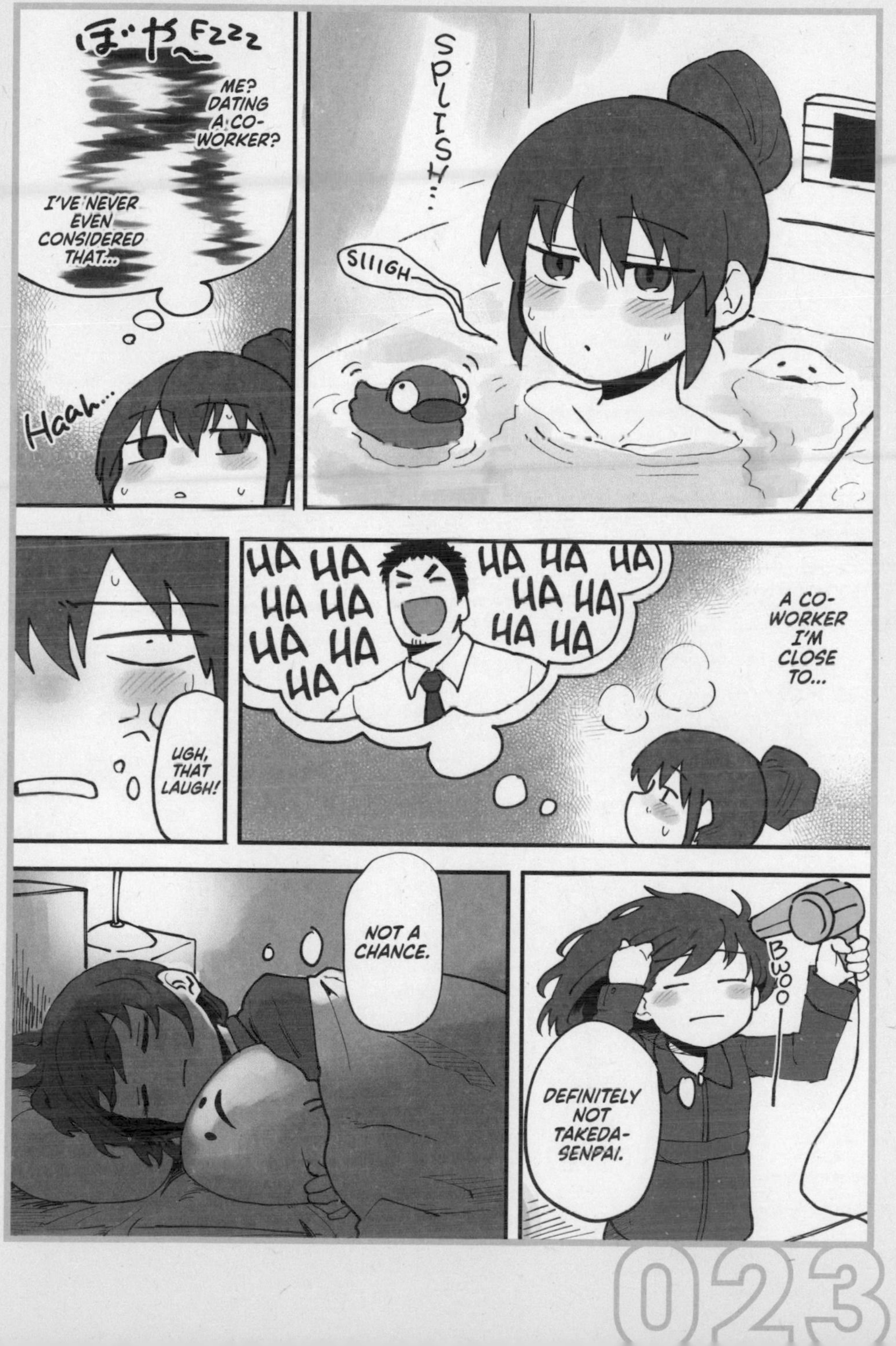
SPLISH...
SIIIGH
ぼや～ Fzzz
ME? DATING A CO-WORKER?
I'VE NEVER EVEN CONSIDERED THAT...
Haah...
A CO-WORKER I'M CLOSE TO...
HA HA HA HA HA HA HA HA HA HA HA HA HA HA HA HA
UGH, THAT LAUGH!
B3OO
DEFINITELY NOT TAKEDA-SENPAI.
NOT A CHANCE.

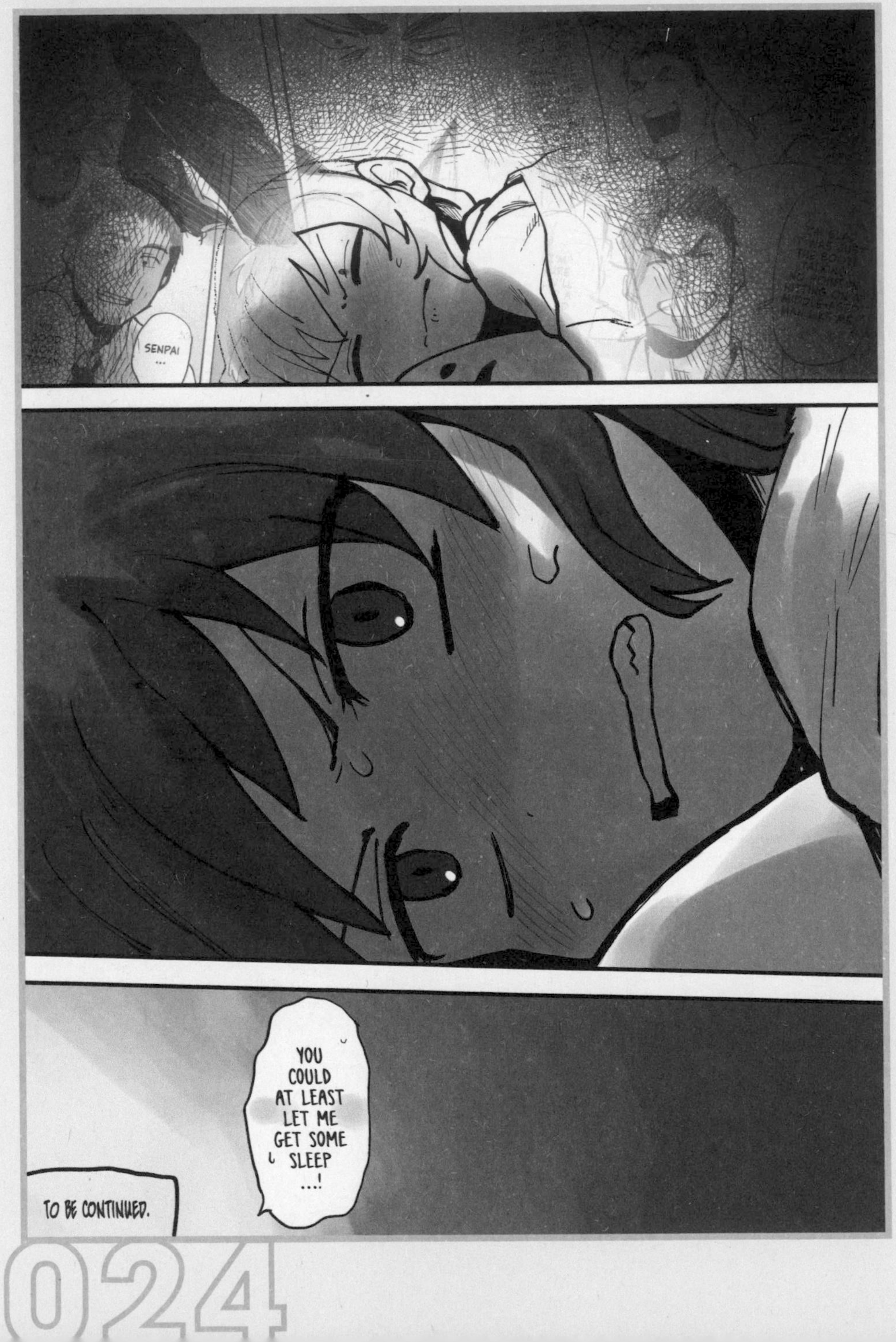
SENPAI ...
YOU COULD AT LEAST LET ME GET SOME SLEEP ...!
TO BE CONTINUED.

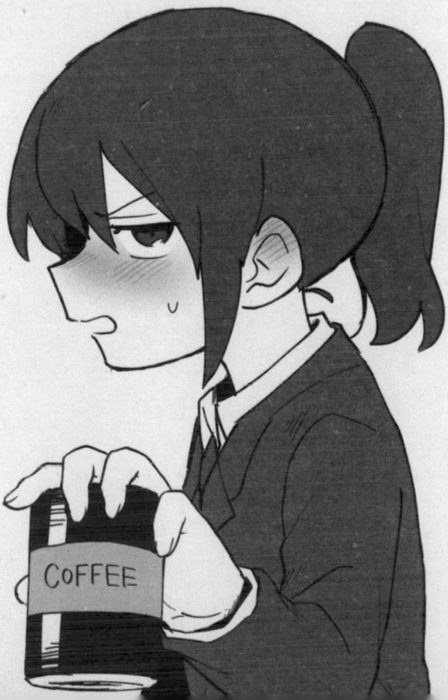
COFFEE

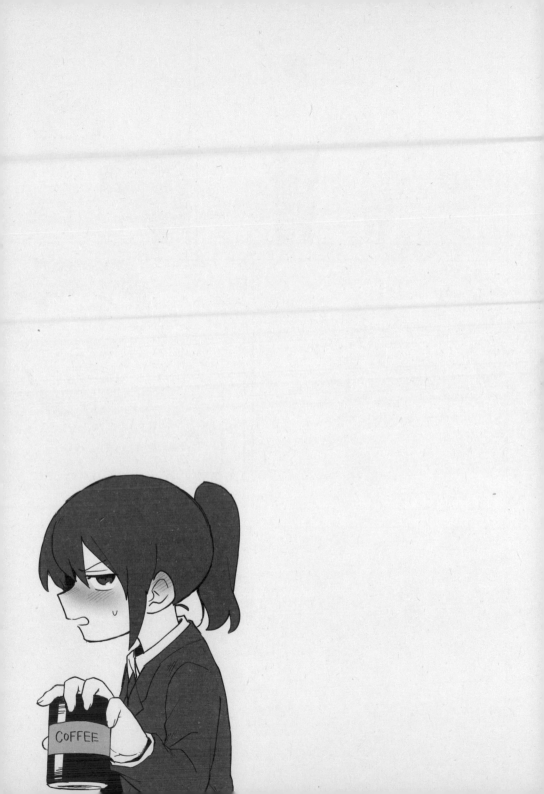

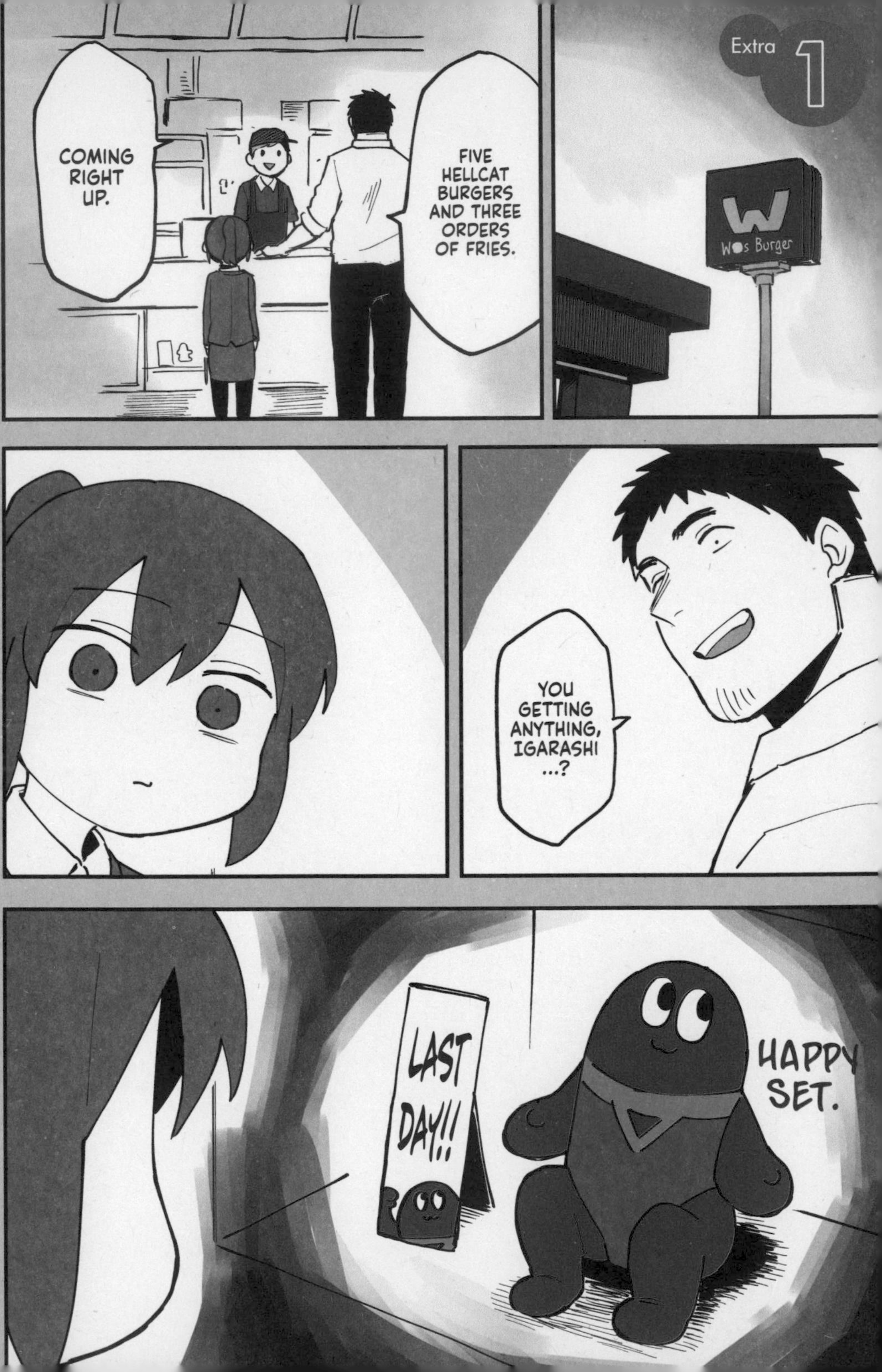
Extra 1
W●s Burger
FIVE HELLCAT BURGERS AND THREE ORDERS OF FRIES.
COMING RIGHT UP.
YOU GETTING ANYTHING, IGARASHI ...?
HAPPY SET.
LAST DAY!!

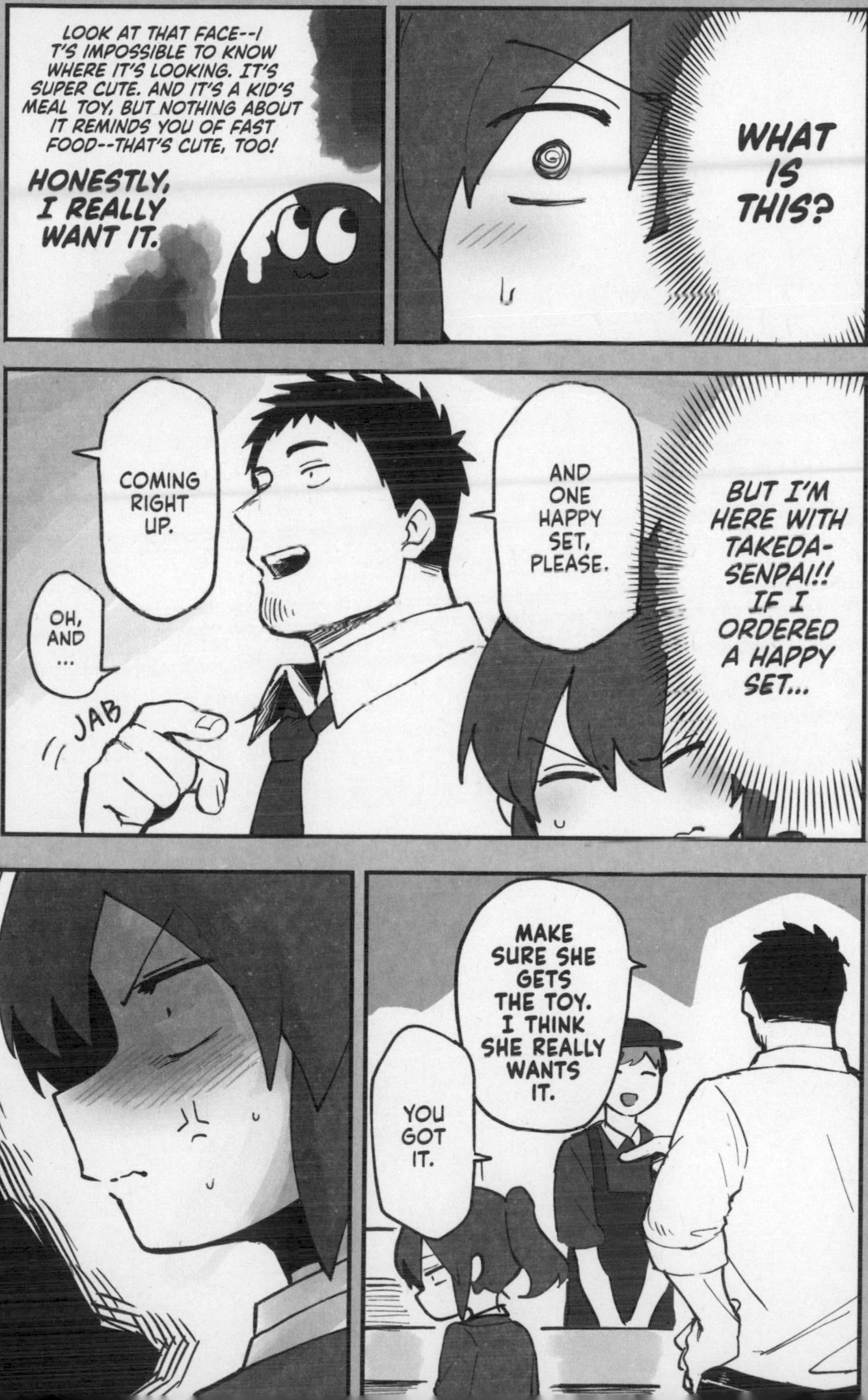
WHAT IS THIS?
LOOK AT THAT FACE--IT'S IMPOSSIBLE TO KNOW WHERE IT'S LOOKING. IT'S SUPER CUTE. AND IT'S A KID'S MEAL TOY, BUT NOTHING ABOUT IT REMINDS YOU OF FAST FOOD--THAT'S CUTE, TOO!
HONESTLY, I REALLY WANT IT.
BUT I'M HERE WITH TAKEDA-SENPAI!! IF I ORDERED A HAPPY SET...
AND ONE HAPPY SET, PLEASE.
COMING RIGHT UP.
OH, AND ...
JAB
MAKE SURE SHE GETS THE TOY. I THINK SHE REALLY WANTS IT.
YOU GOT IT.

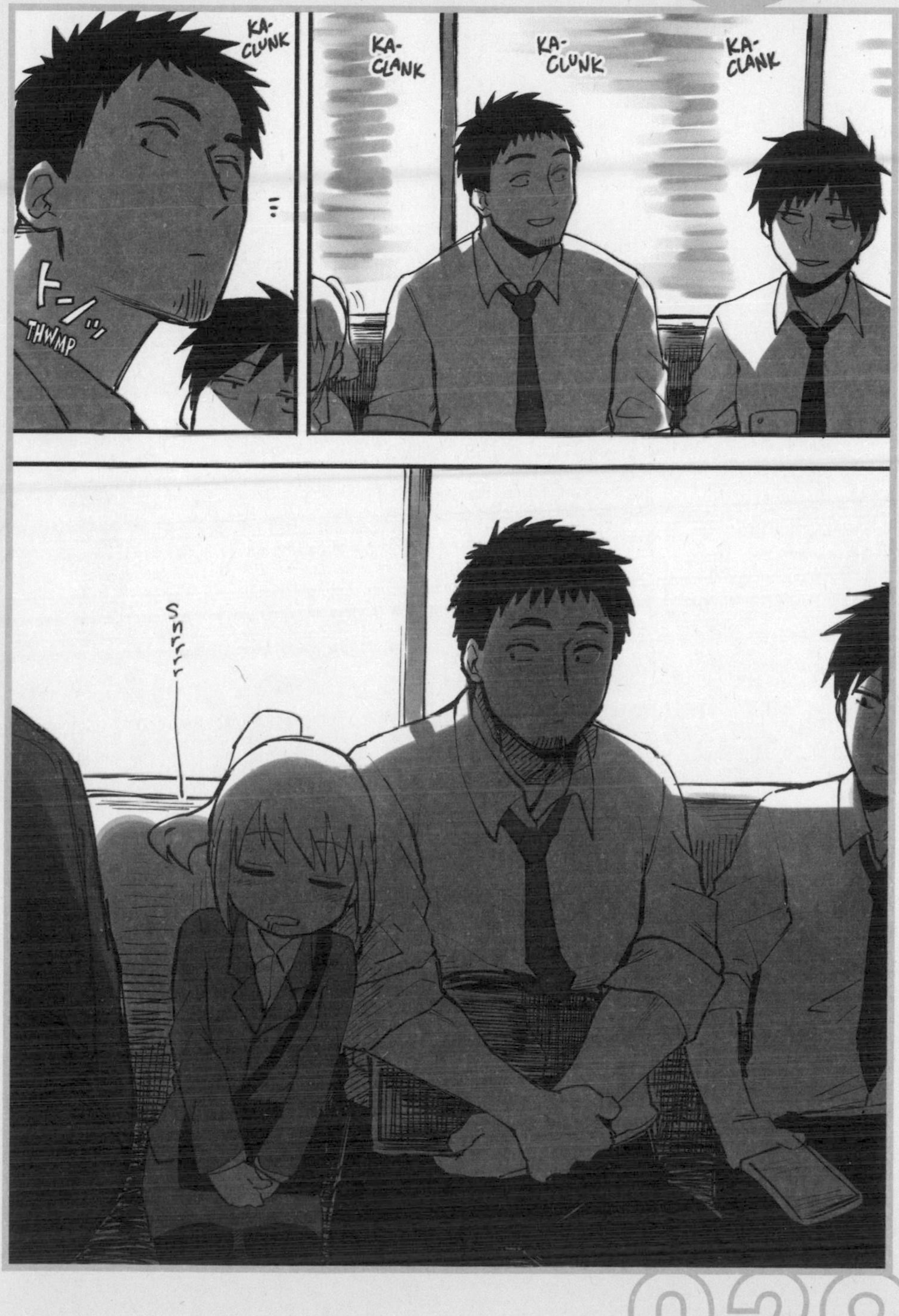
KA-CLANK
KA-CLUNK
KA-CLANK
KA-CLUNK
THWMP
Snrrr

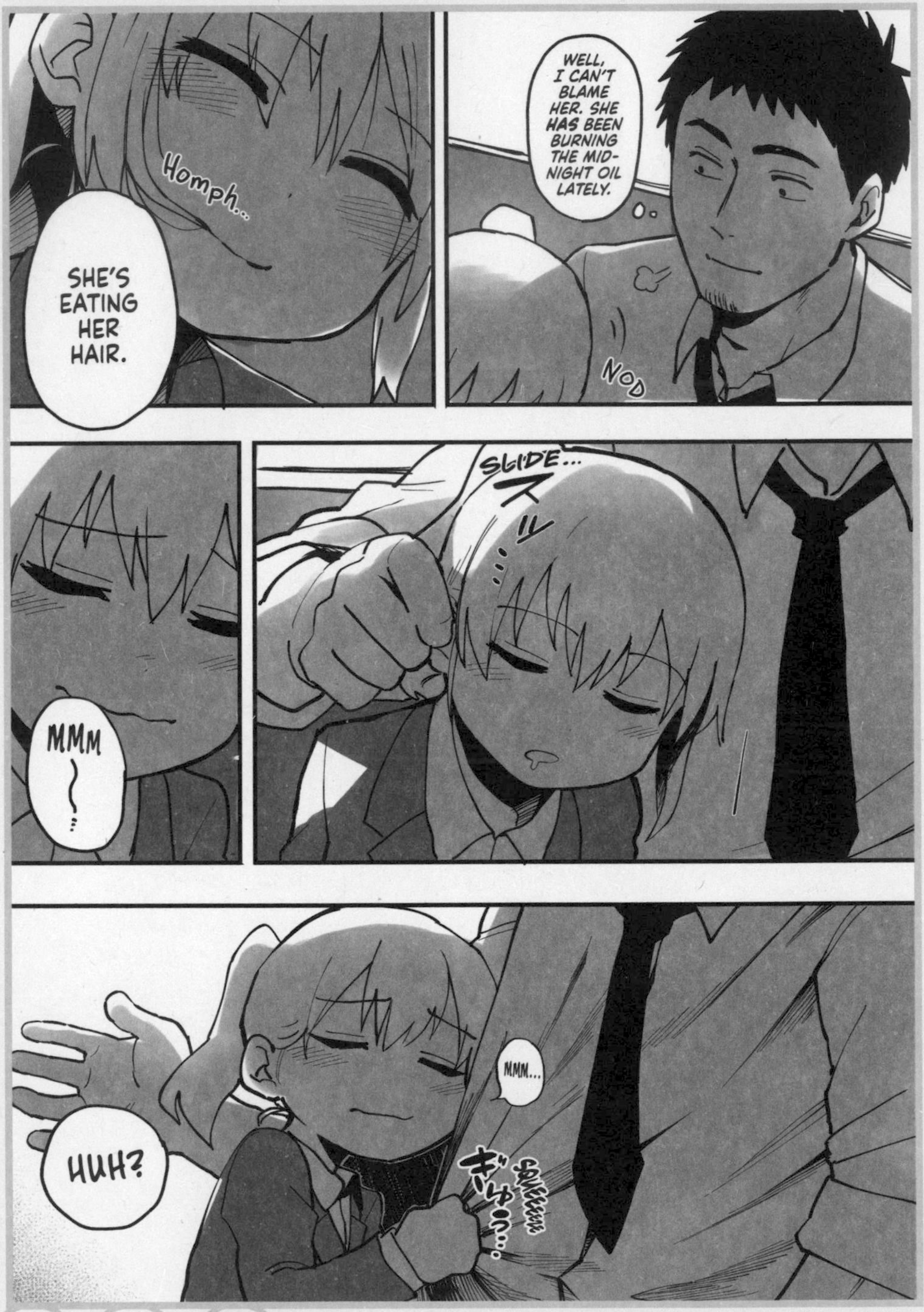
WELL, I CAN'T BLAME HER. SHE HAS BEEN BURNING THE MID-NIGHT OIL LATELY.
NOD
Homph...
SHE'S EATING HER HAIR.
SLIDE...
スル...
MMM~...
MMM...
HUH?
SQUEEEEEZE
ぎゅう...

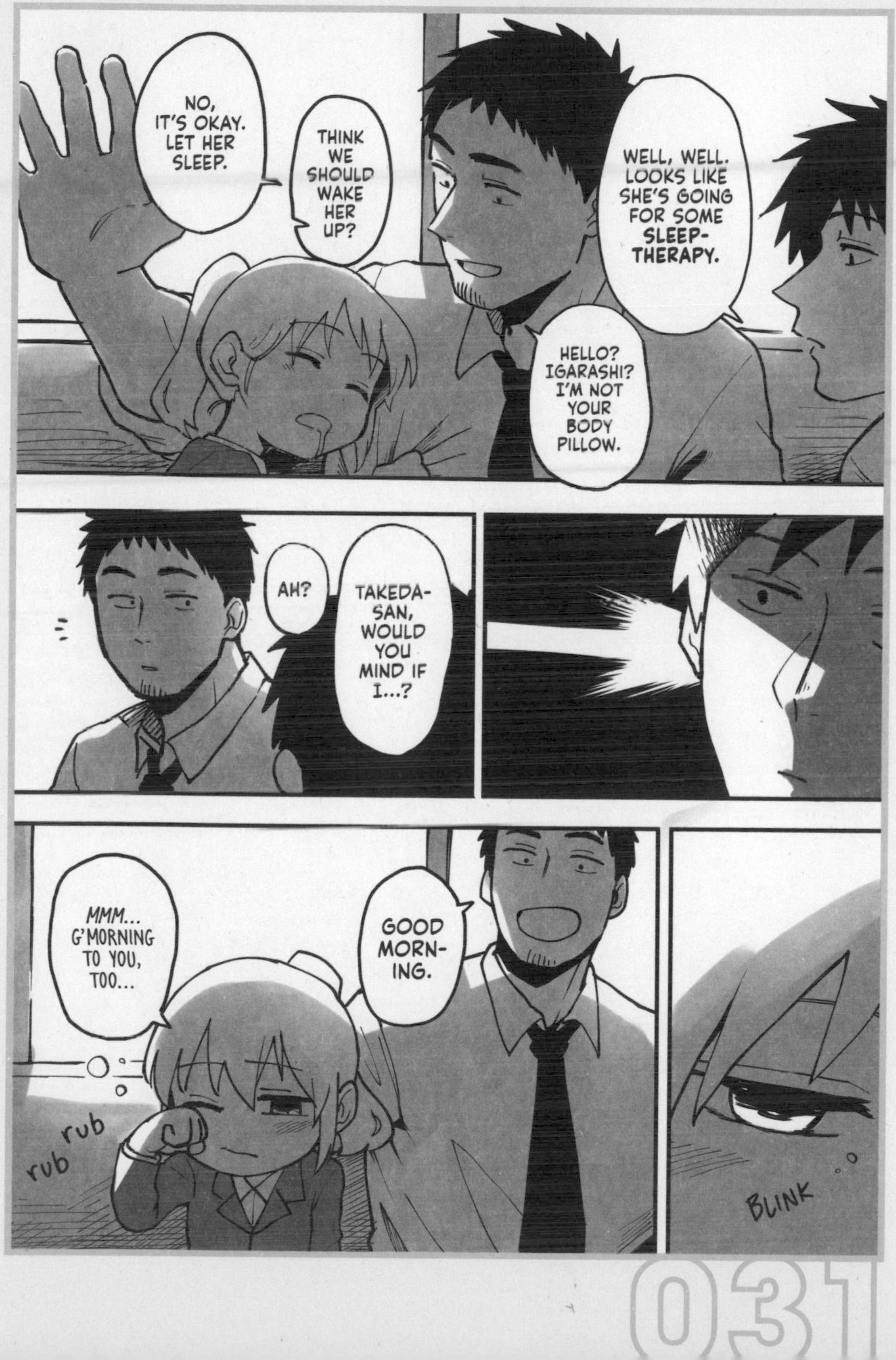

WELL, WELL. LOOKS LIKE SHE'S GOING FOR SOME SLEEP-THERAPY.
HELLO? IGARASHI? I'M NOT YOUR BODY PILLOW.
THINK WE SHOULD WAKE HER UP?
NO, IT'S OKAY. LET HER SLEEP.
TAKEDA-SAN, WOULD YOU MIND IF I...?
AH?
BLINK
GOOD MORNING.
MMM... G'MORNING TO YOU, TOO...
rub rub

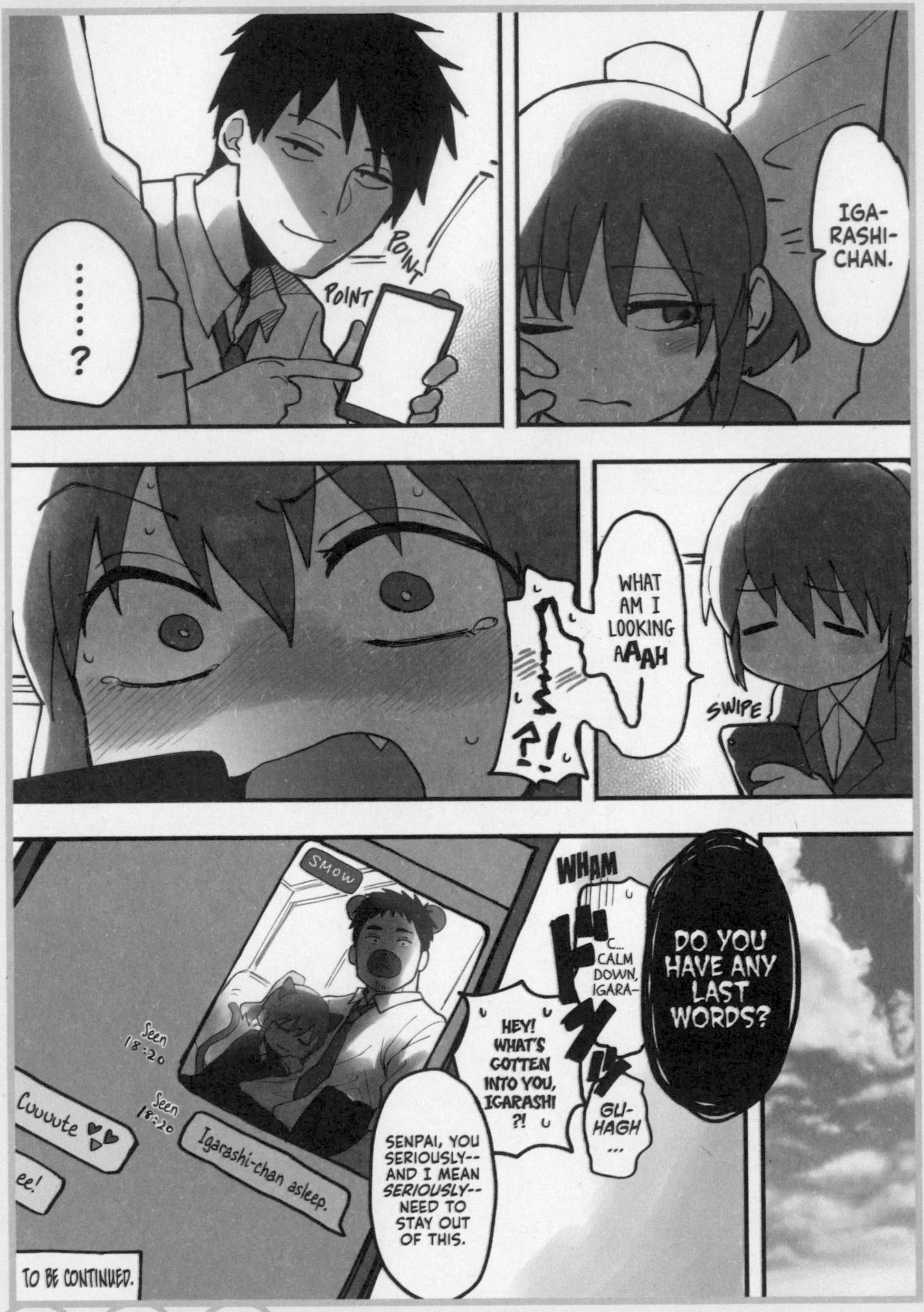
IGA-RASHI-CHAN.
POINT
POINT
……?
SWIPE
WHAT AM I LOOKING AAAH
?!
DO YOU HAVE ANY LAST WORDS?
WHAM
C... CALM DOWN, IGARA-
GU-HAGH ...
HEY! WHAT'S GOTTEN INTO YOU, IGARASHI?!
SENPAI, YOU SERIOUSLY-- AND I MEAN SERIOUSLY-- NEED TO STAY OUT OF THIS.
SMOW
Seen 18:20
Seen 18:20
Igarashi-chan asleep.
Cuuuute
ee!
TO BE CONTINUED.

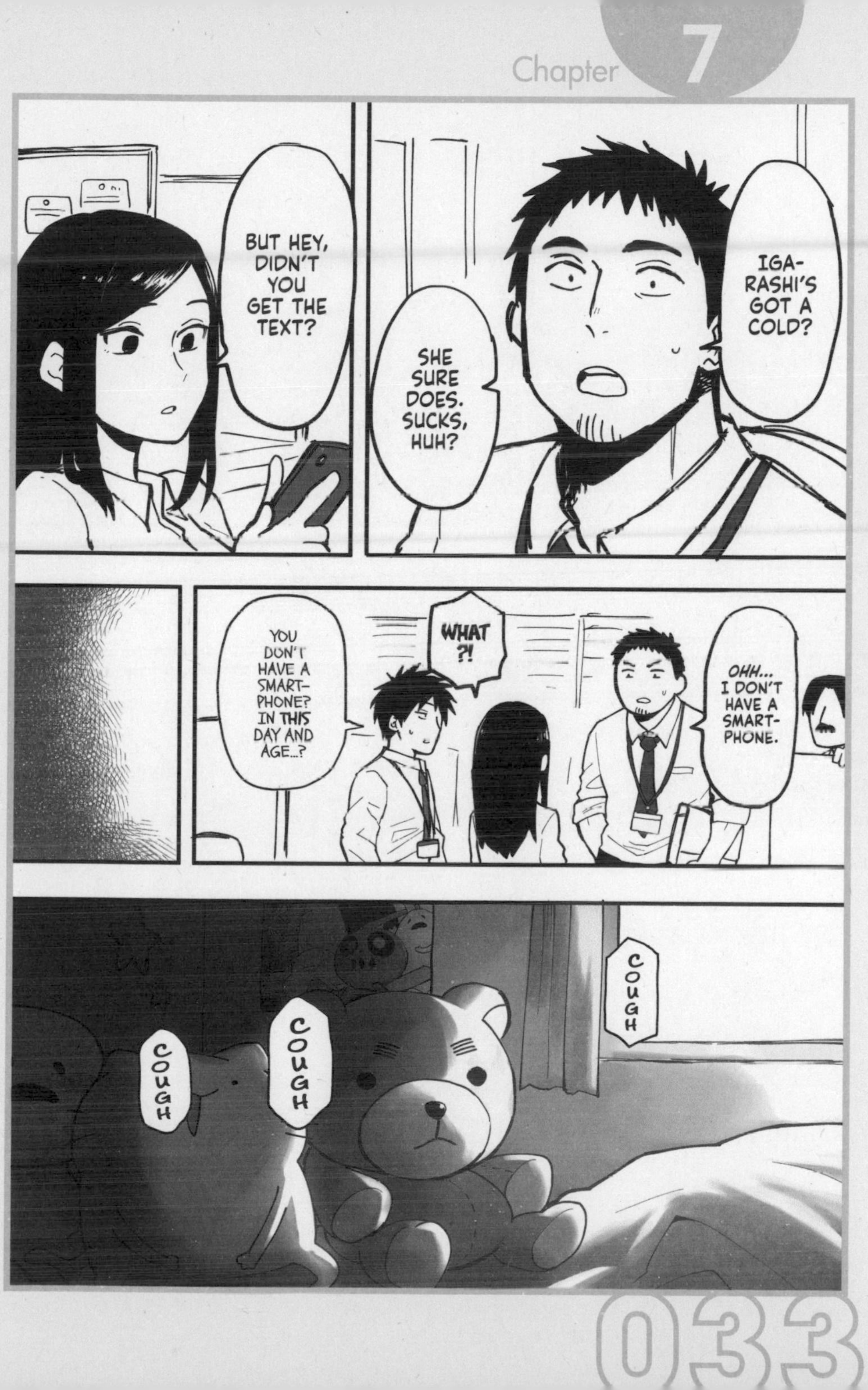
IGA-RASHI'S GOT A COLD?
SHE SURE DOES. SUCKS, HUH?
BUT HEY, DIDN'T YOU GET THE TEXT?
OHH... I DON'T HAVE A SMART-PHONE.
WHAT?!
YOU DON'T HAVE A SMART-PHONE? IN THIS DAY AND AGE...?
COUGH
COUGH
COUGH

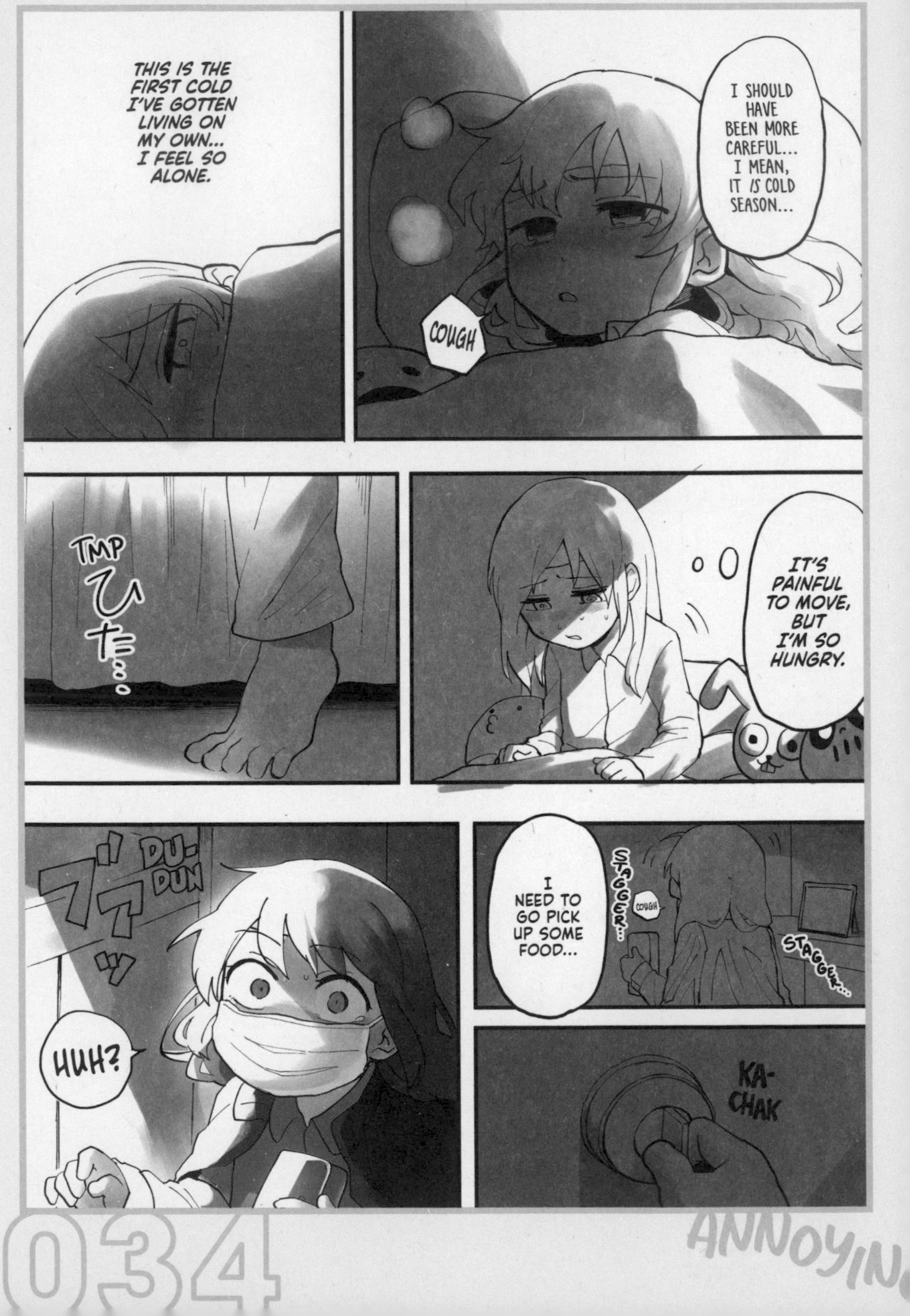
I SHOULD HAVE BEEN MORE CAREFUL... I MEAN, IT IS COLD SEASON...
COUGH
THIS IS THE FIRST COLD I'VE GOTTEN LIVING ON MY OWN... I FEEL SO ALONE.
o O
IT'S PAINFUL TO MOVE, BUT I'M SO HUNGRY.
TMP
ひた…
I NEED TO GO PICK UP SOME FOOD...
STAGGER...
COUGH
STAGGER...
KA-CHAK
ブブッ
DU-DUN
HUH?

034 ANNOYING

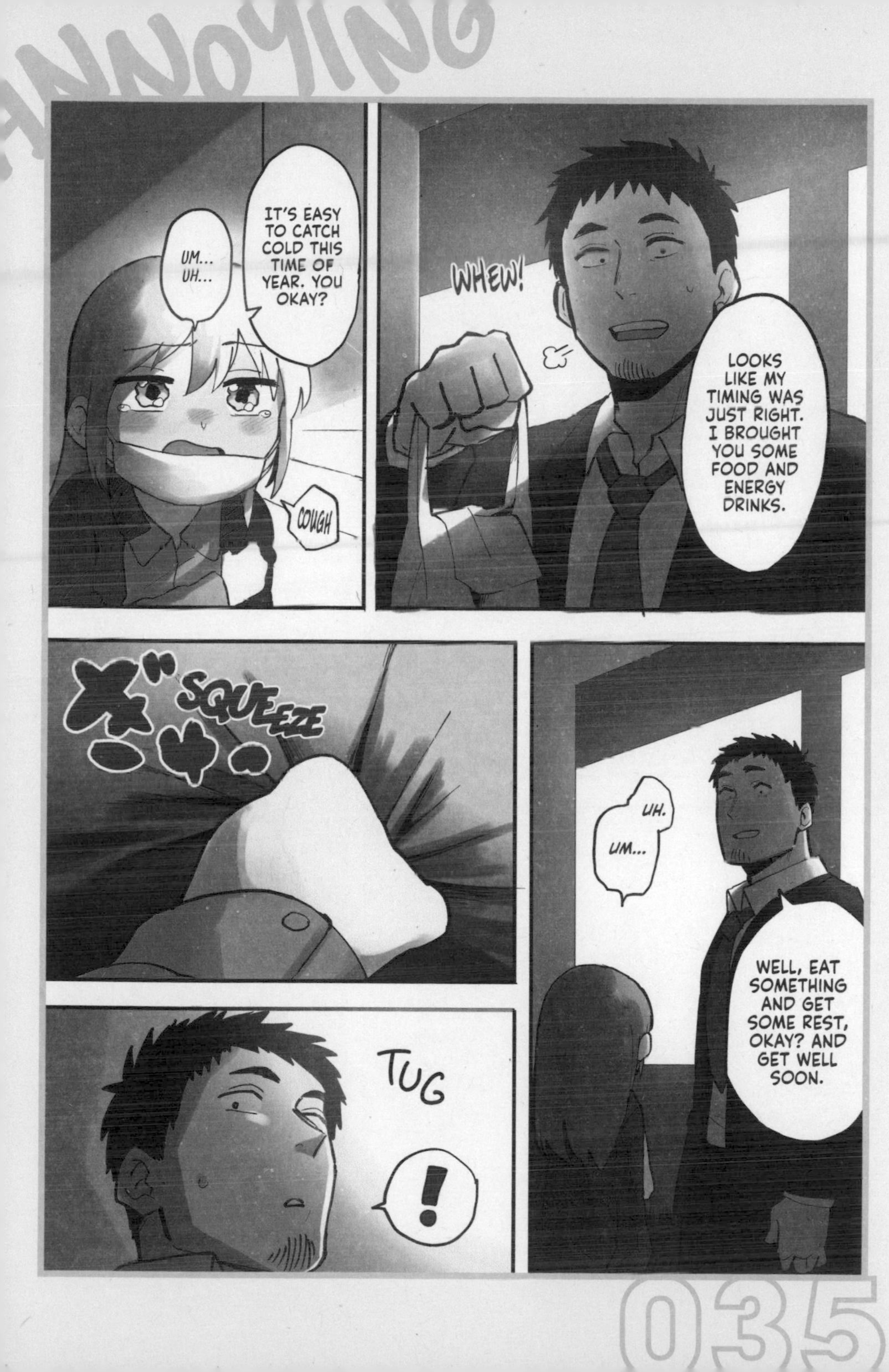
WHEW!
LOOKS LIKE MY TIMING WAS JUST RIGHT. I BROUGHT YOU SOME FOOD AND ENERGY DRINKS.
IT'S EASY TO CATCH COLD THIS TIME OF YEAR. YOU OKAY?
UM... UH...
COUGH
UH. UM...
WELL, EAT SOMETHING AND GET SOME REST, OKAY? AND GET WELL SOON.
SQUEEZE
TUG
!

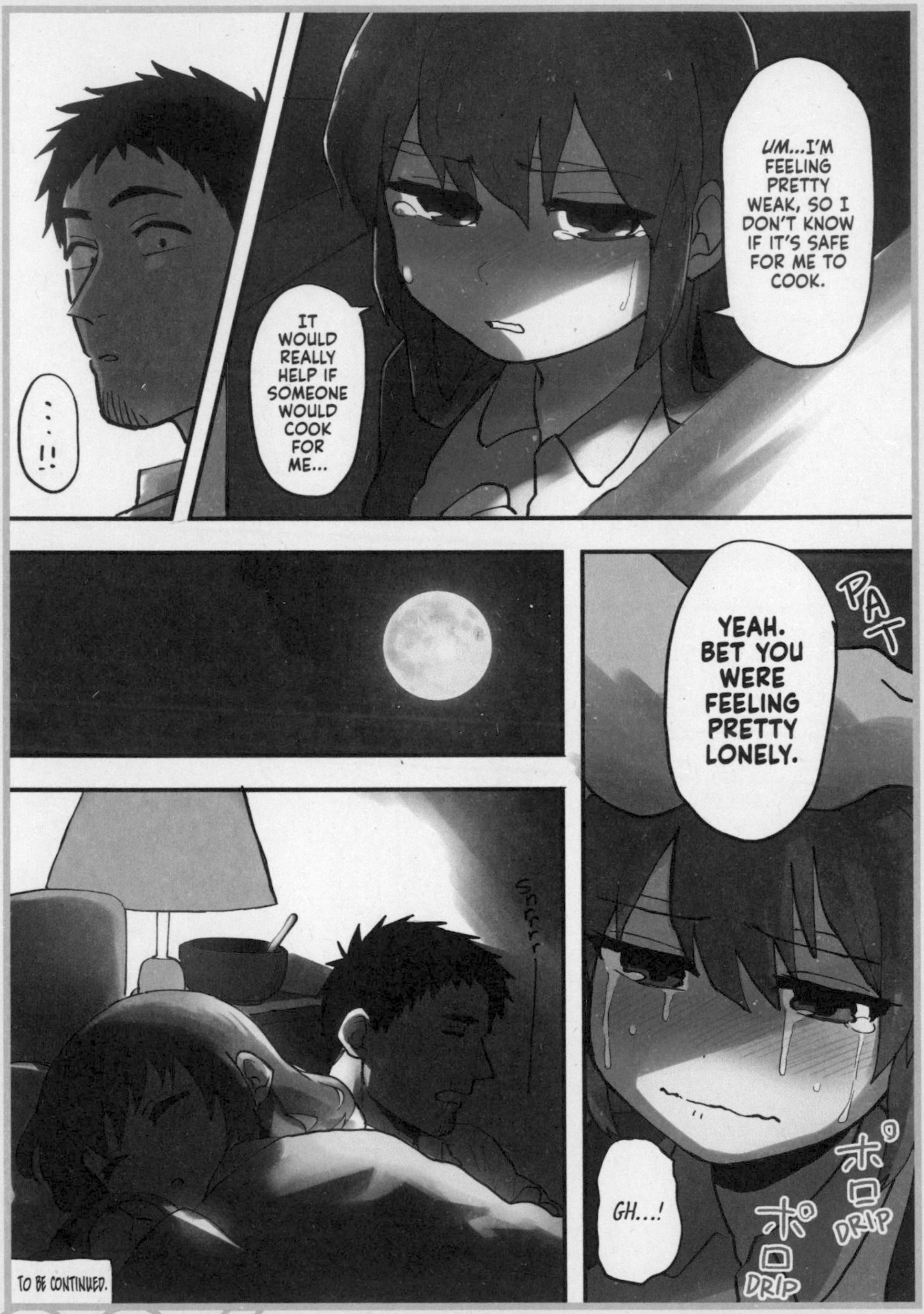
UM...I'M FEELING PRETTY WEAK, SO I DON'T KNOW IF IT'S SAFE FOR ME TO COOK.
IT WOULD REALLY HELP IF SOMEONE WOULD COOK FOR ME...
...!!
PAK
YEAH. BET YOU WERE FEELING PRETTY LONELY.
GH...!
ポロ DRIP
ポロ DRIP
TO BE CONTINUED.

Chapter 8

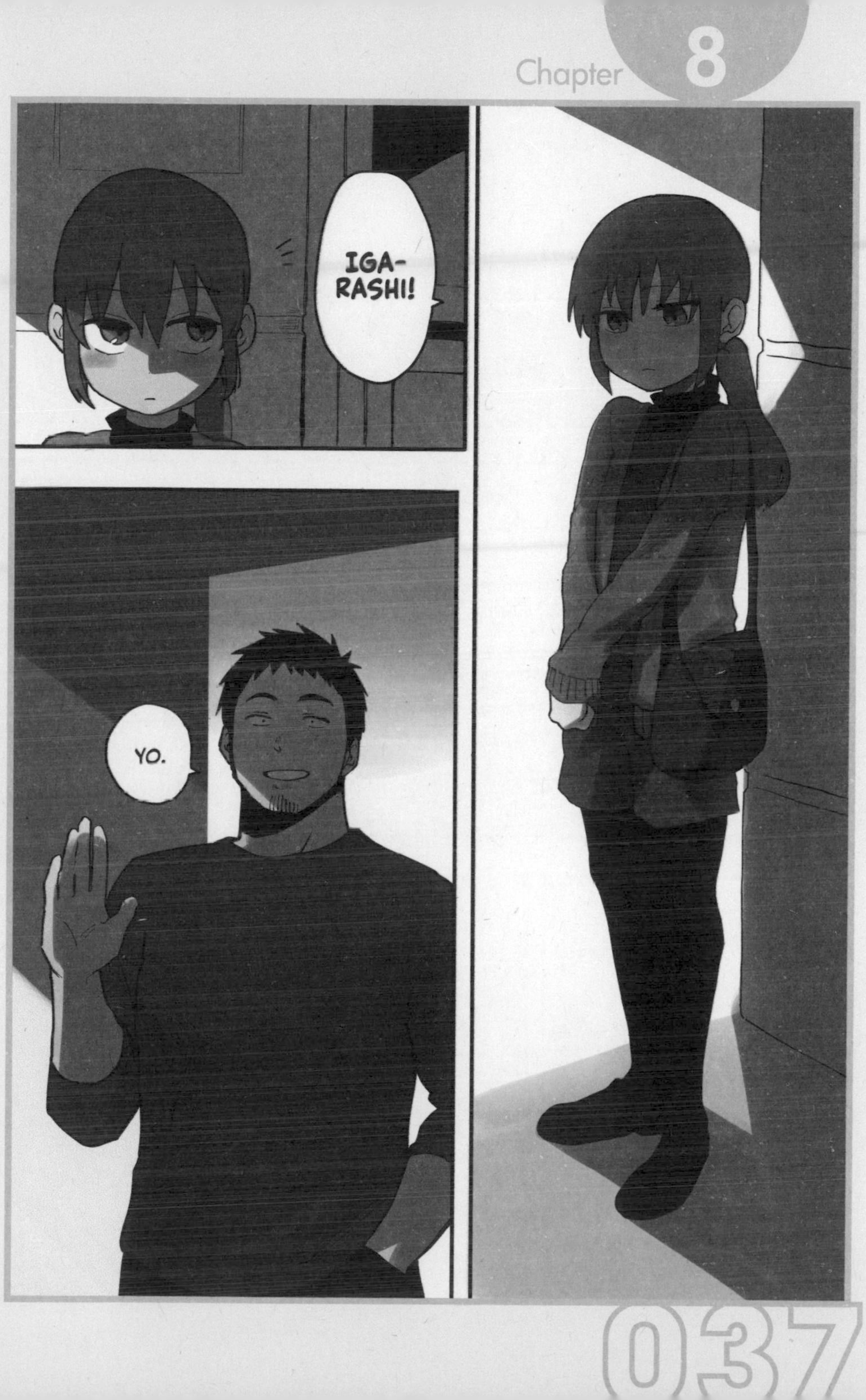
IGA-RASHI!
YO.

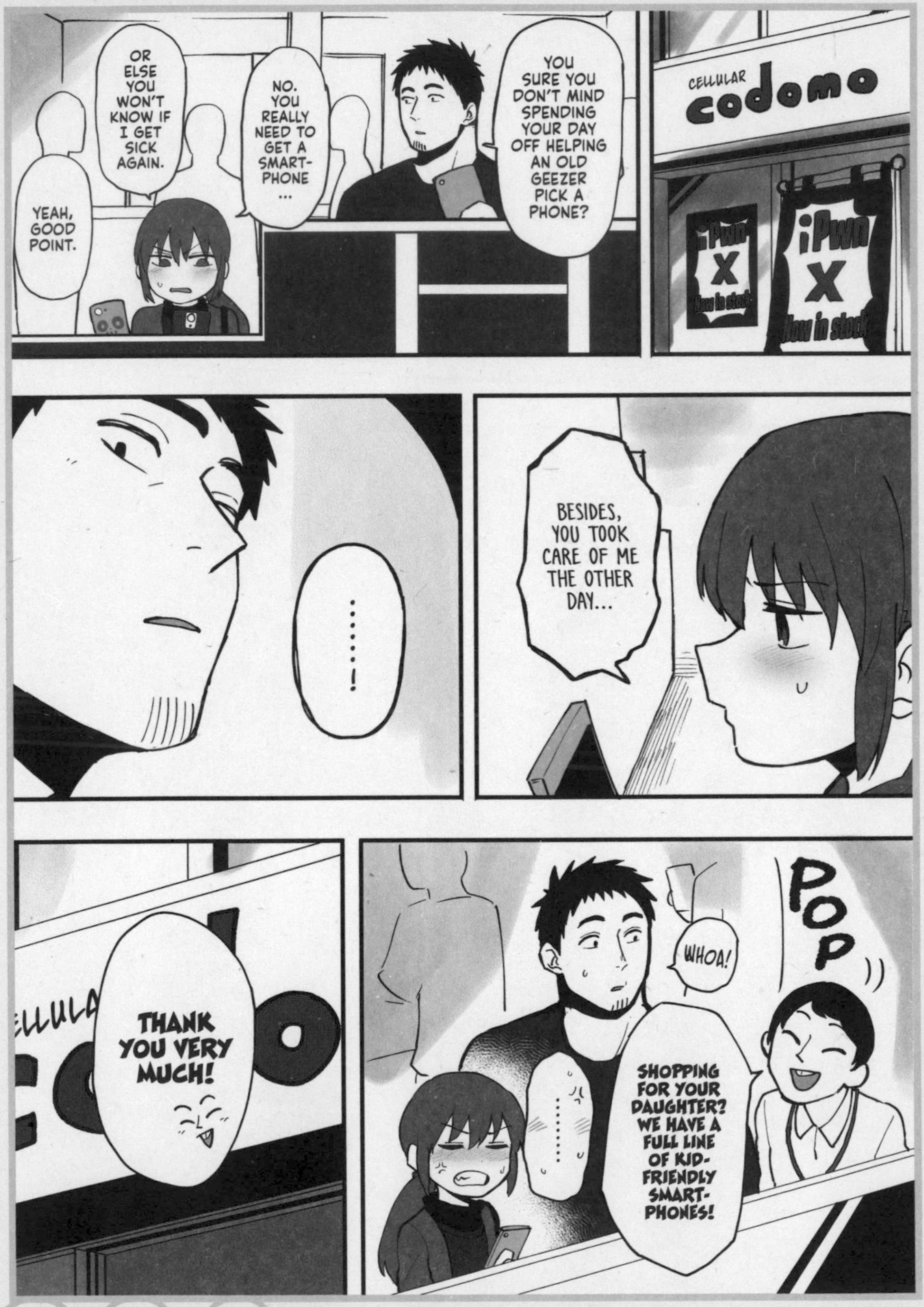
CELLULAR codomo
iPwn X Now in stock
iPwn X Now in stock
YOU SURE YOU DON'T MIND SPENDING YOUR DAY OFF HELPING AN OLD GEEZER PICK A PHONE?
NO. YOU REALLY NEED TO GET A SMART-PHONE ...
OR ELSE YOU WON'T KNOW IF I GET SICK AGAIN.
YEAH, GOOD POINT.
BESIDES, YOU TOOK CARE OF ME THE OTHER DAY...
......!
POP
WHOA!
SHOPPING FOR YOUR DAUGHTER? WE HAVE A FULL LINE OF KID-FRIENDLY SMART-PHONES!
......
CELLULA
THANK YOU VERY MUCH!

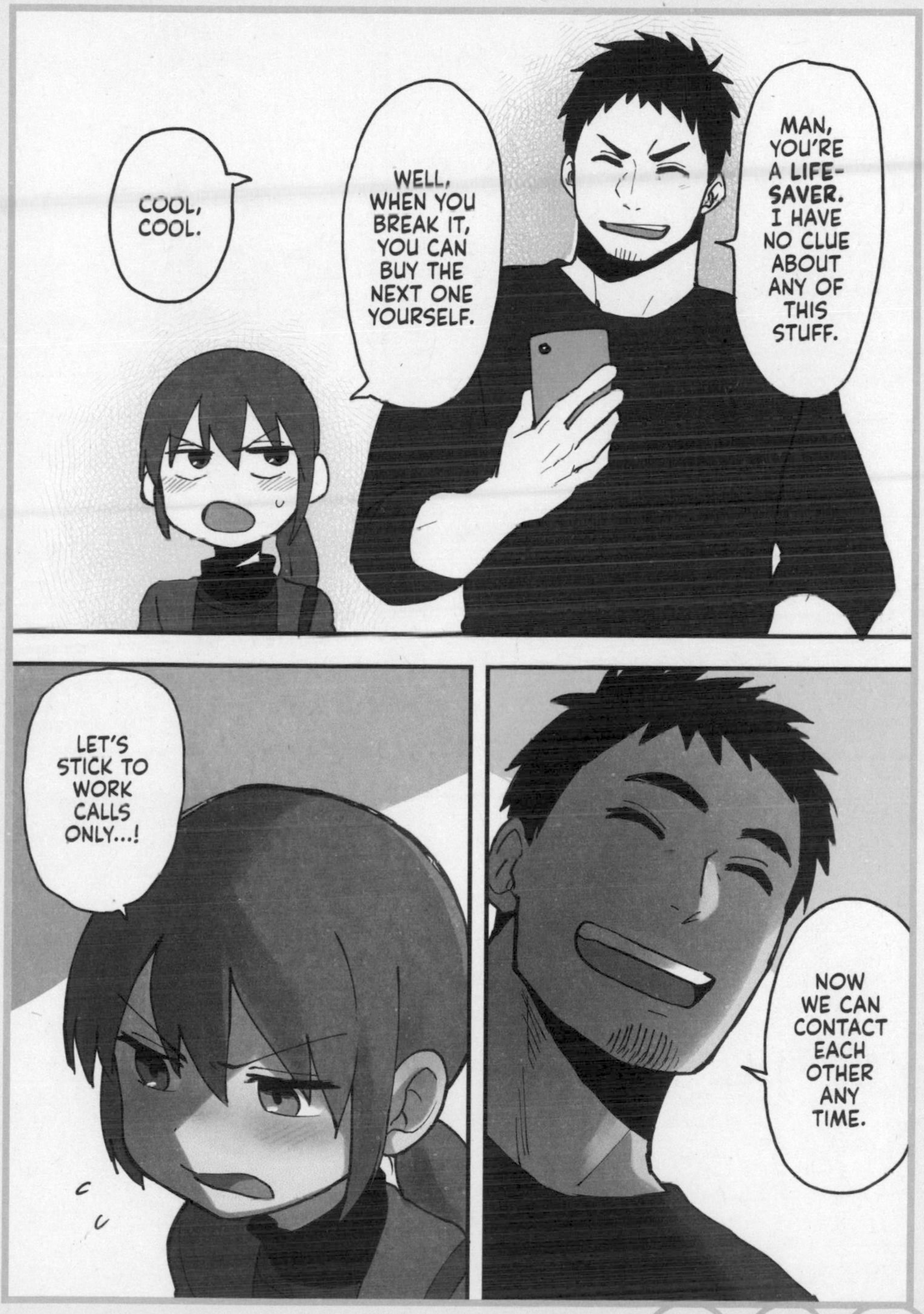
MAN, YOU'RE A LIFE-SAVER. I HAVE NO CLUE ABOUT ANY OF THIS STUFF.
WELL, WHEN YOU BREAK IT, YOU CAN BUY THE NEXT ONE YOURSELF.
COOL, COOL.
NOW WE CAN CONTACT EACH OTHER ANY TIME.
LET'S STICK TO WORK CALLS ONLY...!

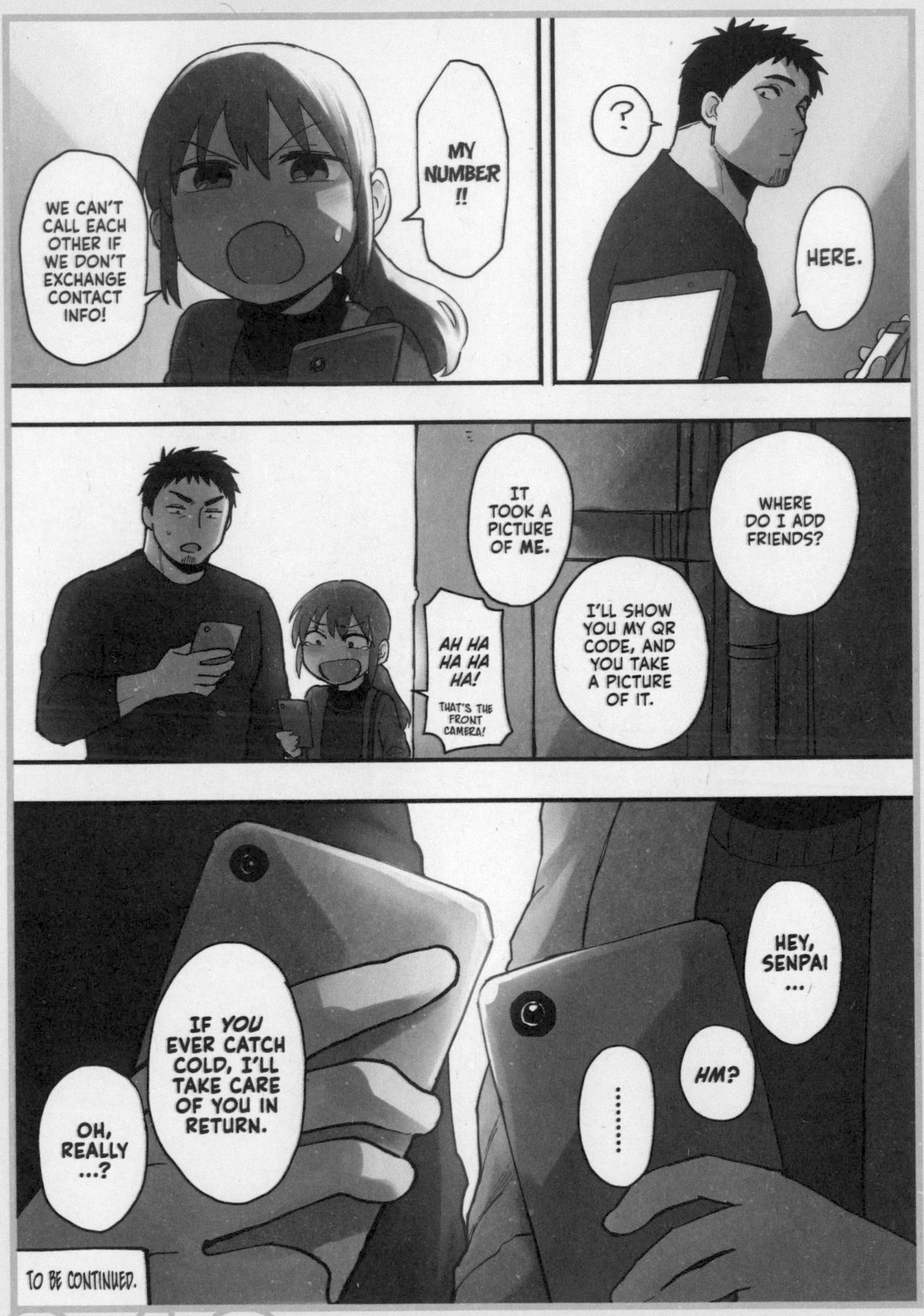
?
HERE.
MY NUMBER !!
WE CAN'T CALL EACH OTHER IF WE DON'T EXCHANGE CONTACT INFO!
WHERE DO I ADD FRIENDS?
I'LL SHOW YOU MY QR CODE, AND YOU TAKE A PICTURE OF IT.
IT TOOK A PICTURE OF ME.
AH HA HA HA HA!
THAT'S THE FRONT CAMERA!
HEY, SENPAI ...
HM?
....
IF *YOU* EVER CATCH COLD, I'LL TAKE CARE OF YOU IN RETURN.
OH, REALLY ...?
TO BE CONTINUED.

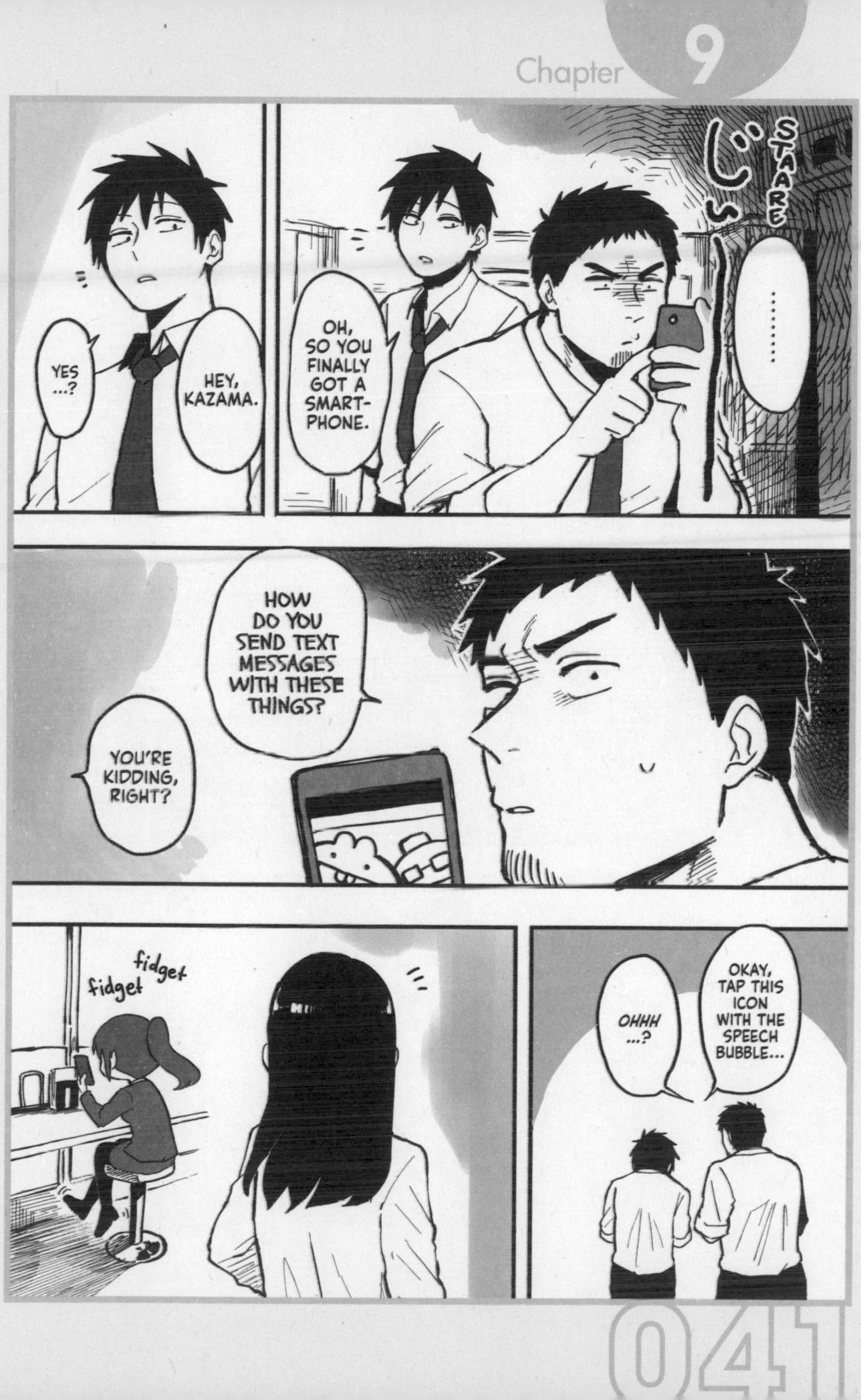
じぃ
STARE
....
OH, SO YOU FINALLY GOT A SMART-PHONE.
HEY, KAZAMA.
YES ...?
HOW DO YOU SEND TEXT MESSAGES WITH THESE THINGS?
YOU'RE KIDDING, RIGHT?
OKAY, TAP THIS ICON WITH THE SPEECH BUBBLE...
OHHH ...?
fidget
fidget

ANNOYING

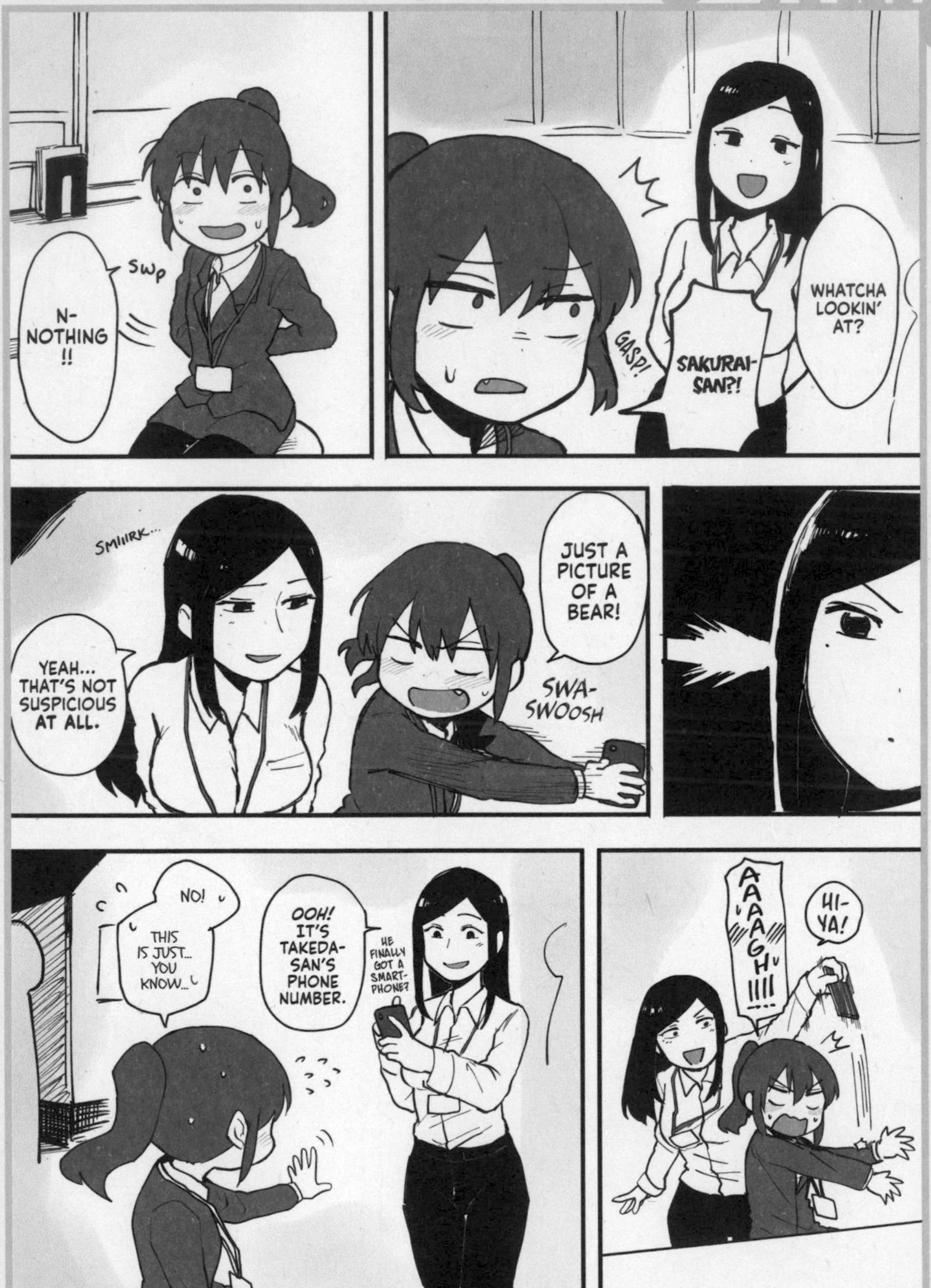

WHATCHA LOOKIN' AT?
GASP!
SAKURAI-SAN?!
SWP
N-NOTHING !!
JUST A PICTURE OF A BEAR!
SWA-SWOOSH
SMIIIRK...
YEAH... THAT'S NOT SUSPICIOUS AT ALL.
HI-YA!
AAAAGH!!!!!
OOH! IT'S TAKEDA-SAN'S PHONE NUMBER.
HE FINALLY GOT A SMART-PHONE?
NO!
THIS IS JUST... YOU KNOW...

042

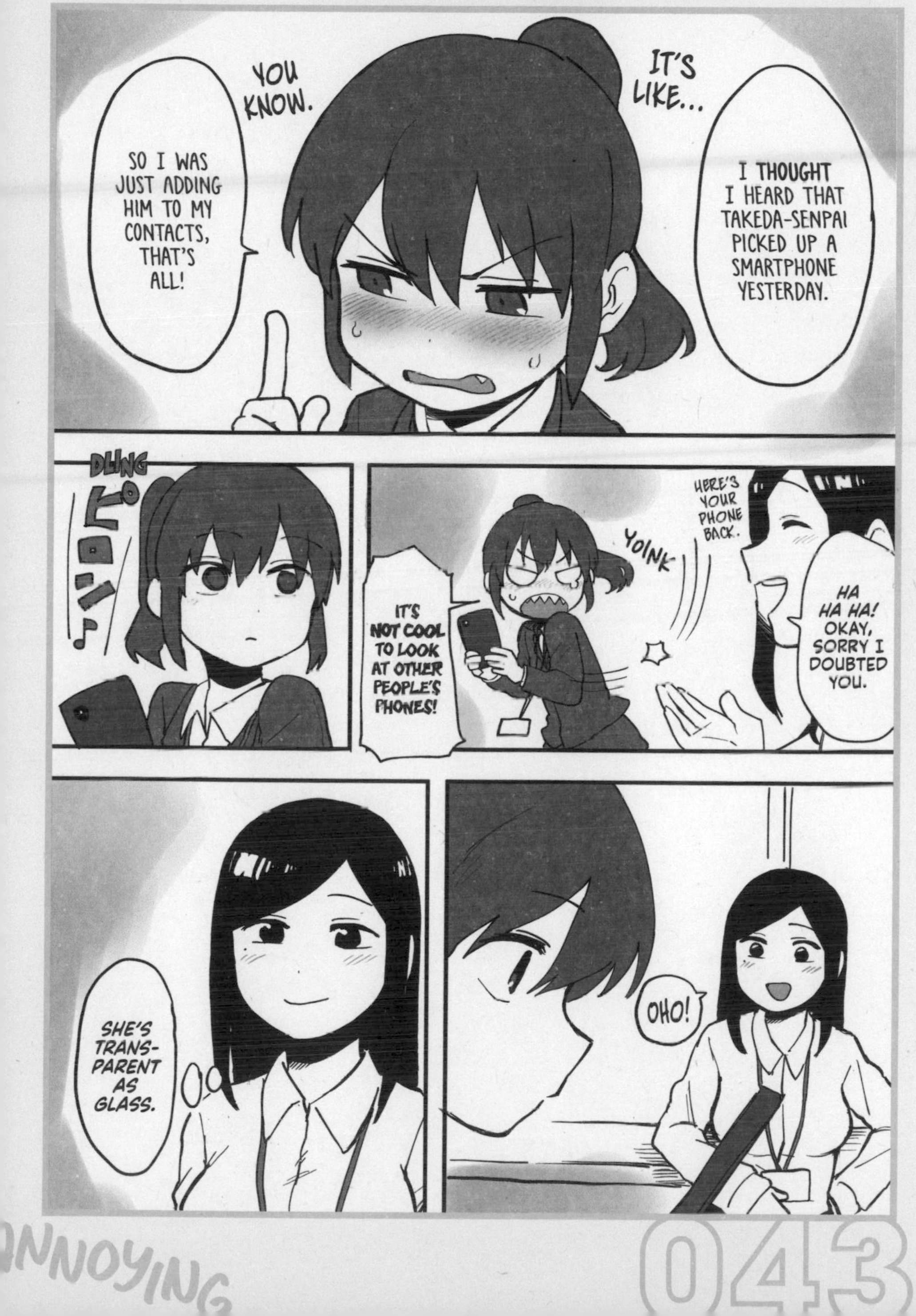
IT'S LIKE...
I THOUGHT I HEARD THAT TAKEDA-SENPAI PICKED UP A SMARTPHONE YESTERDAY.
YOU KNOW.
SO I WAS JUST ADDING HIM TO MY CONTACTS, THAT'S ALL!
HERE'S YOUR PHONE BACK.
HA HA HA! OKAY, SORRY I DOUBTED YOU.
YOINK
IT'S NOT COOL TO LOOK AT OTHER PEOPLE'S PHONES!
DLING
OHO!
SHE'S TRANS-PARENT AS GLASS.

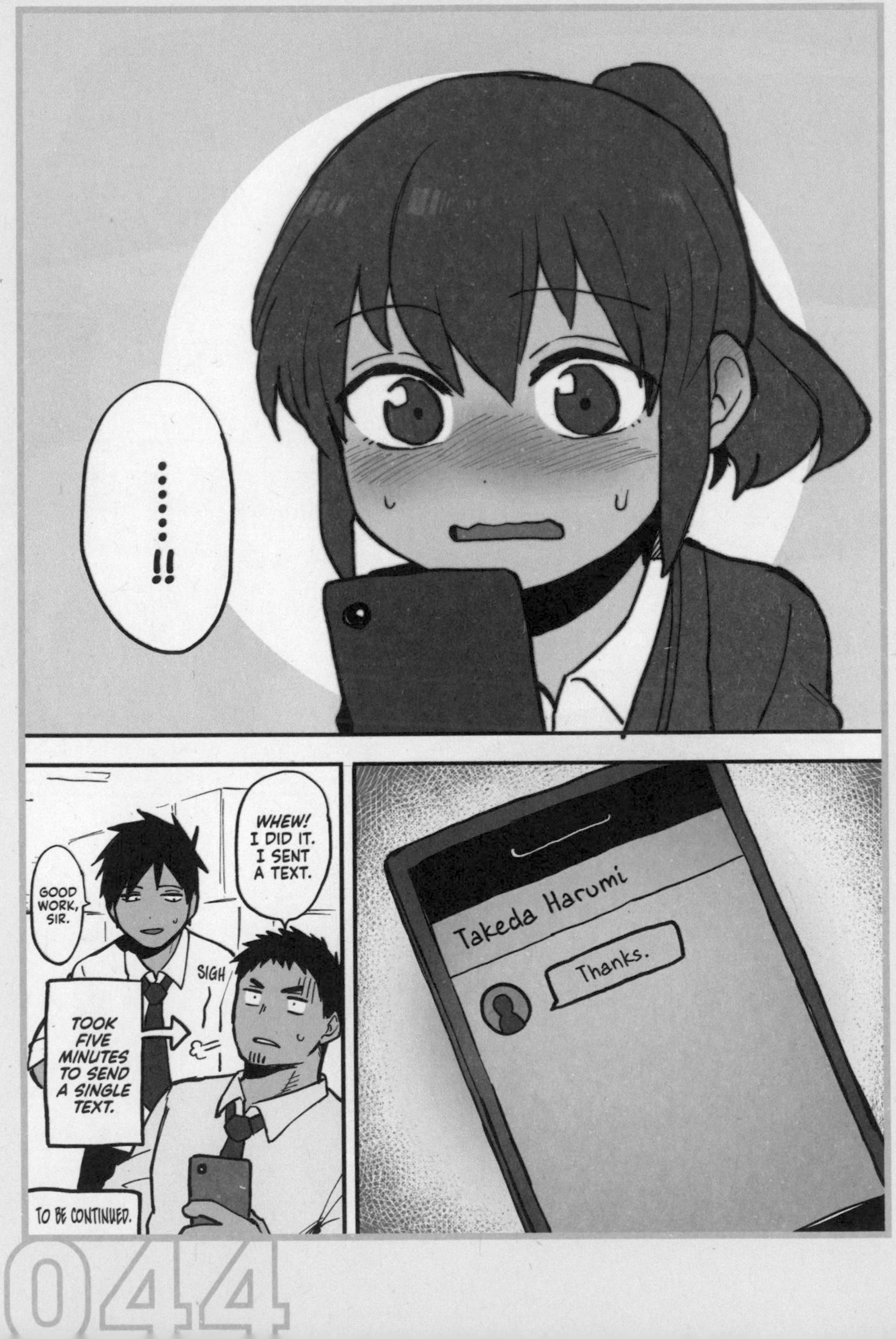
……!!
Takeda Harumi
Thanks.
WHEW! I DID IT. I SENT A TEXT.
GOOD WORK, SIR.
SIGH
TOOK FIVE MINUTES TO SEND A SINGLE TEXT.
TO BE CONTINUED.

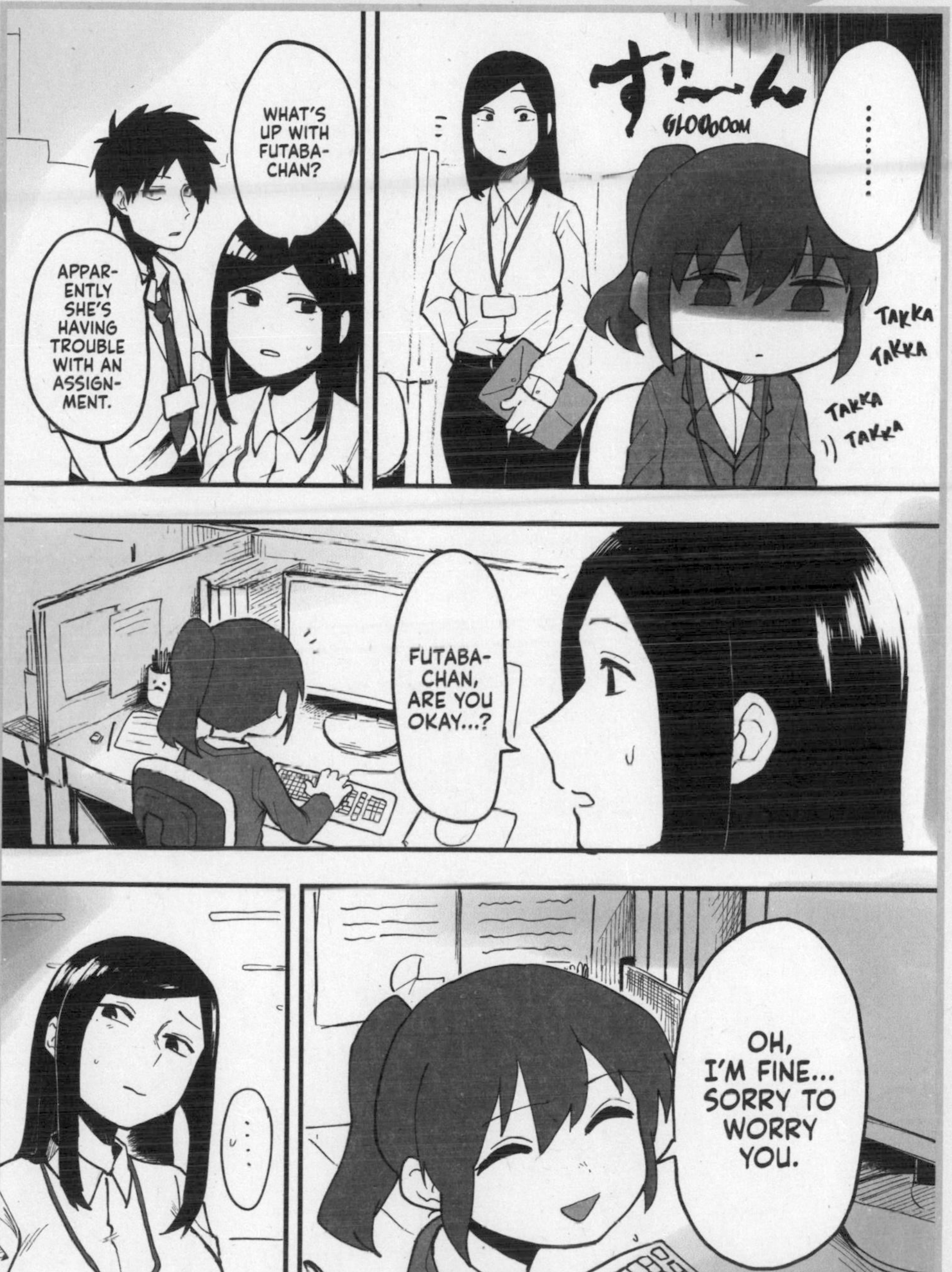
ず〜ん
GLOOOOOM
......
TAKKA
TAKKA
TAKKA
TAKKA
WHAT'S UP WITH FUTABA-CHAN?
APPARENTLY SHE'S HAVING TROUBLE WITH AN ASSIGNMENT.
FUTABA-CHAN, ARE YOU OKAY...?
OH, I'M FINE... SORRY TO WORRY YOU.
...

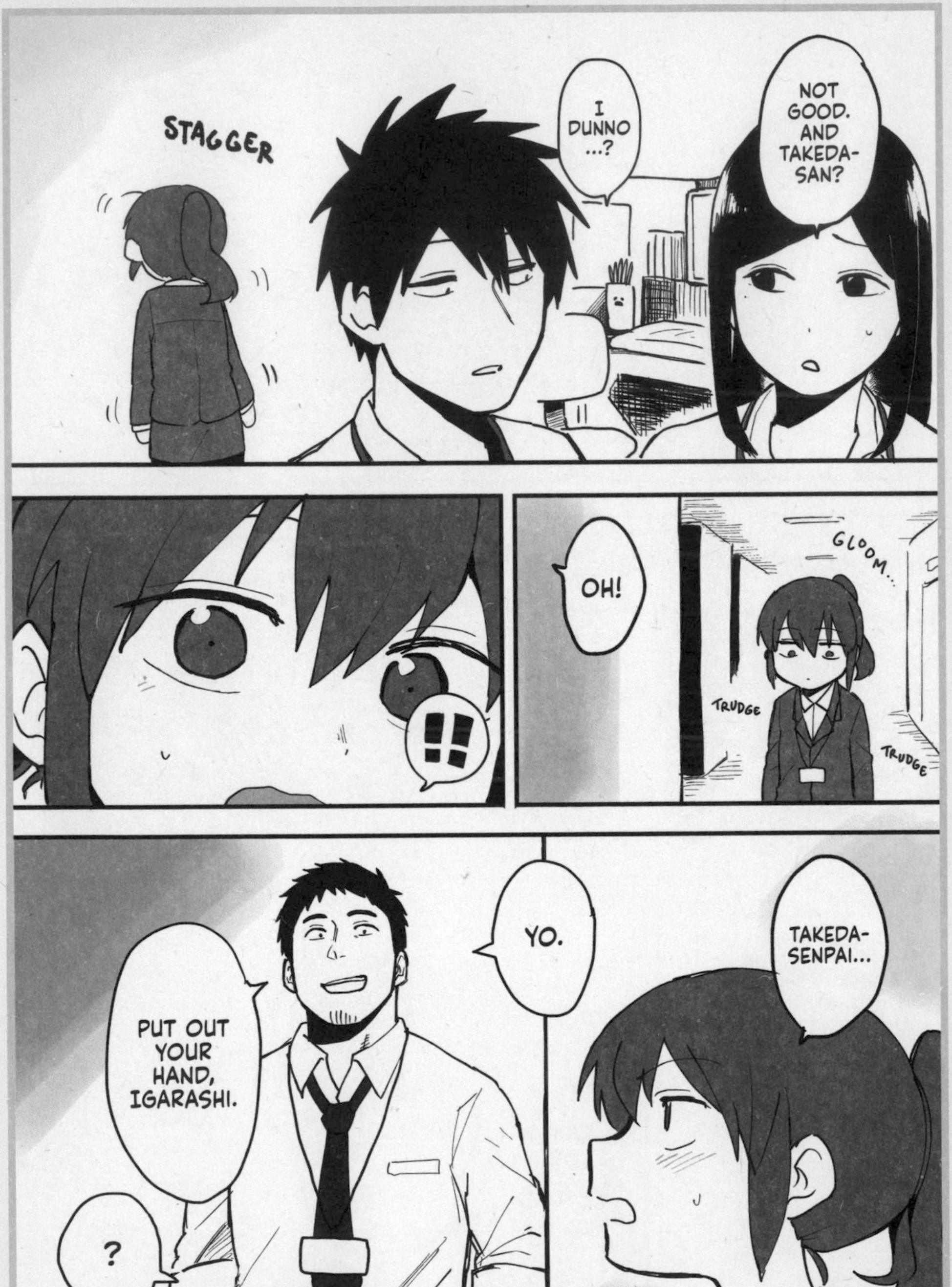
NOT GOOD. AND TAKEDA-SAN?
I DUNNO ...?
STAGGER
GLOOM...
OH!
TRUDGE
TRUDGE
!!
TAKEDA-SENPAI...
YO.
PUT OUT YOUR HAND, IGARASHI.
?

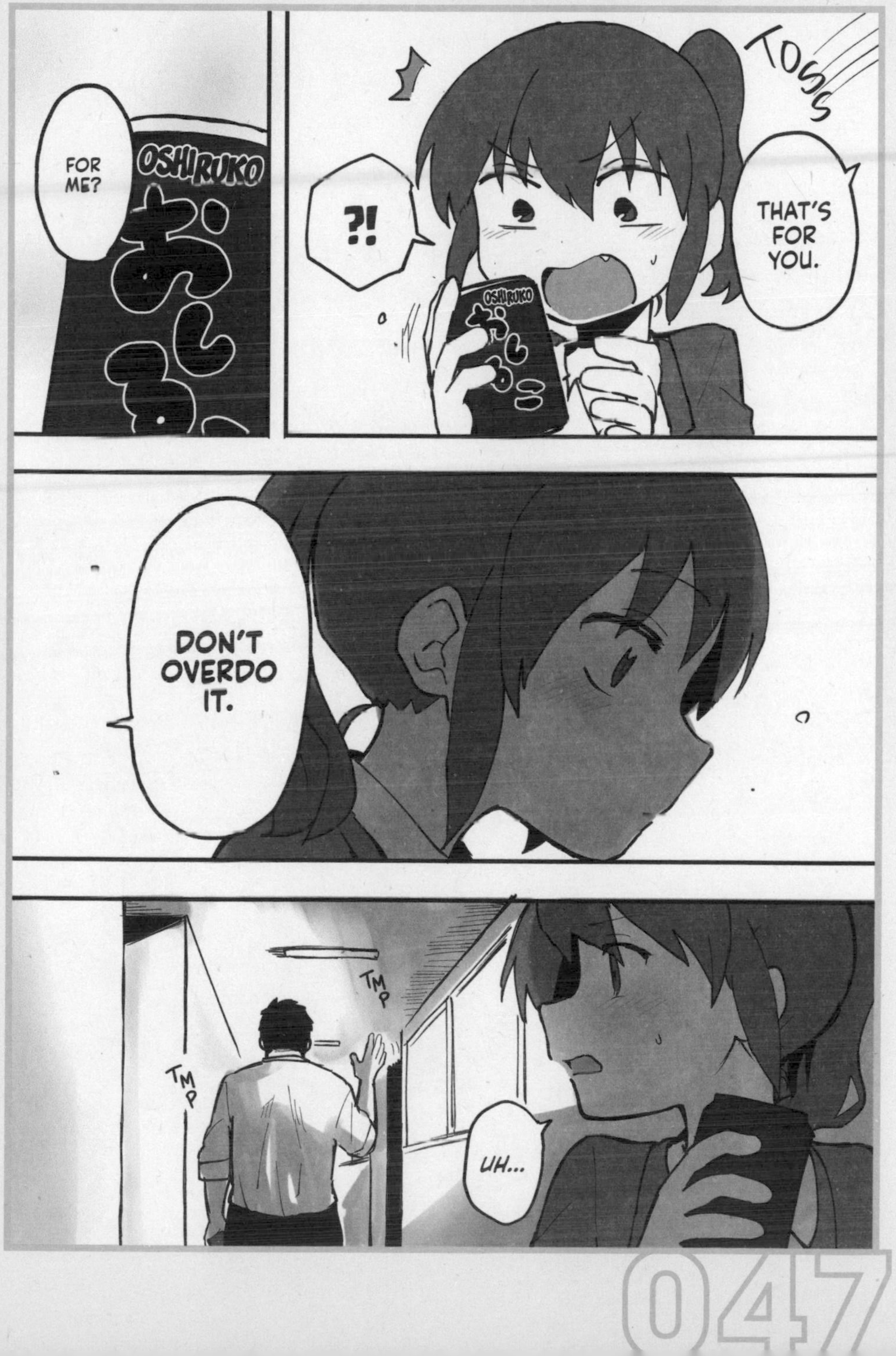
TOSS
THAT'S FOR YOU.
?!
OSHIRUKO
おしるこ
FOR ME?
OSHIRUKO
DON'T OVERDO IT.
TMP
TMP
UH...

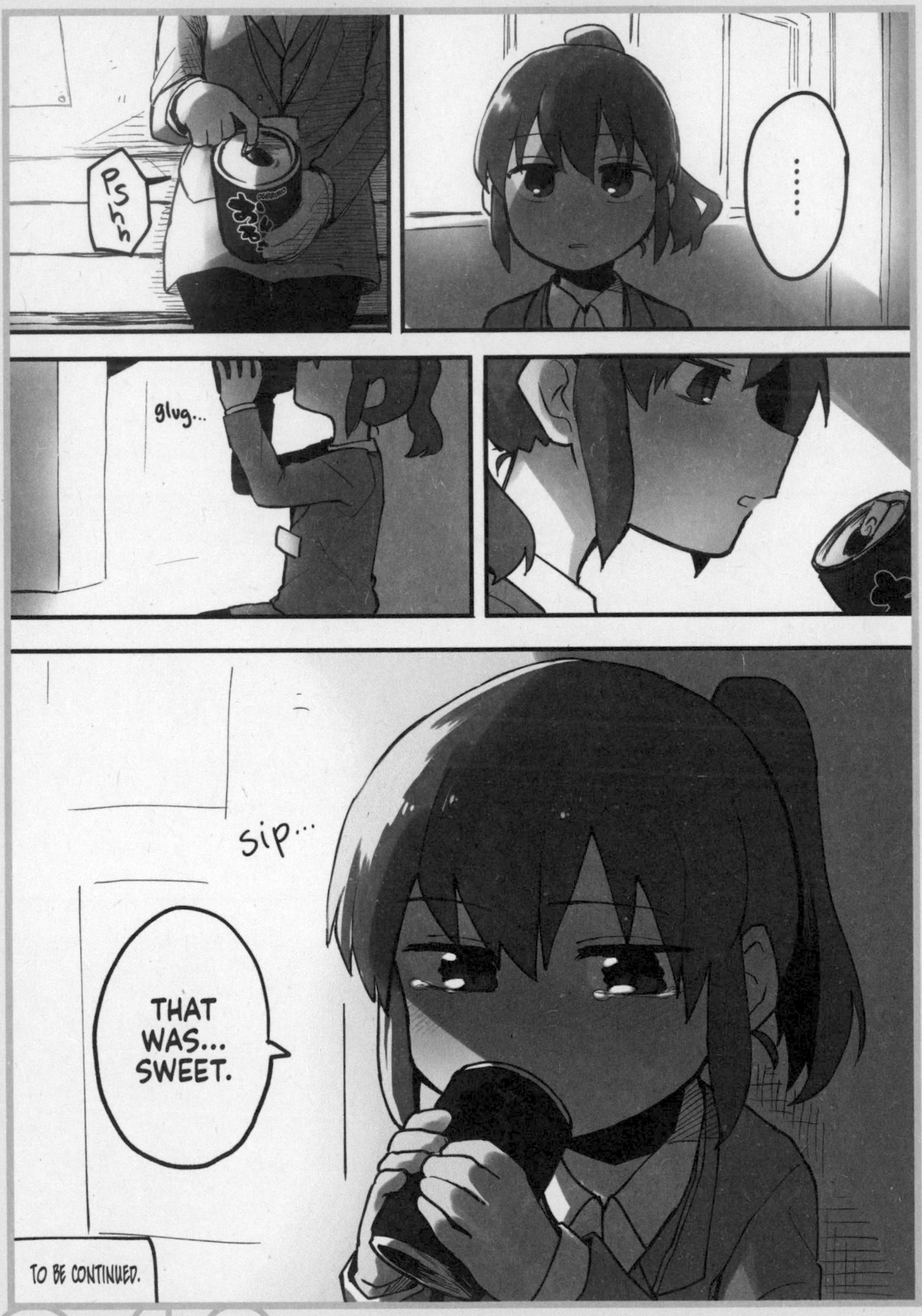

......
Pshh
glug...
sip...
THAT WAS... SWEET.
TO BE CONTINUED.

048

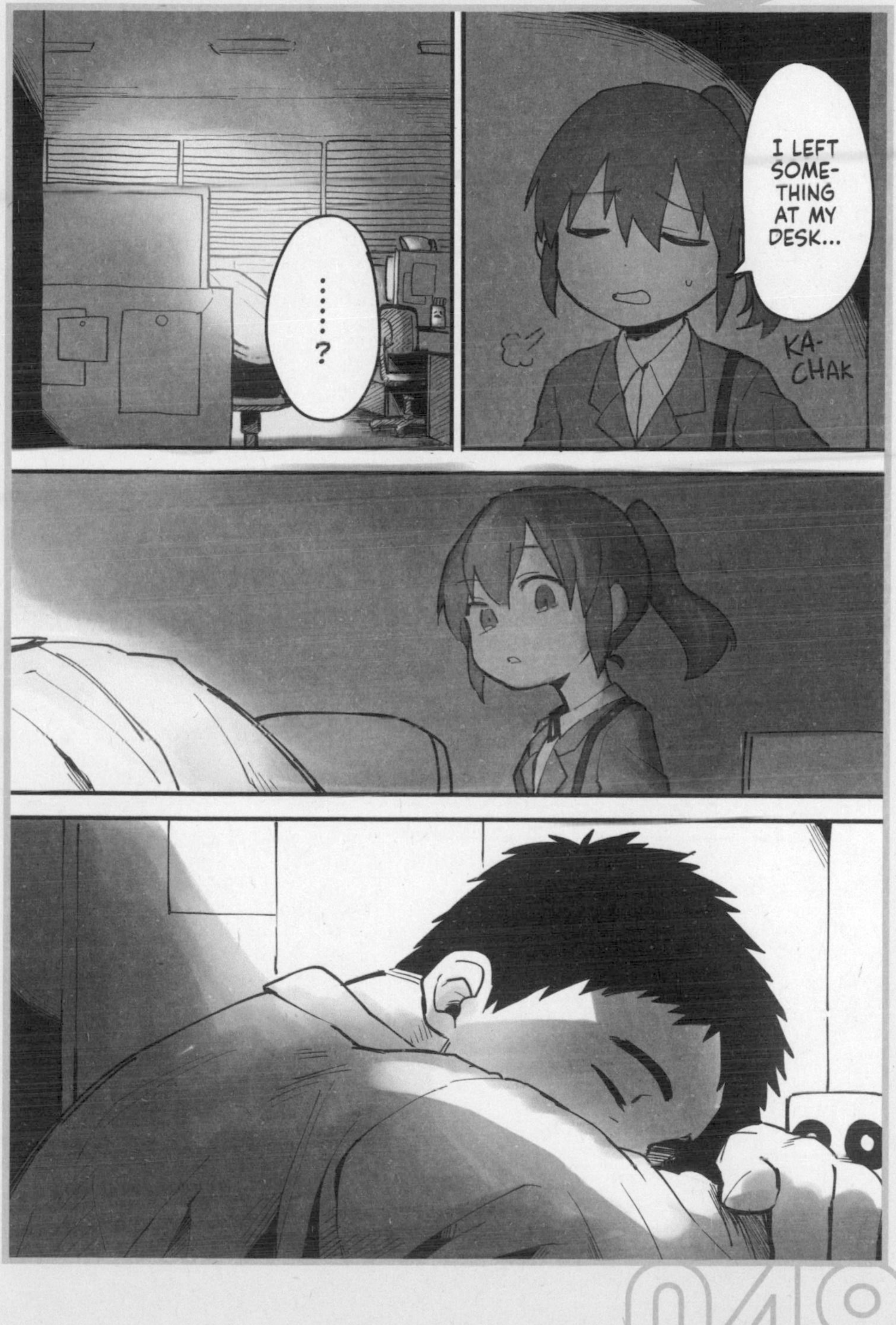
I LEFT SOMETHING AT MY DESK...
KA-CHAK
......?

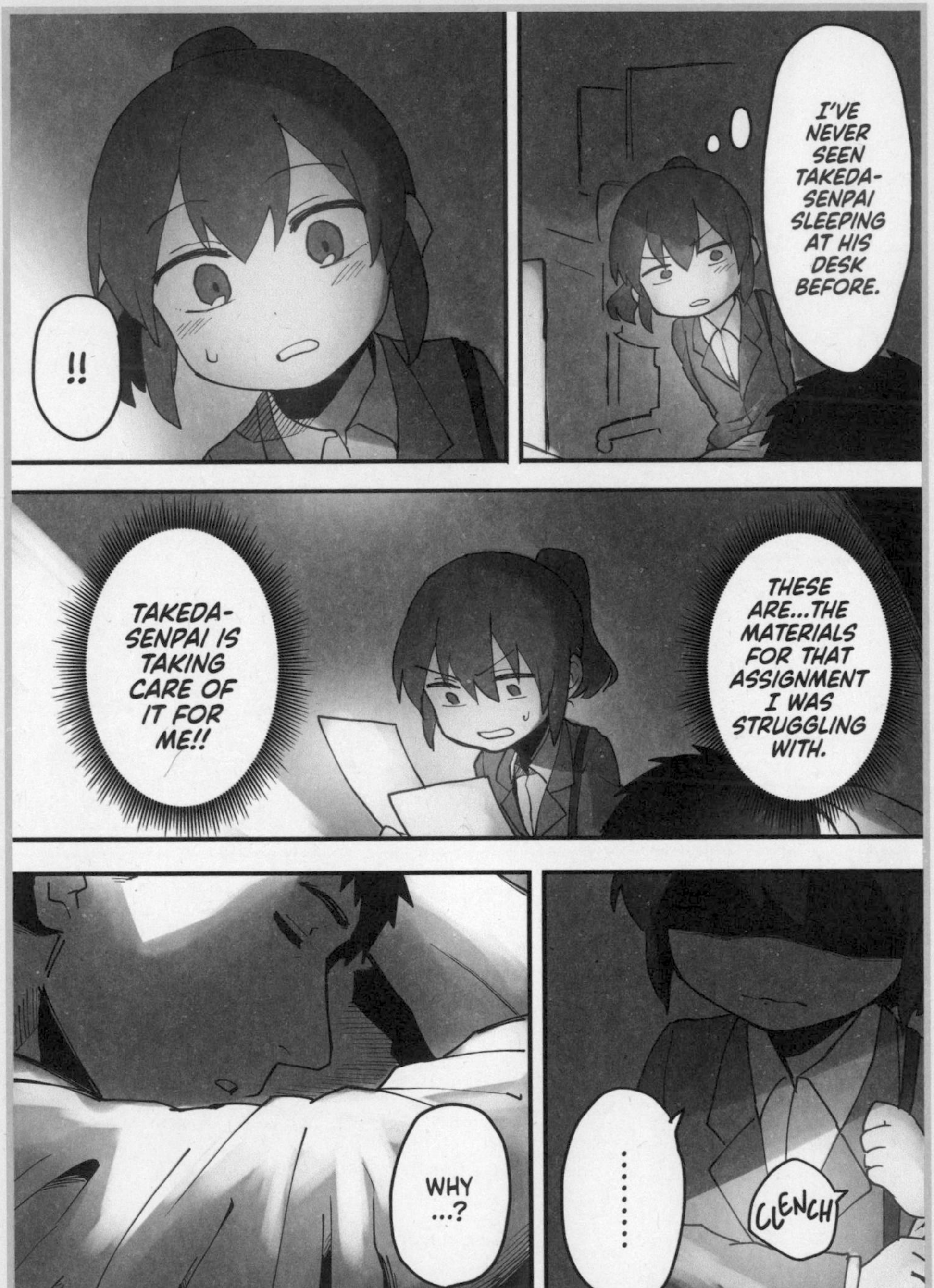
I'VE NEVER SEEN TAKEDA-SENPAI SLEEPING AT HIS DESK BEFORE.
!!
THESE ARE...THE MATERIALS FOR THAT ASSIGNMENT I WAS STRUGGLING WITH.
TAKEDA-SENPAI IS TAKING CARE OF IT FOR ME!!
......
CLENCH
WHY ...?

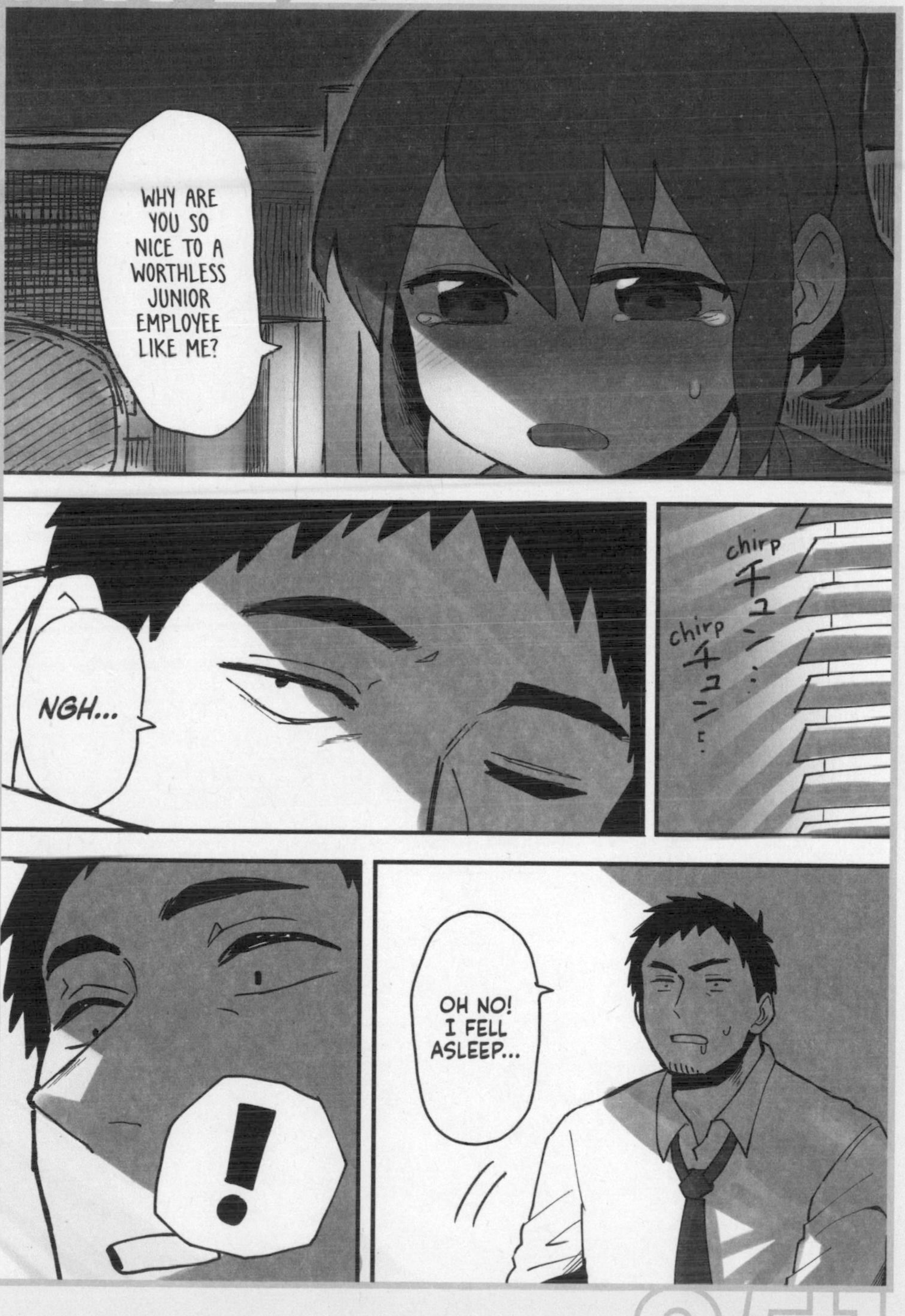
WHY ARE YOU SO NICE TO A WORTHLESS JUNIOR EMPLOYEE LIKE ME?
chirp
チュン…
chirp
チュン…
NGH...
OH NO! I FELL ASLEEP...
!

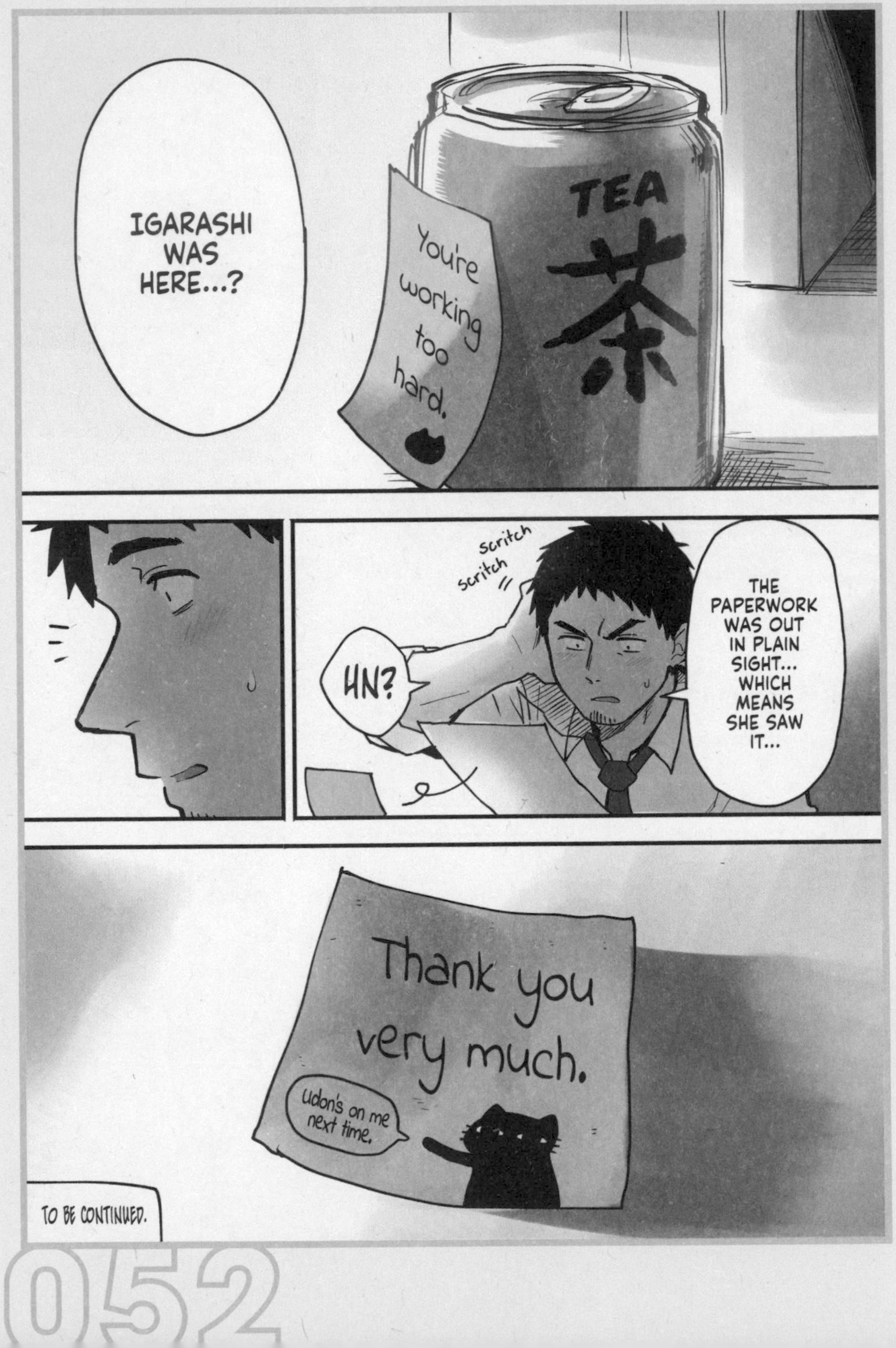
TEA
茶
You're working too hard.
IGARASHI WAS HERE...?
scritch scritch
THE PAPERWORK WAS OUT IN PLAIN SIGHT... WHICH MEANS SHE SAW IT...
HN?
Thank you very much.
udon's on me next time.
TO BE CONTINUED.

TEA
茶

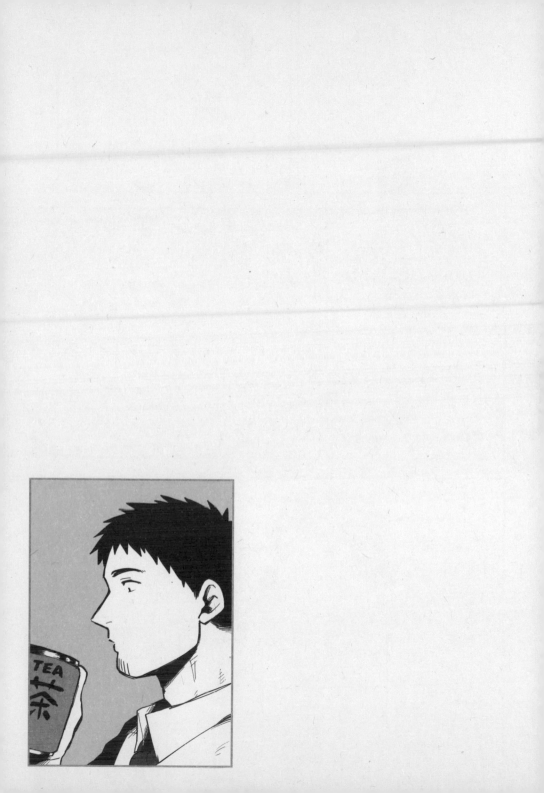

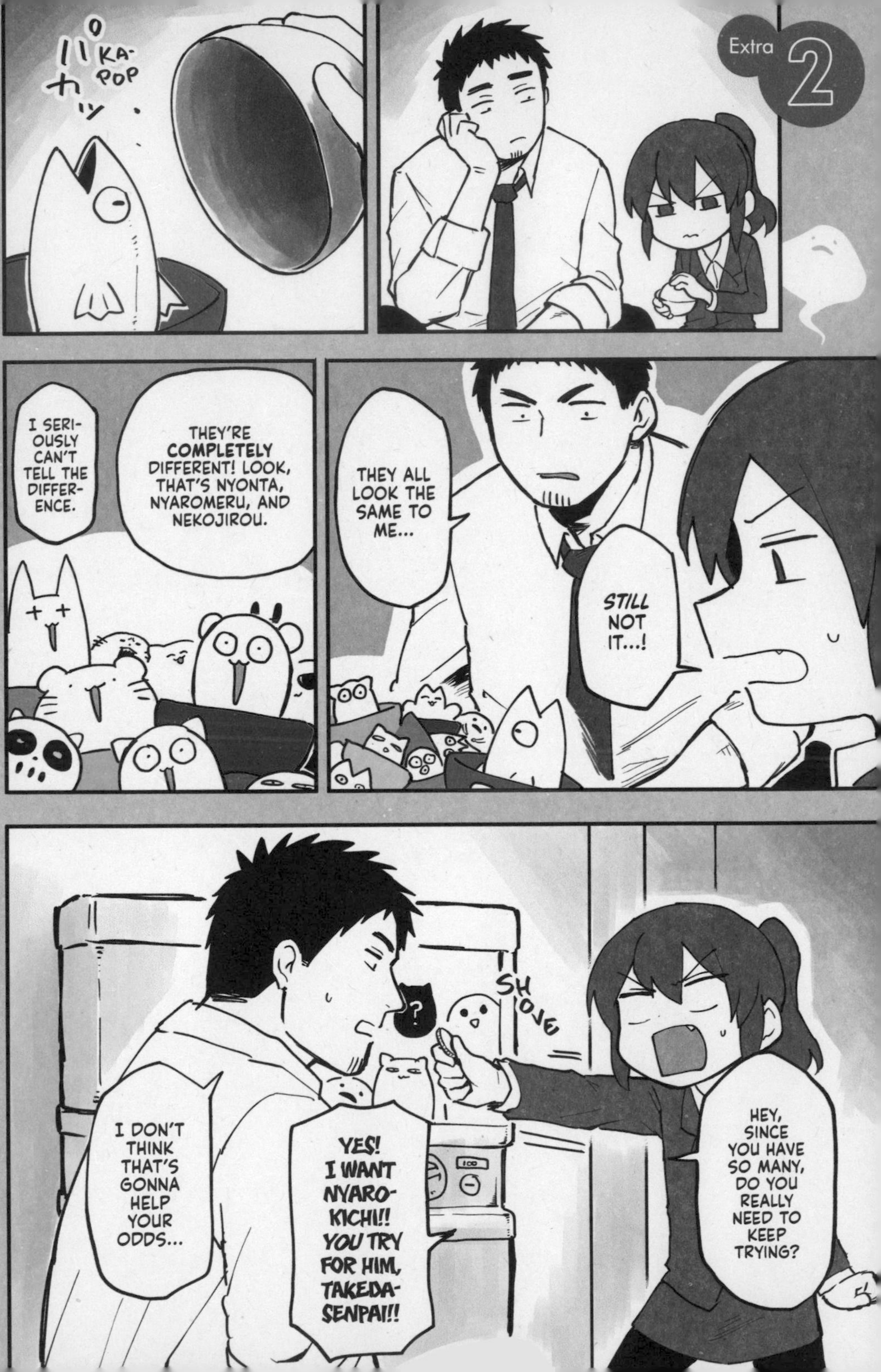
Extra 2
KA-POP
カッ
STILL NOT IT...!
THEY ALL LOOK THE SAME TO ME...
THEY'RE COMPLETELY DIFFERENT! LOOK, THAT'S NYONTA, NYAROMERU, AND NEKOJIROU.
I SERIOUSLY CAN'T TELL THE DIFFERENCE.
HEY, SINCE YOU HAVE SO MANY, DO YOU REALLY NEED TO KEEP TRYING?
SHOVE
YES! I WANT NYAROKICHI!! YOU TRY FOR HIM, TAKEDA-SENPAI!!
I DON'T THINK THAT'S GONNA HELP YOUR ODDS...

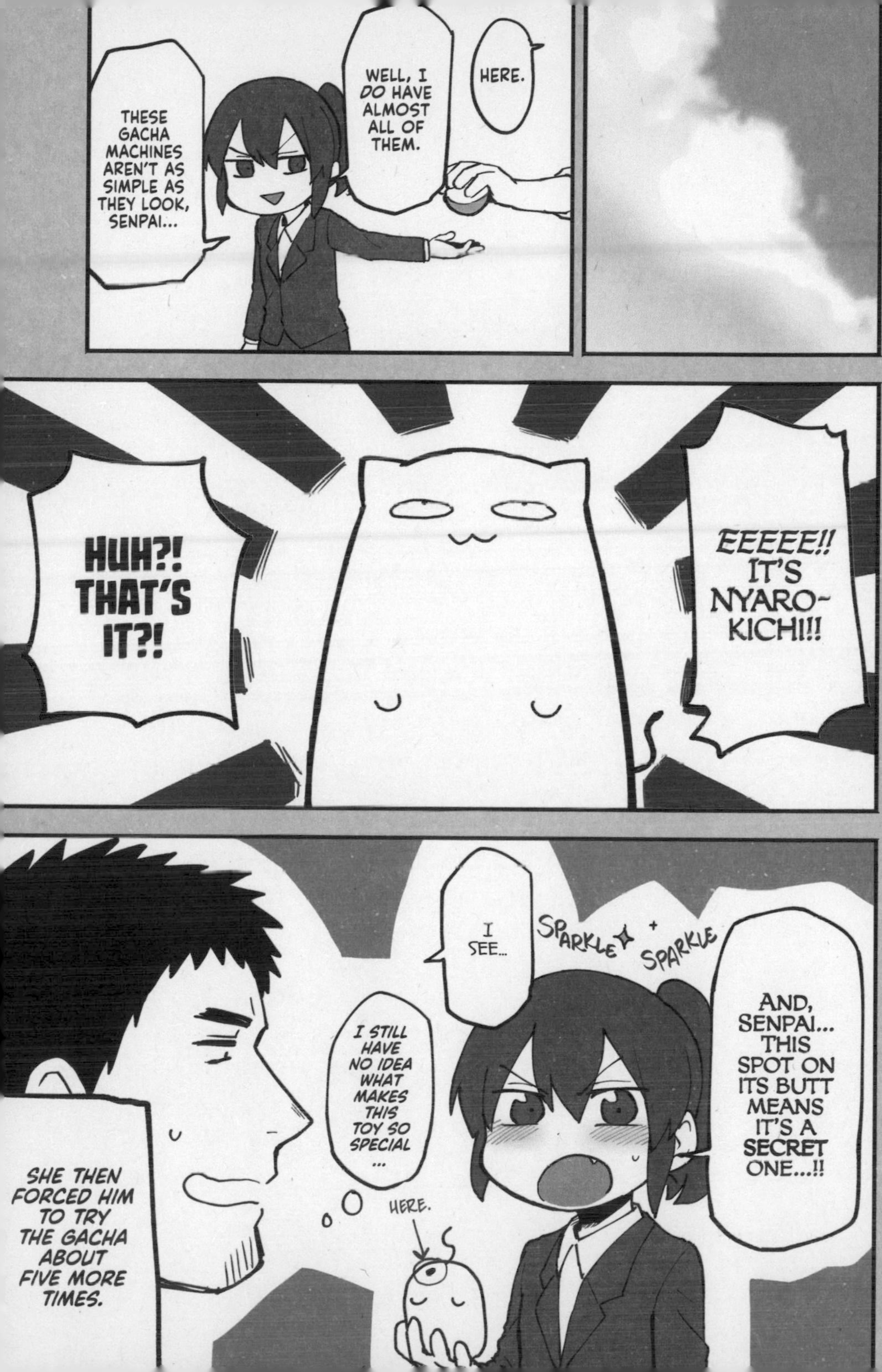
HERE.
WELL, I DO HAVE ALMOST ALL OF THEM.
THESE GACHA MACHINES AREN'T AS SIMPLE AS THEY LOOK, SENPAI...
EEEEE!! IT'S NYARO-KICHI!!!
HUH?! THAT'S IT?!
AND, SENPAI... THIS SPOT ON ITS BUTT MEANS IT'S A SECRET ONE...!!
SPARKLE SPARKLE
I SEE...
I STILL HAVE NO IDEA WHAT MAKES THIS TOY SO SPECIAL...
HERE.
SHE THEN FORCED HIM TO TRY THE GACHA ABOUT FIVE MORE TIMES.

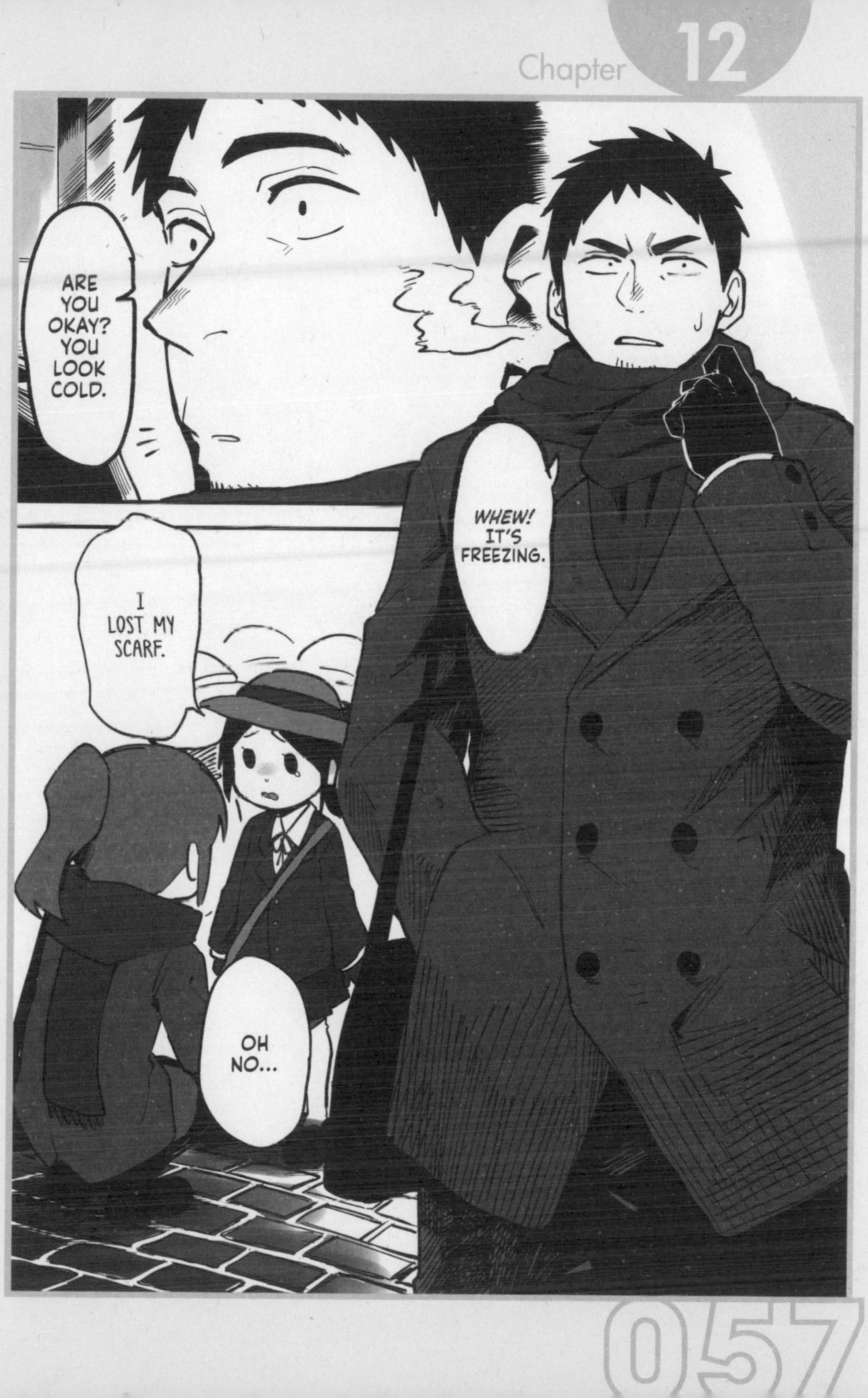
WHEW! IT'S FREEZING.
ARE YOU OKAY? YOU LOOK COLD.
I LOST MY SCARF.
OH NO...

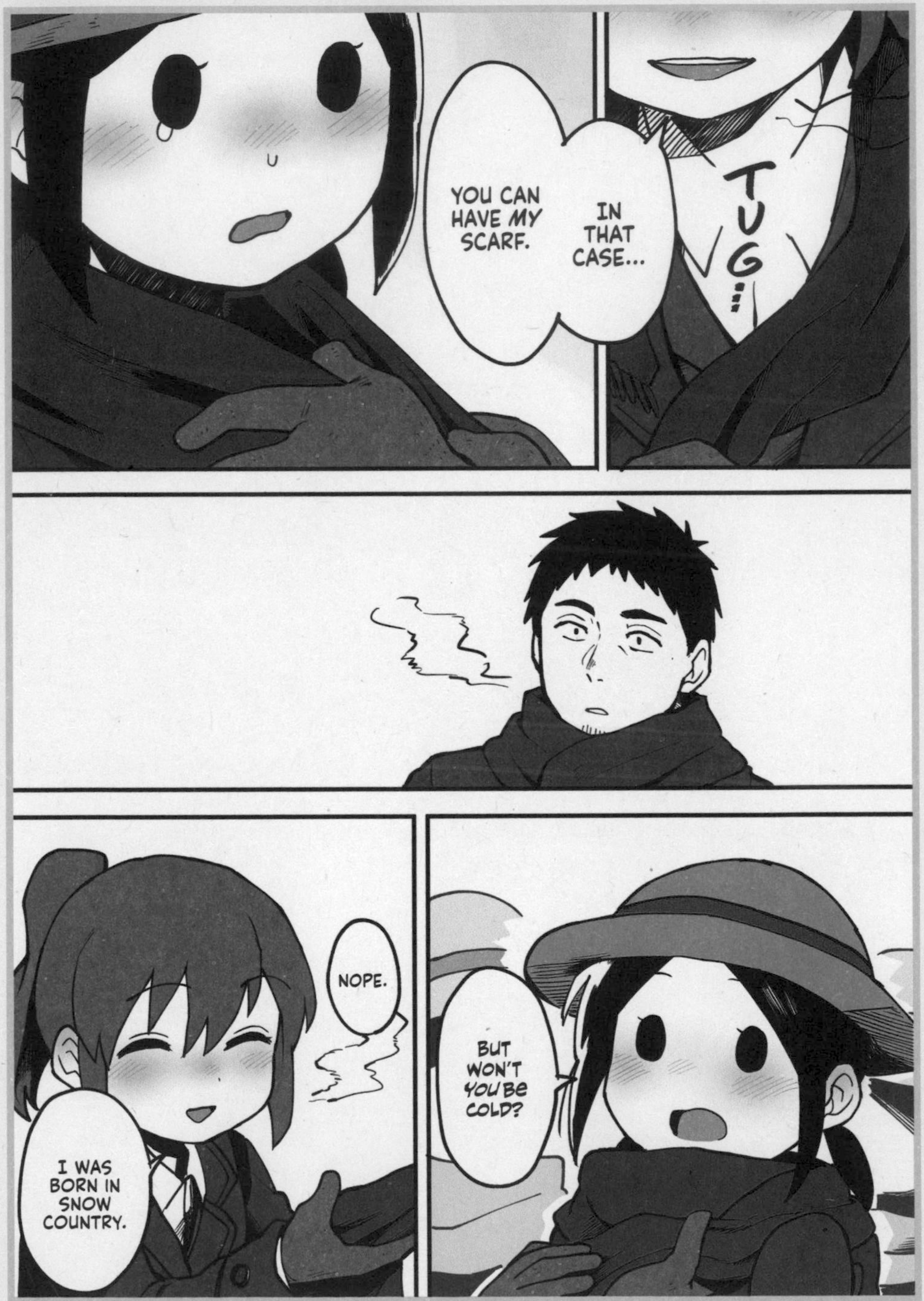
TUG...
IN THAT CASE...
YOU CAN HAVE MY SCARF.
BUT WON'T YOU BE COLD?
NOPE.
I WAS BORN IN SNOW COUNTRY.

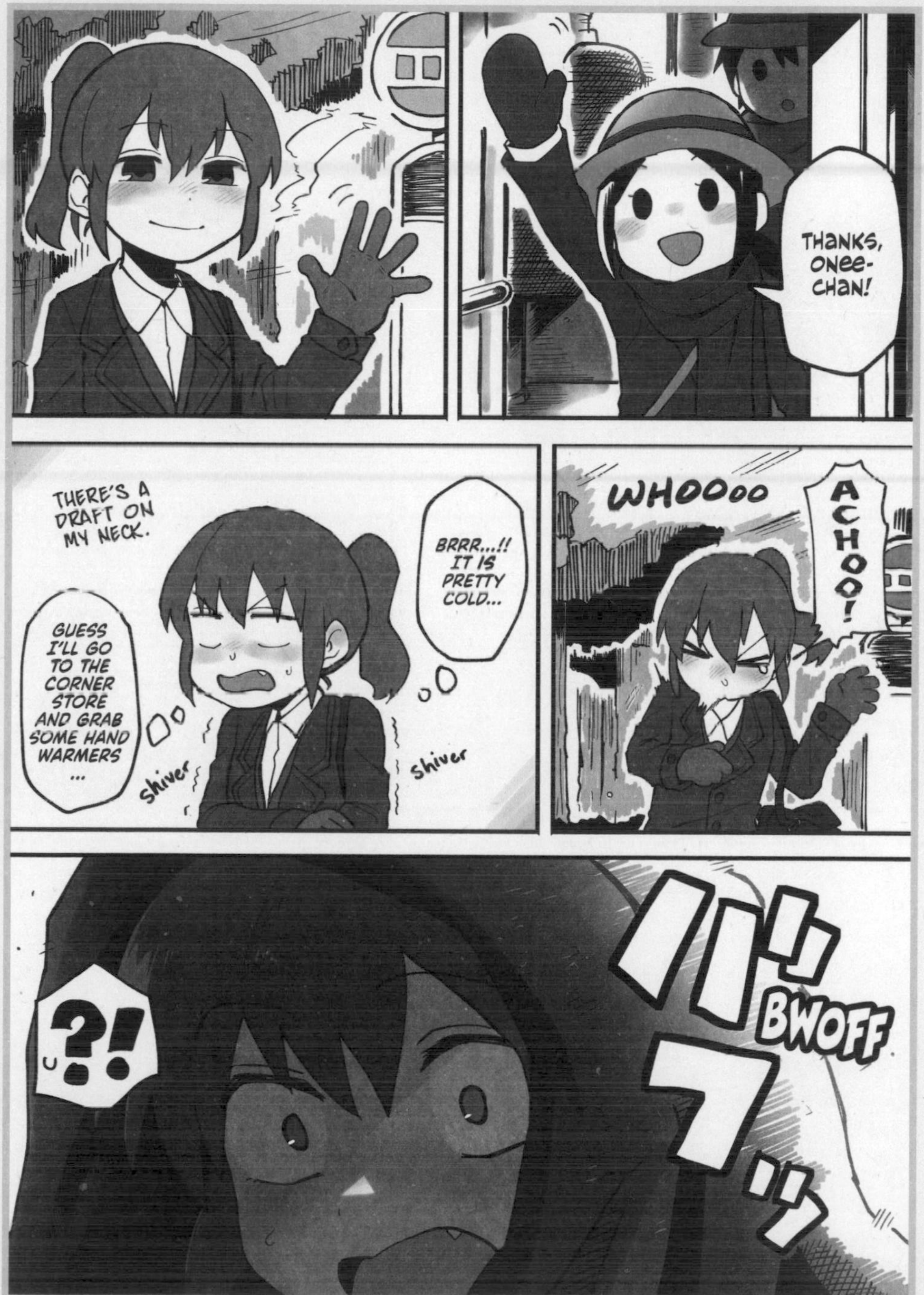
THANKS, ONEE-CHAN!
WHOOooo
ACHOO!
BRRR...!! IT IS PRETTY COLD...
THERE'S A DRAFT ON MY NECK.
GUESS I'LL GO TO THE CORNER STORE AND GRAB SOME HAND WARMERS ...
shiver
shiver
BWOFF
?!

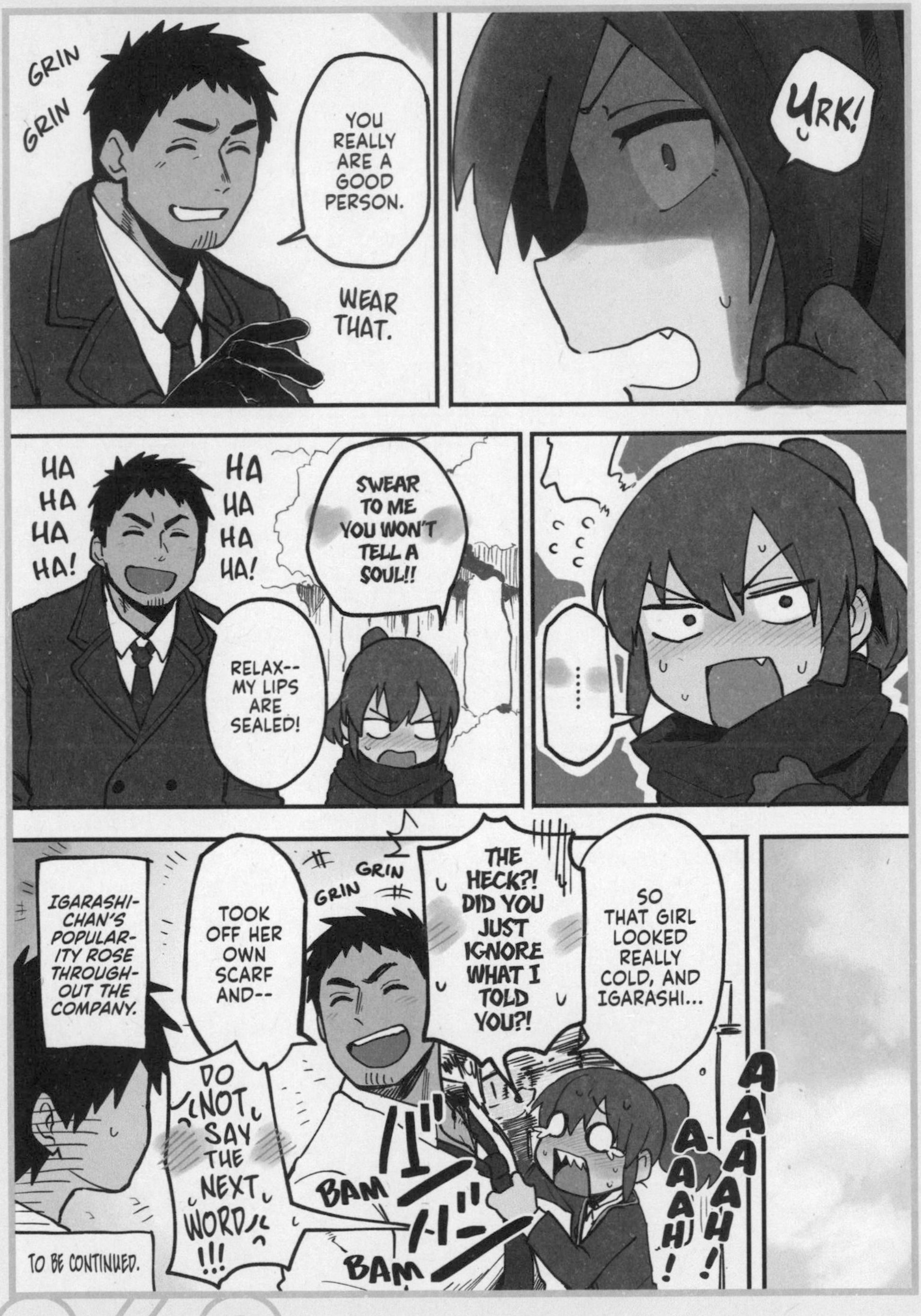
URK!
YOU REALLY ARE A GOOD PERSON.
GRIN GRIN
WEAR THAT.
......
SWEAR TO ME YOU WON'T TELL A SOUL!!
HA HA HA HA!
HA HA HA HA!
RELAX-- MY LIPS ARE SEALED!
AAAAH!
AAAAH!
SO THAT GIRL LOOKED REALLY COLD, AND IGARASHI...
THE HECK?! DID YOU JUST IGNORE WHAT I TOLD YOU?!
GRIN GRIN
TOOK OFF HER OWN SCARF AND--
IGARASHI-CHAN'S POPULAR-ITY ROSE THROUGH-OUT THE COMPANY.
BAM
BAM
DO NOT SAY THE NEXT WORD!!!
TO BE CONTINUED.

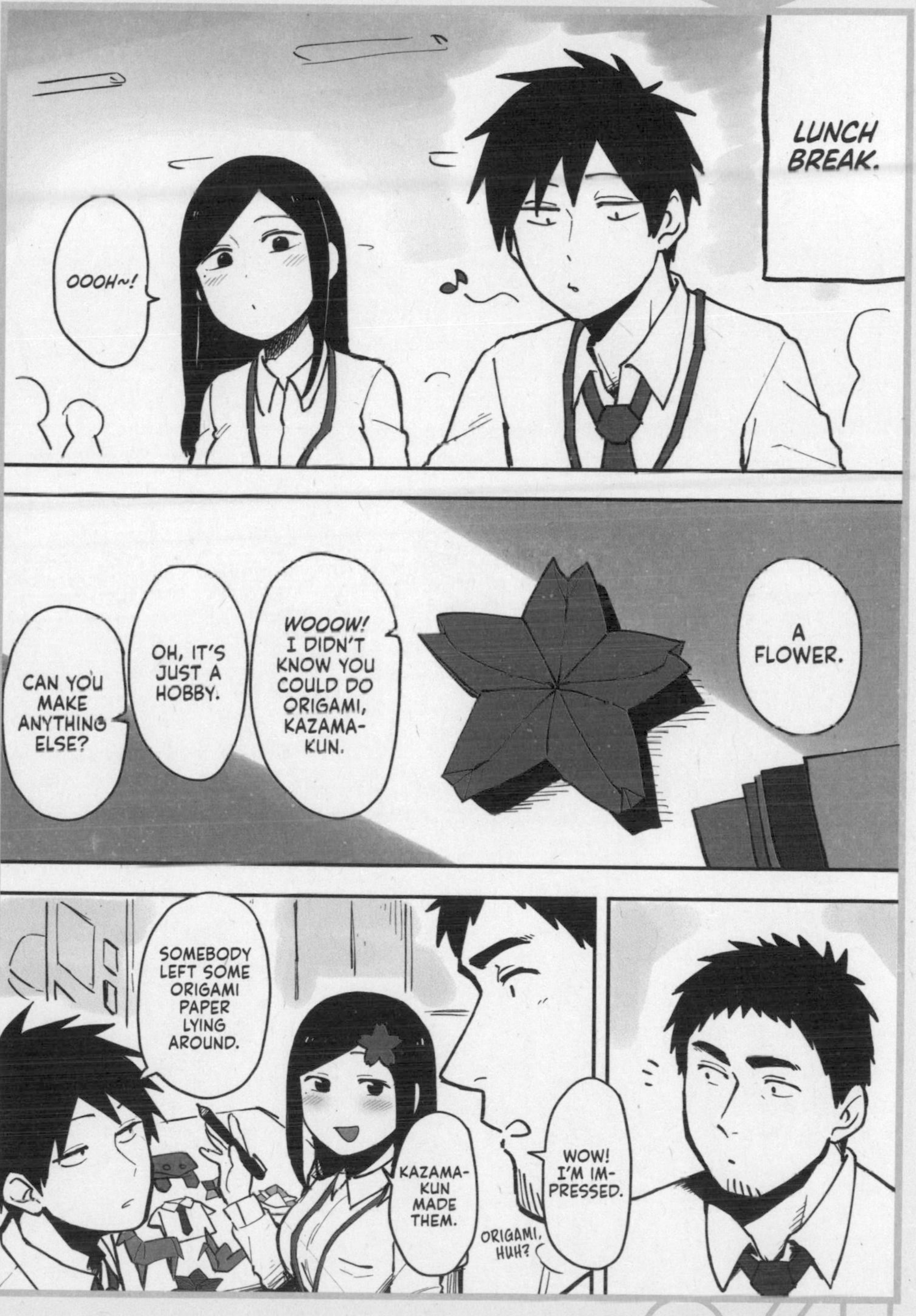
LUNCH BREAK.
OOOH~!
A FLOWER.
WOOOW! I DIDN'T KNOW YOU COULD DO ORIGAMI, KAZAMA-KUN.
OH, IT'S JUST A HOBBY.
CAN YOU MAKE ANYTHING ELSE?
WOW! I'M IM-PRESSED.
SOMEBODY LEFT SOME ORIGAMI PAPER LYING AROUND.
KAZAMA-KUN MADE THEM.
ORIGAMI, HUH?

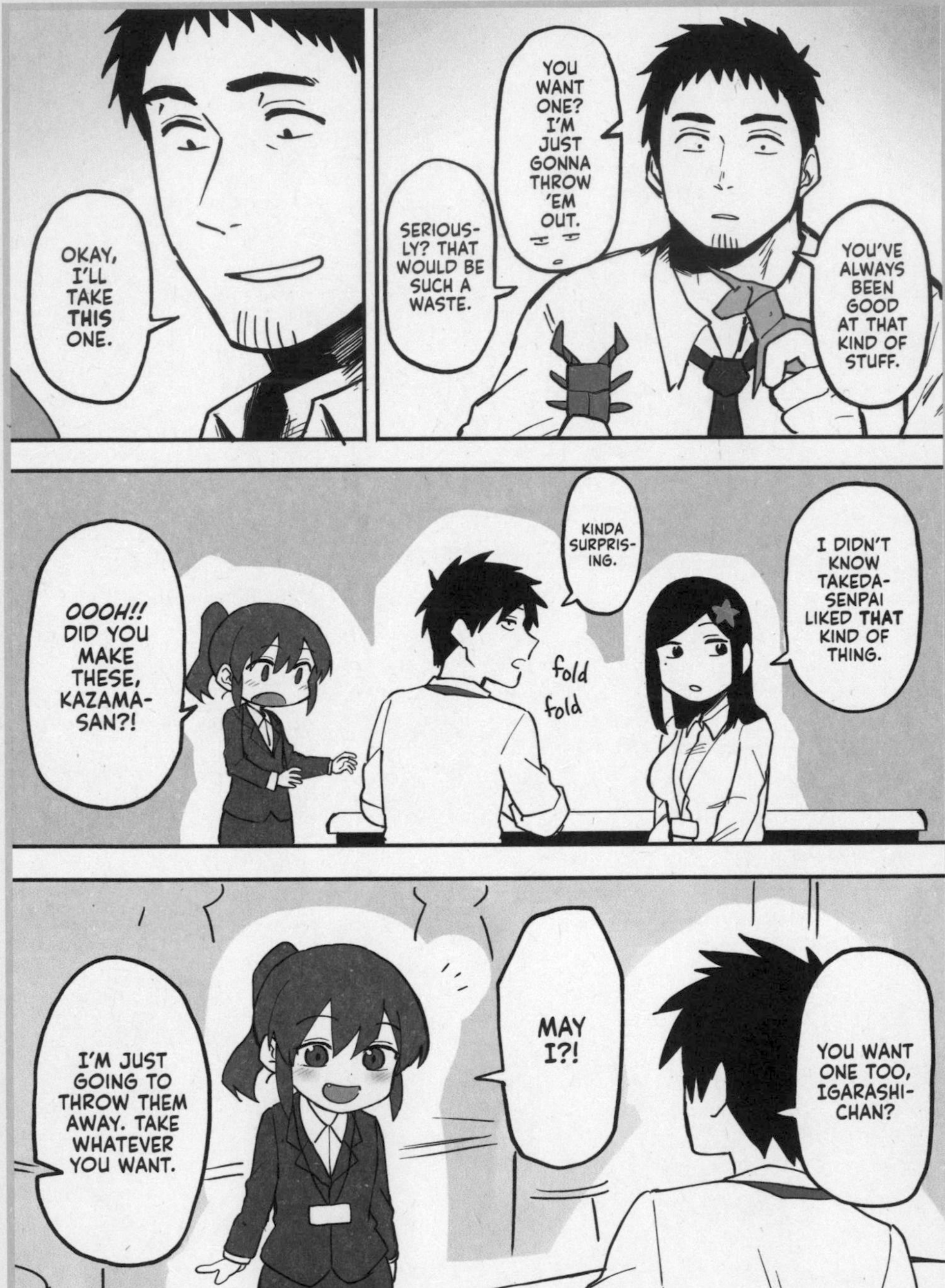
YOU'VE ALWAYS BEEN GOOD AT THAT KIND OF STUFF.
YOU WANT ONE? I'M JUST GONNA THROW 'EM OUT.
SERIOUSLY? THAT WOULD BE SUCH A WASTE.
OKAY, I'LL TAKE THIS ONE.
I DIDN'T KNOW TAKEDA-SENPAI LIKED THAT KIND OF THING.
KINDA SURPRISING.
fold fold
OOOH!! DID YOU MAKE THESE, KAZAMA-SAN?!
YOU WANT ONE TOO, IGARASHI-CHAN?
MAY I?!
I'M JUST GOING TO THROW THEM AWAY. TAKE WHATEVER YOU WANT.

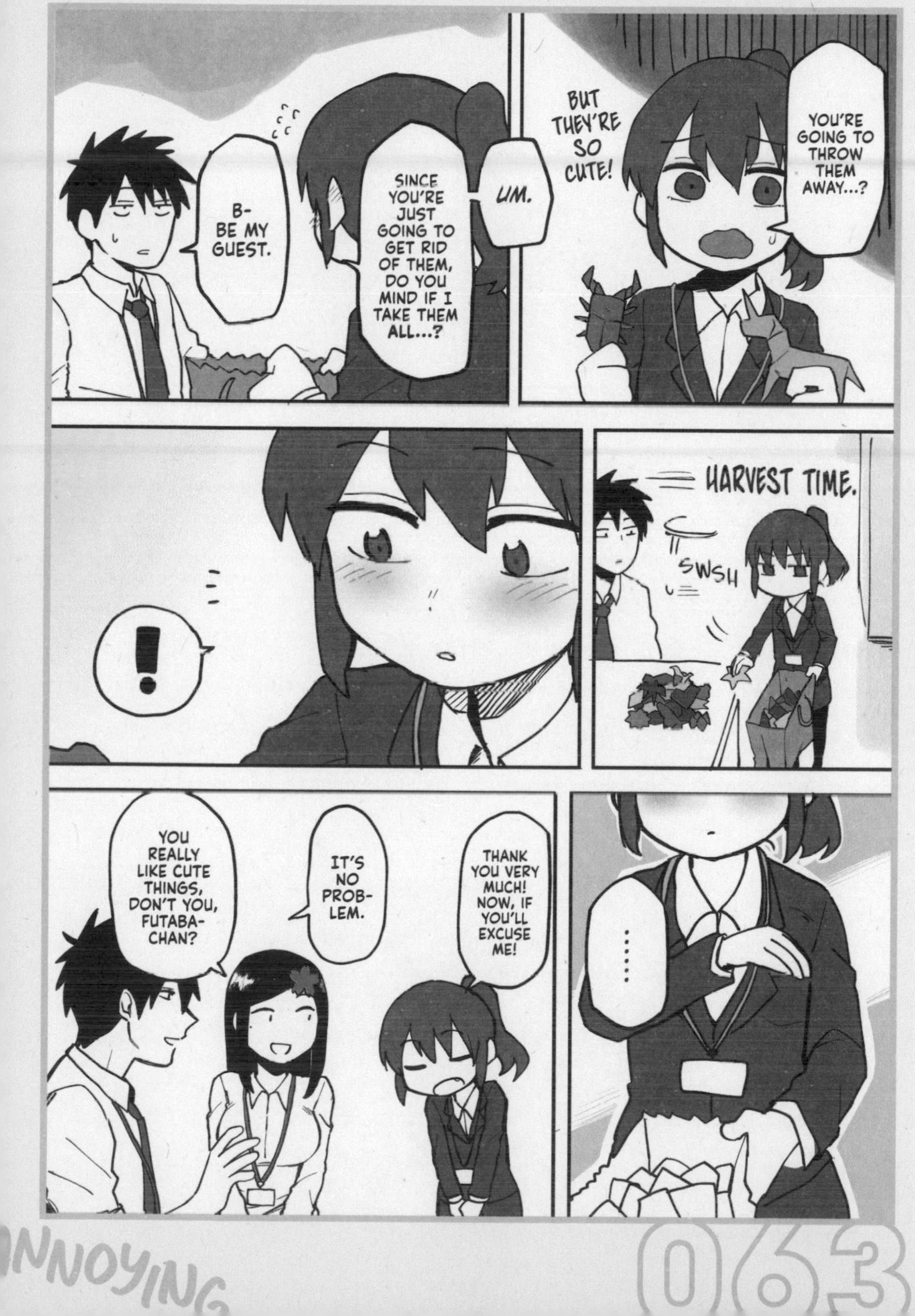
YOU'RE GOING TO THROW THEM AWAY...?
BUT THEY'RE SO CUTE!
UM.
SINCE YOU'RE JUST GOING TO GET RID OF THEM, DO YOU MIND IF I TAKE THEM ALL...?
B- BE MY GUEST.
HARVEST TIME.
SWSH
!
......
THANK YOU VERY MUCH! NOW, IF YOU'LL EXCUSE ME!
IT'S NO PROBLEM.
YOU REALLY LIKE CUTE THINGS, DON'T YOU, FUTABA-CHAN?

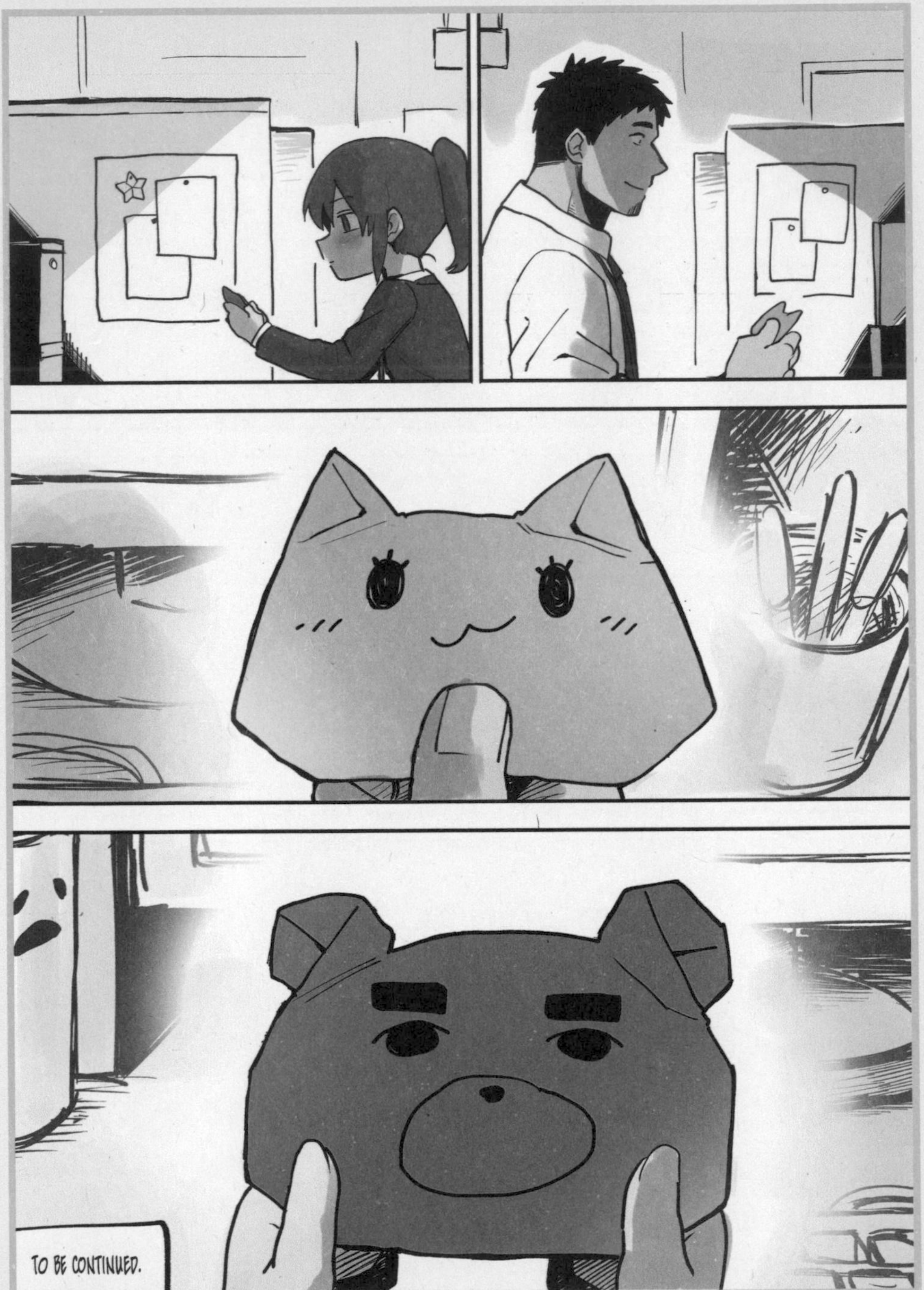
TO BE CONTINUED.

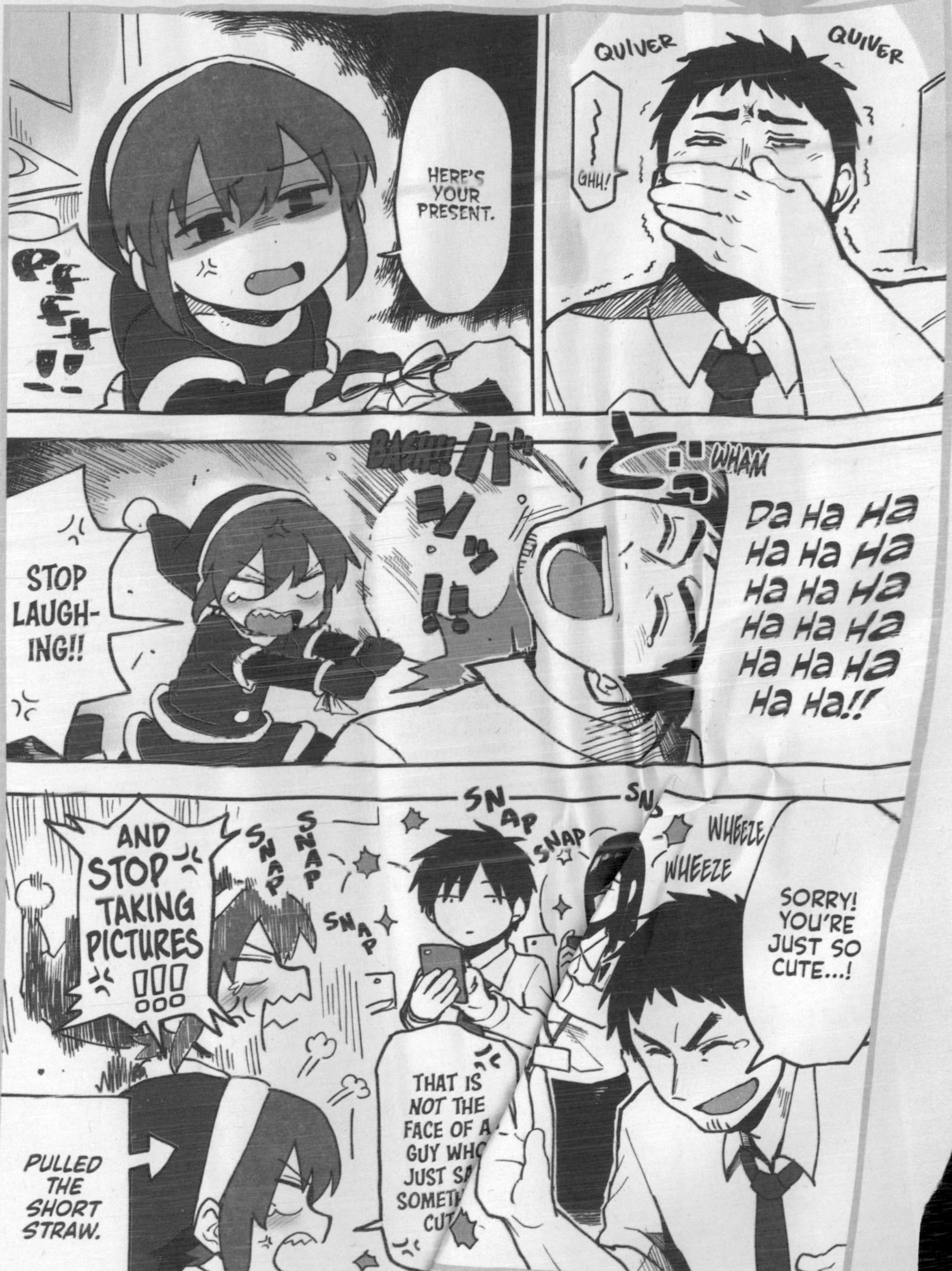
QUIVER
QUIVER
GHH!
HERE'S YOUR PRESENT.
PFFFT!!
WHAM
Da Ha Ha Ha Ha Ha Ha Ha Ha Ha Ha Ha Ha Ha Ha Ha Ha!!
BASH!!
STOP LAUGHING!!
SNAP
SNAP
WHEEZE
WHEEZE
SORRY! YOU'RE JUST SO CUTE...!
SNAP
SNAP
SNAP
SNAP
AND STOP TAKING PICTURES!!!
THAT IS NOT THE FACE OF A GUY WHO JUST SA SOMETH CUT
PULLED THE SHORT STRAW.

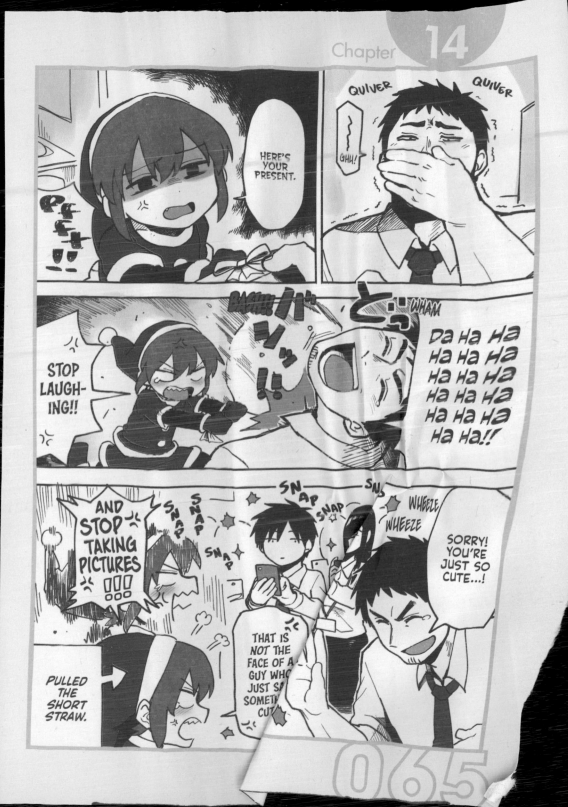

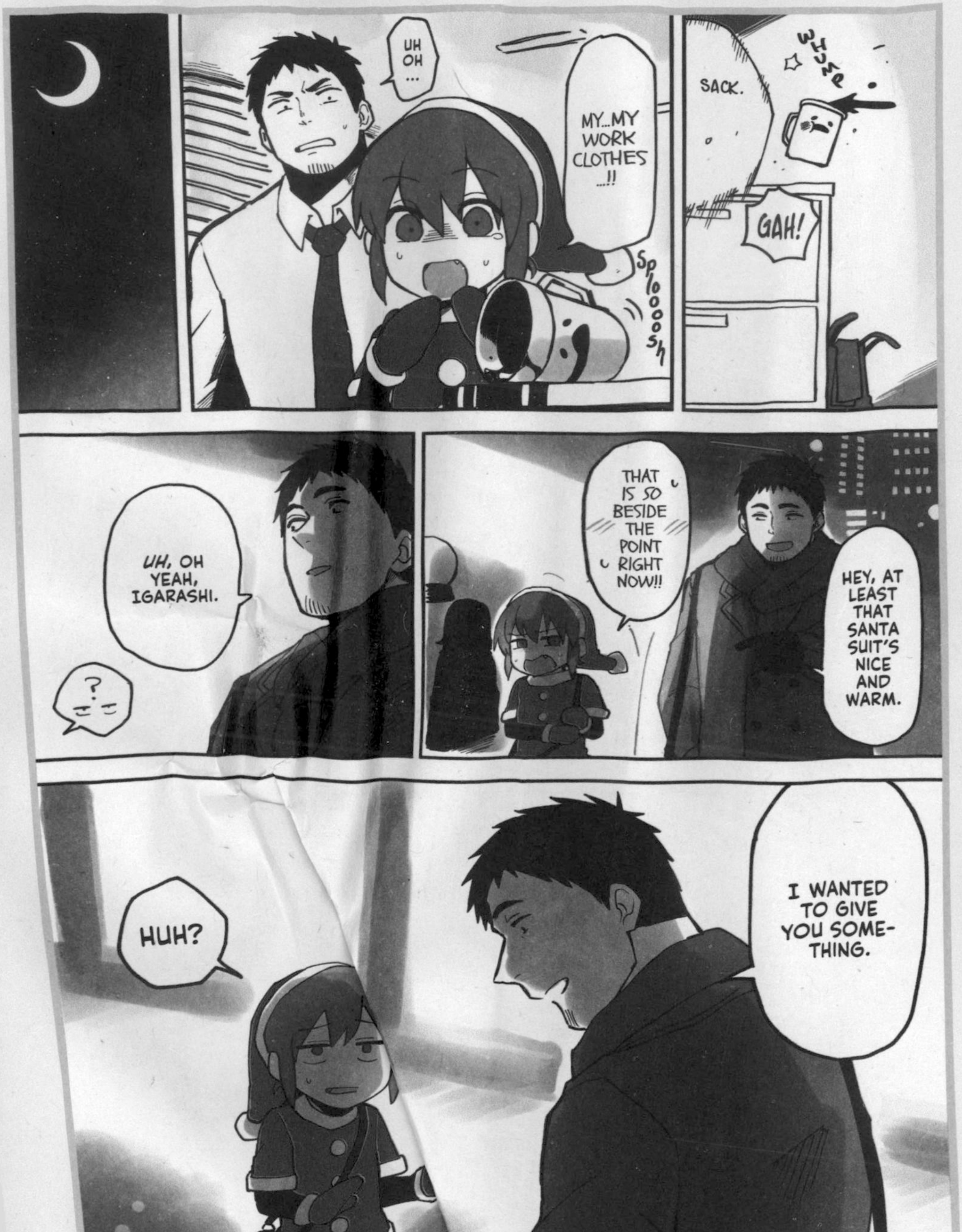
SACK.
WHUMP
GAH!
MY...MY WORK CLOTHES ...!!
UH OH ...
SPLOOOOOSH
HEY, AT LEAST THAT SANTA SUIT'S NICE AND WARM.
THAT IS SO BESIDE THE POINT RIGHT NOW!!
UH, OH YEAH, IGARASHI.
?
I WANTED TO GIVE YOU SOME-THING.
HUH?

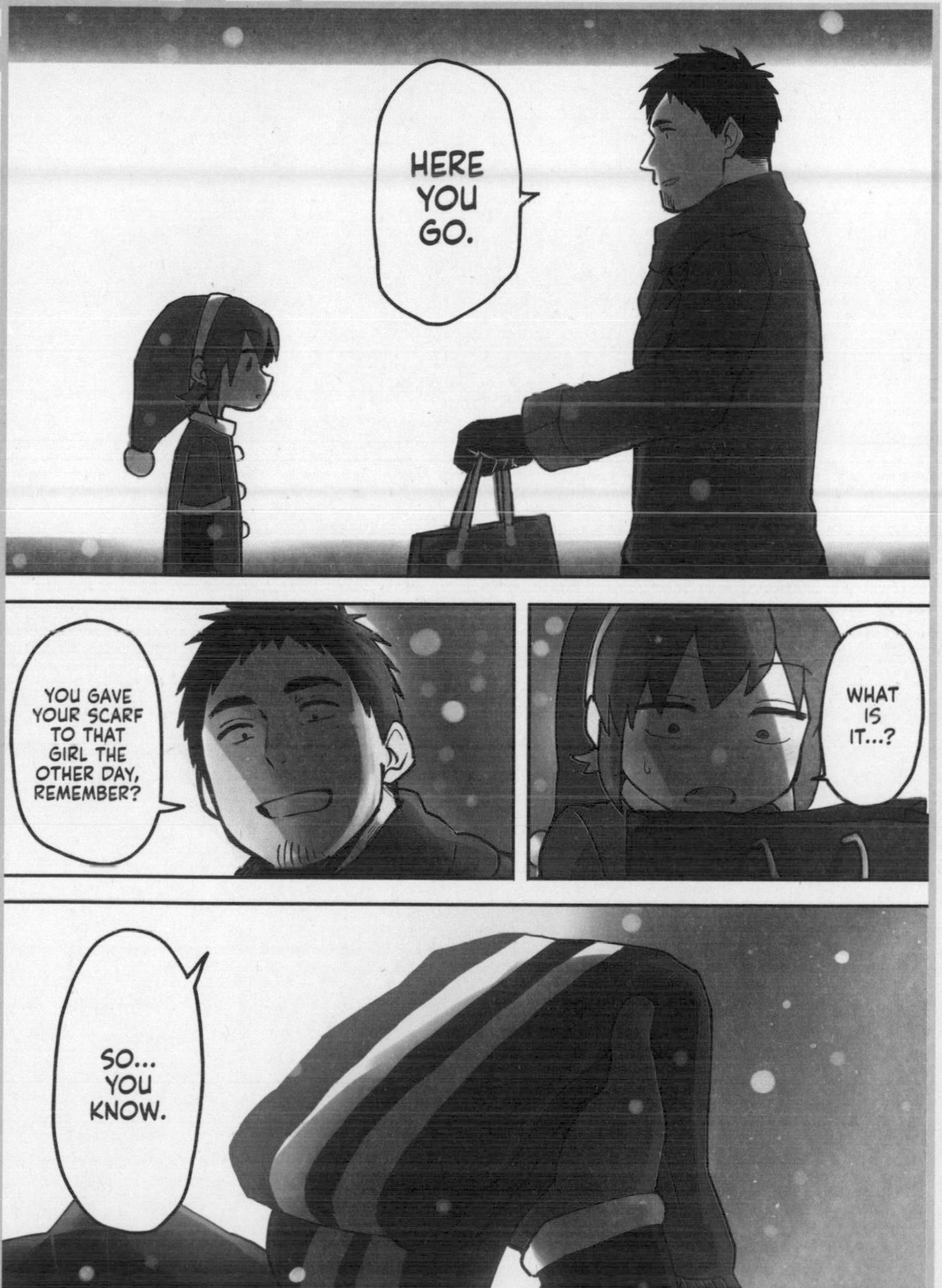
HERE YOU GO.
WHAT IS IT...?
YOU GAVE YOUR SCARF TO THAT GIRL THE OTHER DAY, REMEMBER?
SO... YOU KNOW.

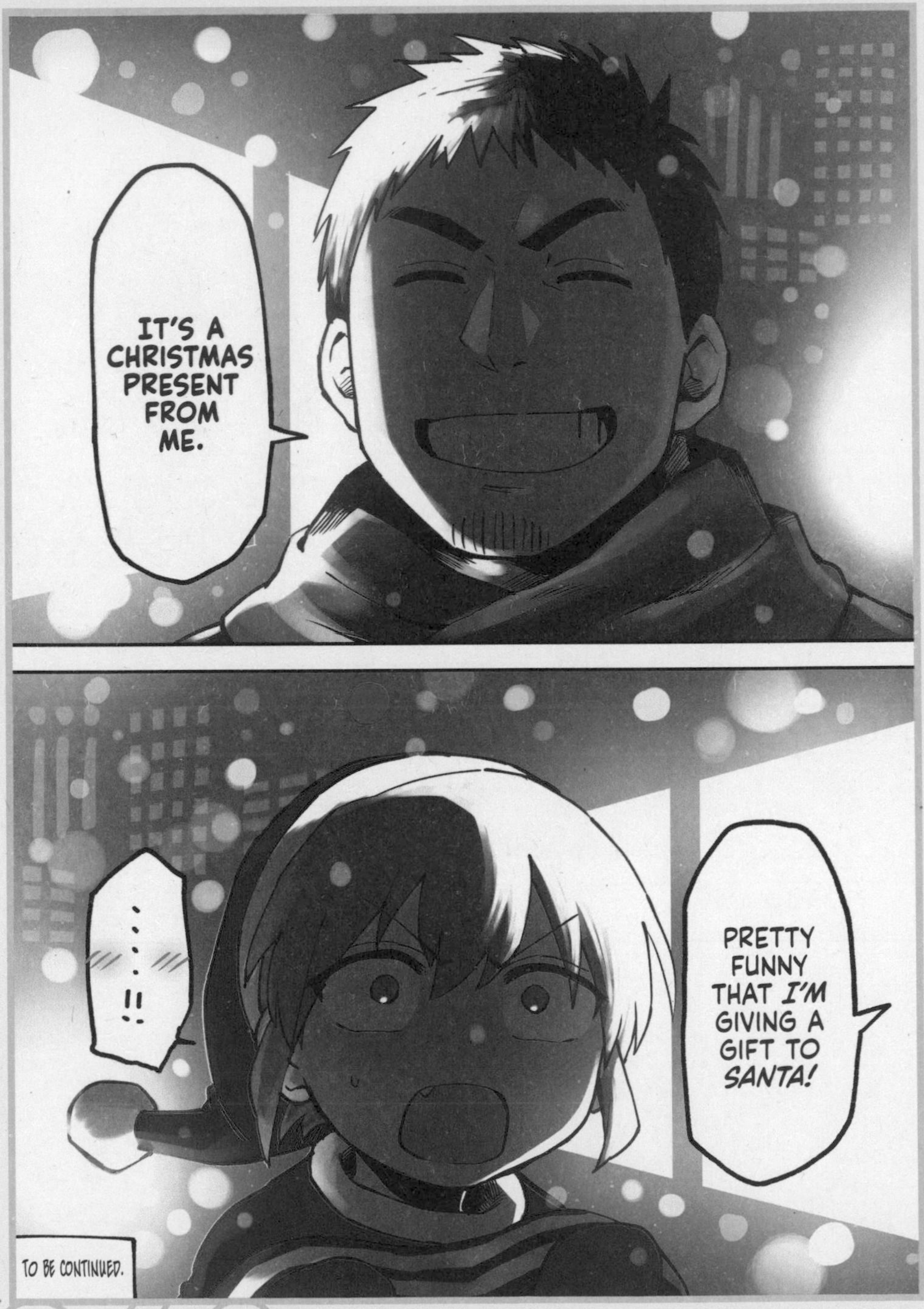
IT'S A CHRISTMAS PRESENT FROM ME.
PRETTY FUNNY THAT *I'M* GIVING A GIFT TO *SANTA!*
......!!
TO BE CONTINUED.

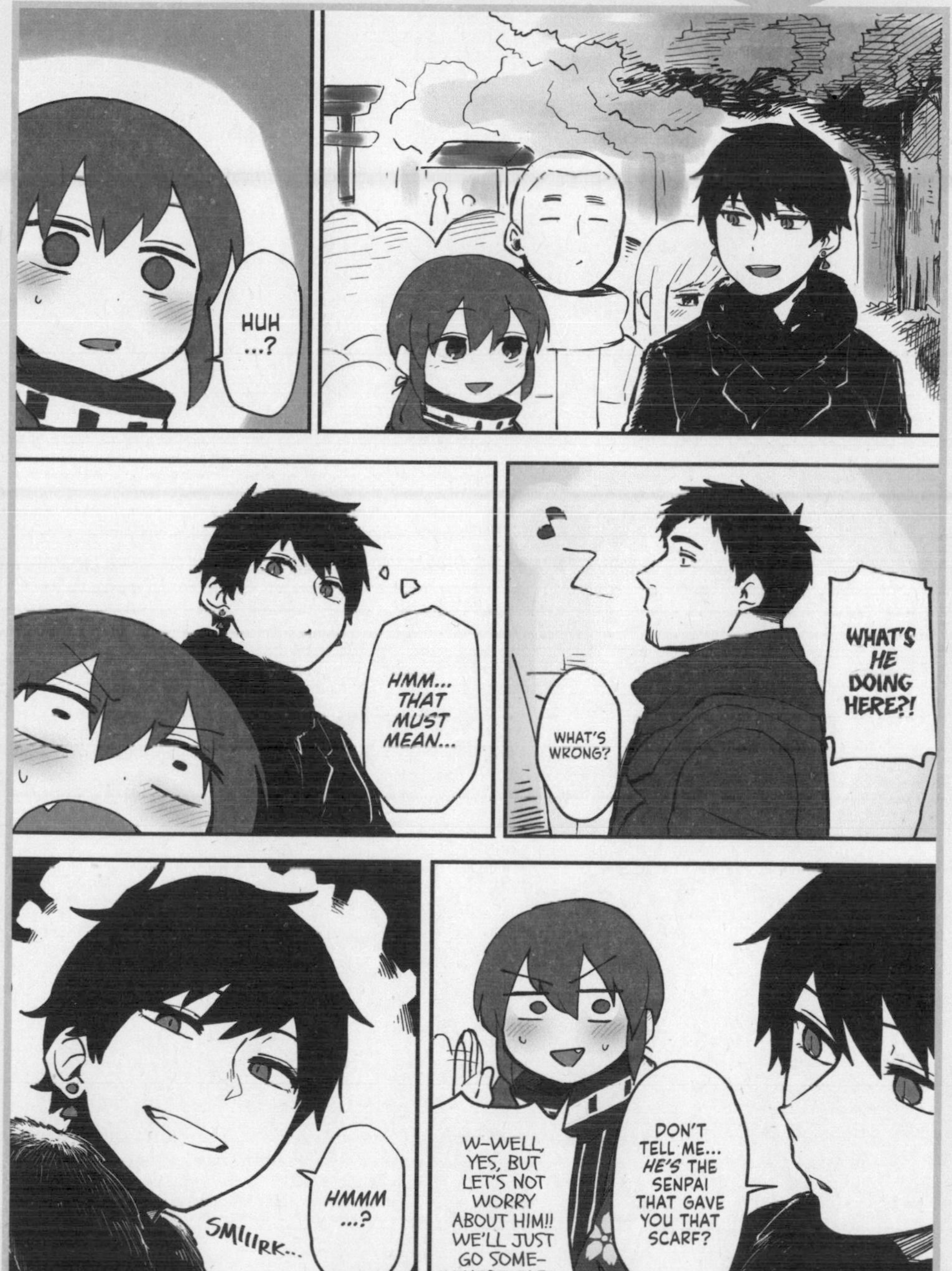
HUH ...?
WHAT'S HE DOING HERE?!
WHAT'S WRONG?
HMM... THAT MUST MEAN...
DON'T TELL ME... HE'S THE SENPAI THAT GAVE YOU THAT SCARF?
W-WELL, YES, BUT LET'S NOT WORRY ABOUT HIM!! WE'LL JUST GO SOME-WHERE ELSE, OKAY...?!
HMMM ...?
SMIIIRK...

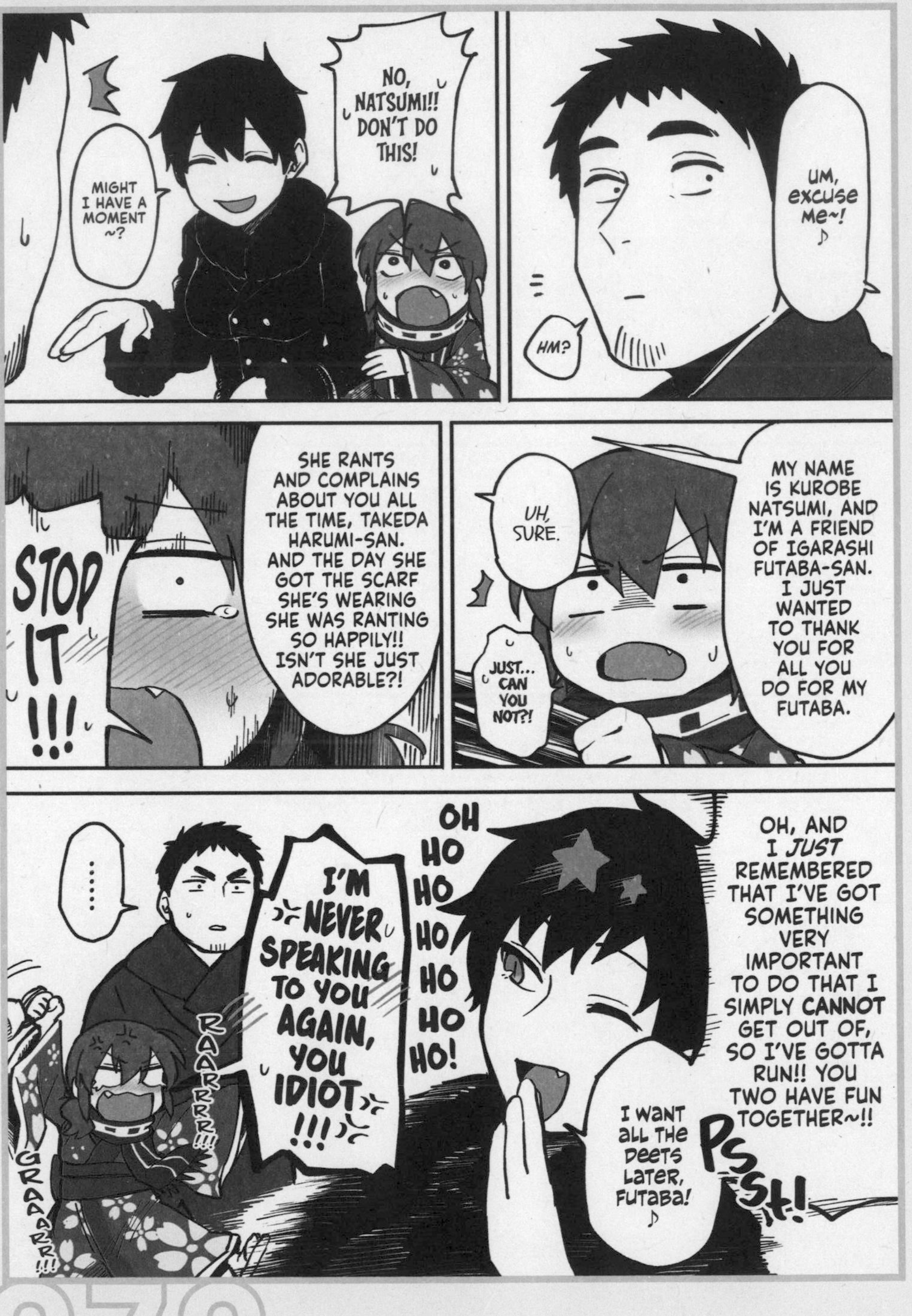
UM, excuse me~! ♪
HM?
NO, NATSUMI!! DON'T DO THIS!
MIGHT I HAVE A MOMENT ~?
MY NAME IS KUROBE NATSUMI, AND I'M A FRIEND OF IGARASHI FUTABA-SAN. I JUST WANTED TO THANK YOU FOR ALL YOU DO FOR MY FUTABA.
UH, SURE.
JUST... CAN YOU NOT?!
SHE RANTS AND COMPLAINS ABOUT YOU ALL THE TIME, TAKEDA HARUMI-SAN. AND THE DAY SHE GOT THE SCARF SHE'S WEARING SHE WAS RANTING SO HAPPILY!! ISN'T SHE JUST ADORABLE?!
STOP IT !!!
OH, AND I *JUST* REMEMBERED THAT I'VE GOT SOMETHING VERY IMPORTANT TO DO THAT I SIMPLY CANNOT GET OUT OF, SO I'VE GOTTA RUN!! YOU TWO HAVE FUN TOGETHER~!!
I want all the deets later, Futaba! ♪
PSST!
OH HO HO HO HO HO HO HO!
I'M NEVER SPEAKING TO YOU AGAIN, YOU IDIOT!!!
RAAARRRR!!!
GRAAARR!!!
......

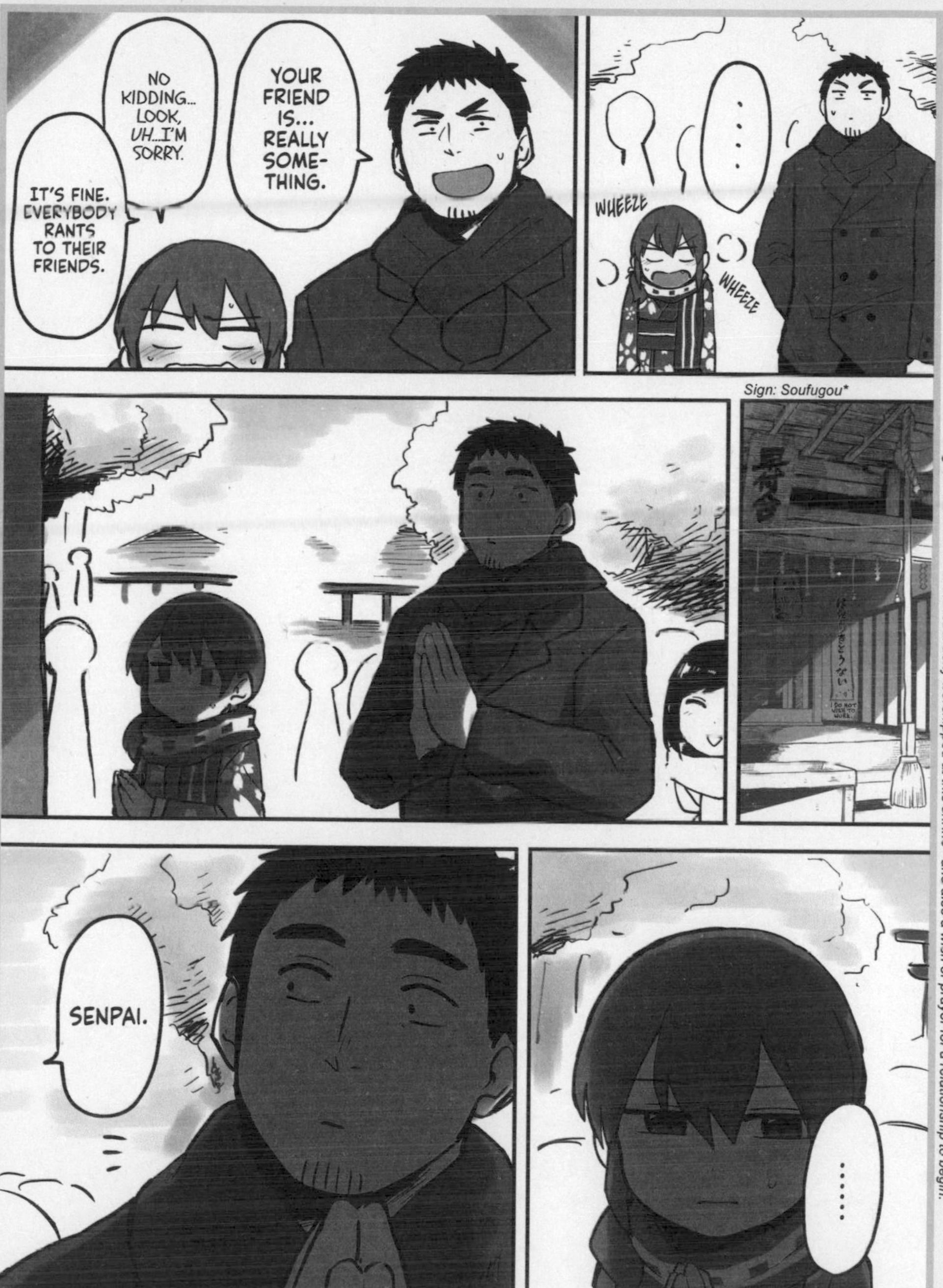
. . . .
WHEEZE
WHEEZE
YOUR FRIEND IS... REALLY SOME-THING.
NO KIDDING... LOOK, UH...I'M SORRY.
IT'S FINE. EVERYBODY RANTS TO THEIR FRIENDS.
......
SENPAI.

Chapter 15

Sign: Soufugou*

*"Soufugou" is the name of the local deity worshipped at this shrine--and also a wish or prayer for a relationship to begin.

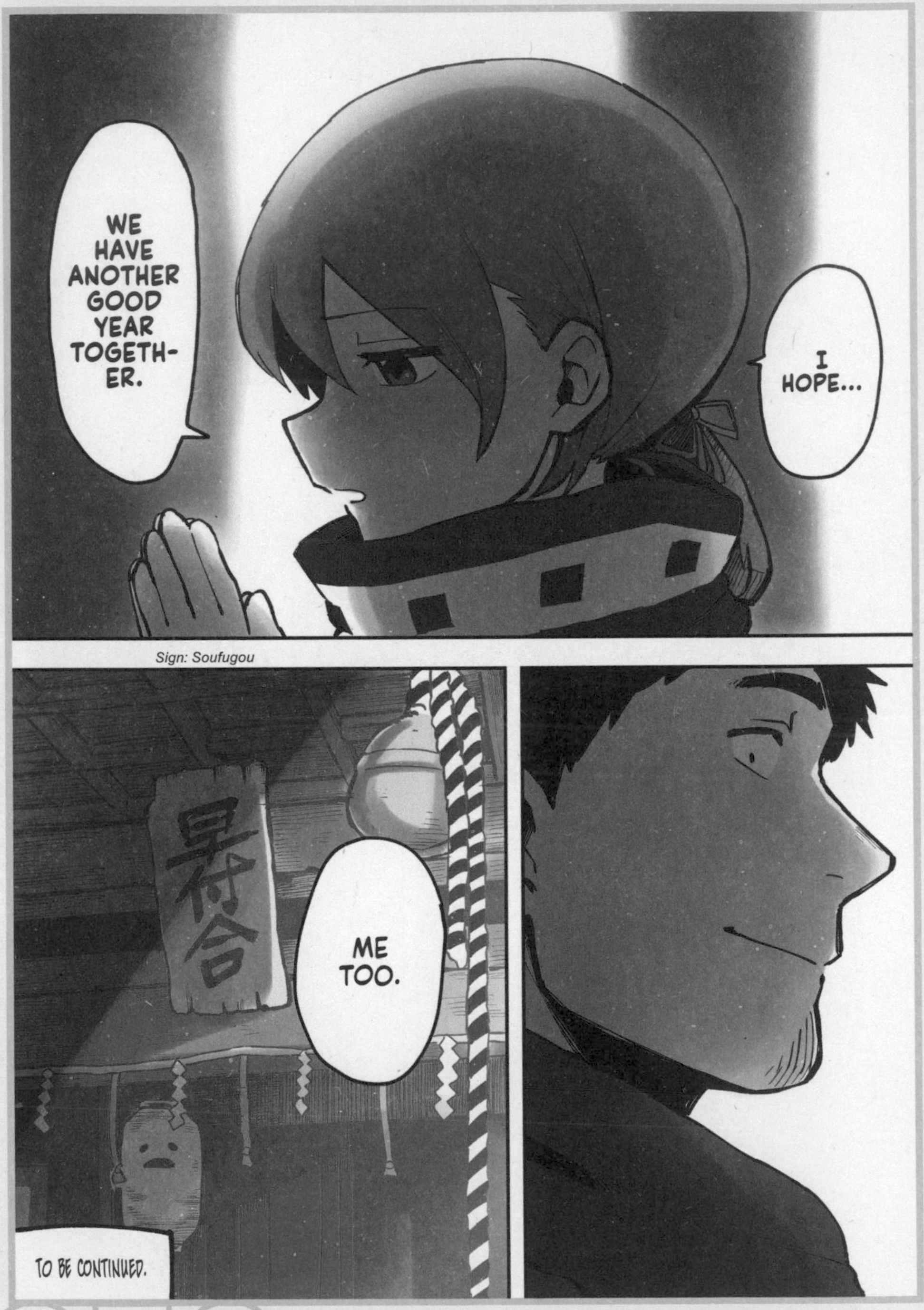
I HOPE...
WE HAVE ANOTHER GOOD YEAR TOGETHER.
ME TOO.
TO BE CONTINUED.
Sign: Soufugou

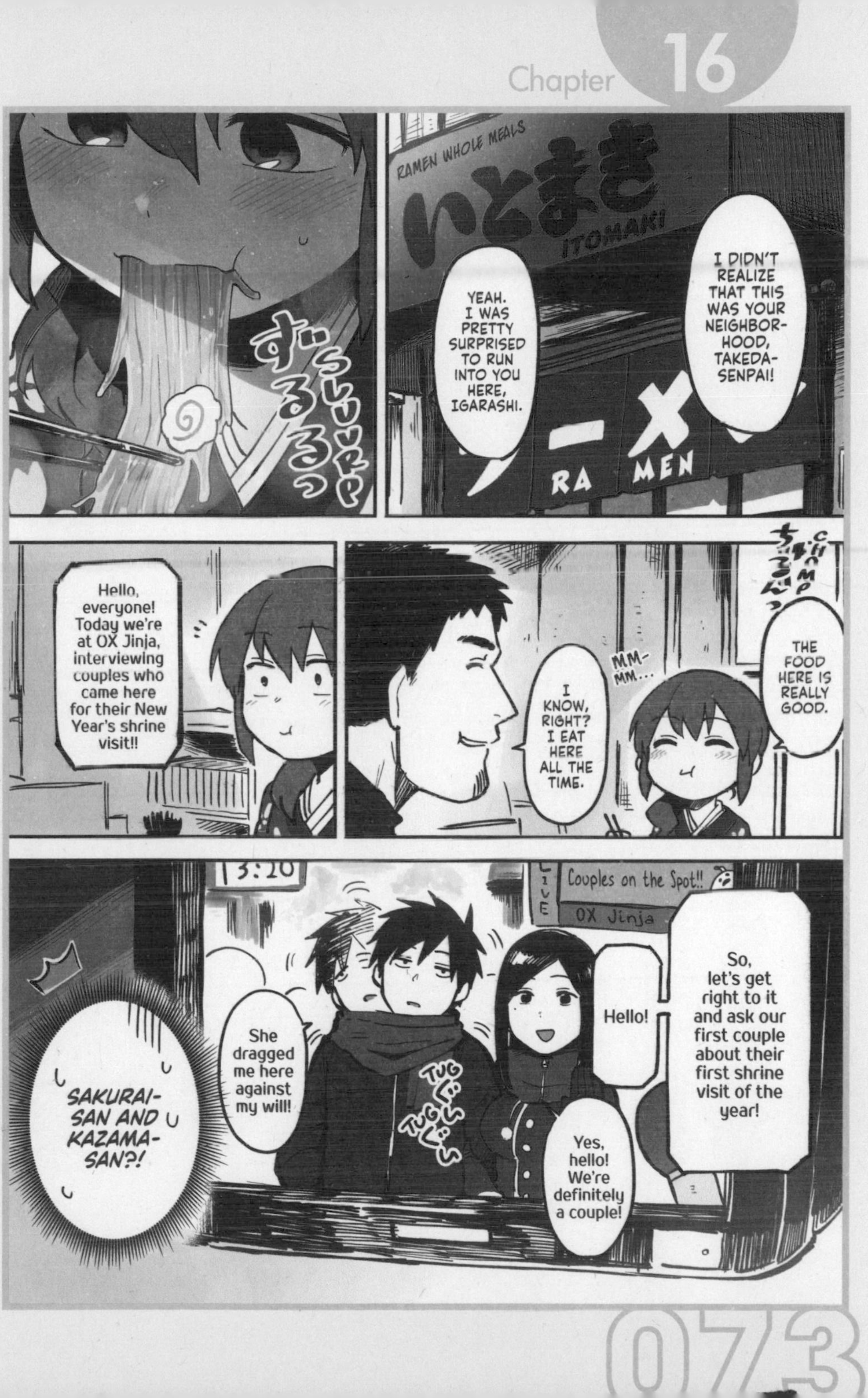
RAMEN WHOLE MEALS
いとまき
ITOMAKI
I DIDN'T REALIZE THAT THIS WAS YOUR NEIGHBOR-HOOD, TAKEDA-SENPAI!
YEAH. I WAS PRETTY SURPRISED TO RUN INTO YOU HERE, IGARASHI.
RA MEN
ずるるっ
SLUURP
CHOMP
THE FOOD HERE IS REALLY GOOD.
MM-MM...
I KNOW, RIGHT? I EAT HERE ALL THE TIME.
Hello, everyone! Today we're at OX Jinja, interviewing couples who came here for their New Year's shrine visit!!
3:20
LIVE
Couples on the Spot!!
OX Jinja
So, let's get right to it and ask our first couple about their first shrine visit of the year!
Hello!
Yes, hello! We're definitely a couple!
She dragged me here against my will!
TUG TUG
SAKURAI-SAN AND KAZAMA-SAN?!

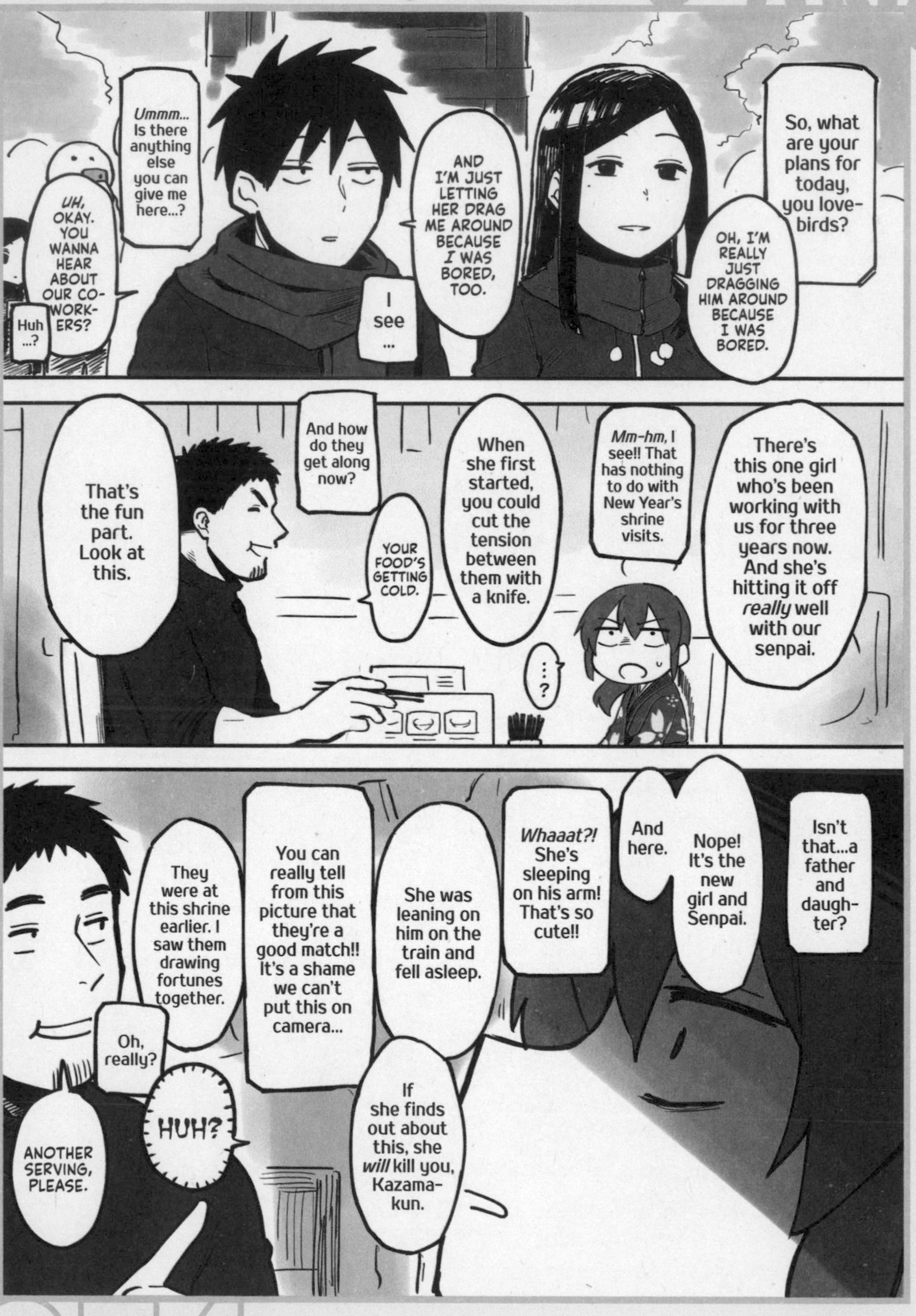
So, what are your plans for today, you love-birds?
OH, I'M REALLY JUST DRAGGING HIM AROUND BECAUSE I WAS BORED.
AND I'M JUST LETTING HER DRAG ME AROUND BECAUSE *I* WAS BORED, TOO.
I see...
Ummm... Is there anything else you can give me here...?
UH, OKAY. YOU WANNA HEAR ABOUT OUR CO-WORKERS?
Huh...?
There's this one girl who's been working with us for three years now. And she's hitting it off *really* well with our senpai.
Mm-hm, I see!! That has nothing to do with New Year's shrine visits.
When she first started, you could cut the tension between them with a knife.
And how do they get along now?
YOUR FOOD'S GETTING COLD.
...?
That's the fun part. Look at this.
Isn't that...a father and daughter?
Nope! It's the new girl and Senpai.
And here.
Whaaat?! She's sleeping on his arm! That's so cute!!
She was leaning on him on the train and fell asleep.
You can really tell from this picture that they're a good match!! It's a shame we can't put this on camera...
They were at this shrine earlier. I saw them drawing fortunes together.
Oh, really?
If she finds out about this, she *will* kill you, Kazama-kun.
HUH?
ANOTHER SERVING, PLEASE.

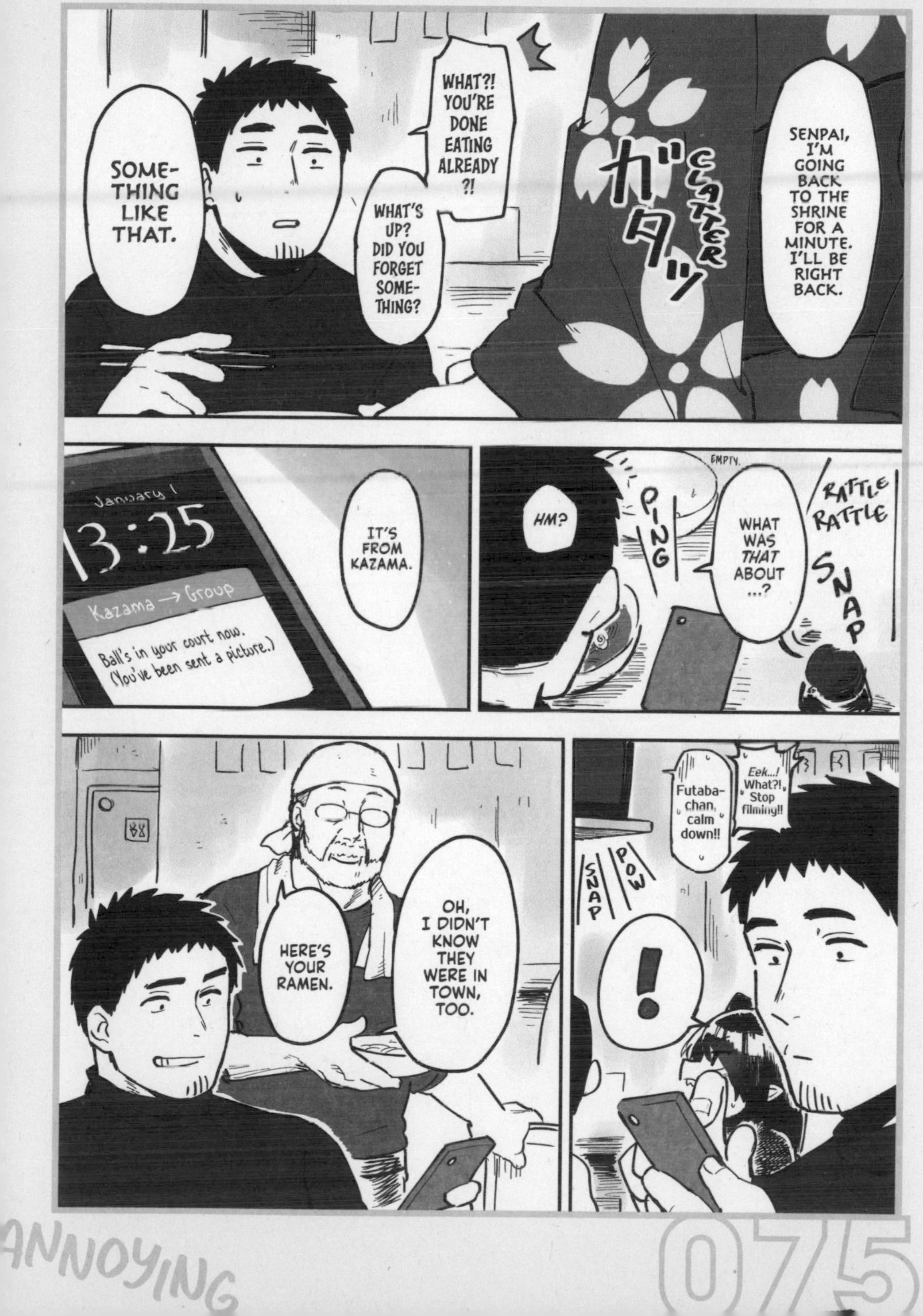
SENPAI, I'M GOING BACK TO THE SHRINE FOR A MINUTE. I'LL BE RIGHT BACK.
ガタッ
CLATTER
WHAT?! YOU'RE DONE EATING ALREADY?!
WHAT'S UP? DID YOU FORGET SOME-THING?
SOME-THING LIKE THAT.
RATTLE RATTLE
SNAP
WHAT WAS THAT ABOUT ...?
EMPTY.
PING
HM?
IT'S FROM KAZAMA.
January 1
13:25
Kazama → Group
Ball's in your court now. (You've been sent a picture.)
Eek...! What?! Stop filming!!
Futaba-chan, calm down!!
POW
SNAP
!
OH, I DIDN'T KNOW THEY WERE IN TOWN, TOO.
HERE'S YOUR RAMEN.

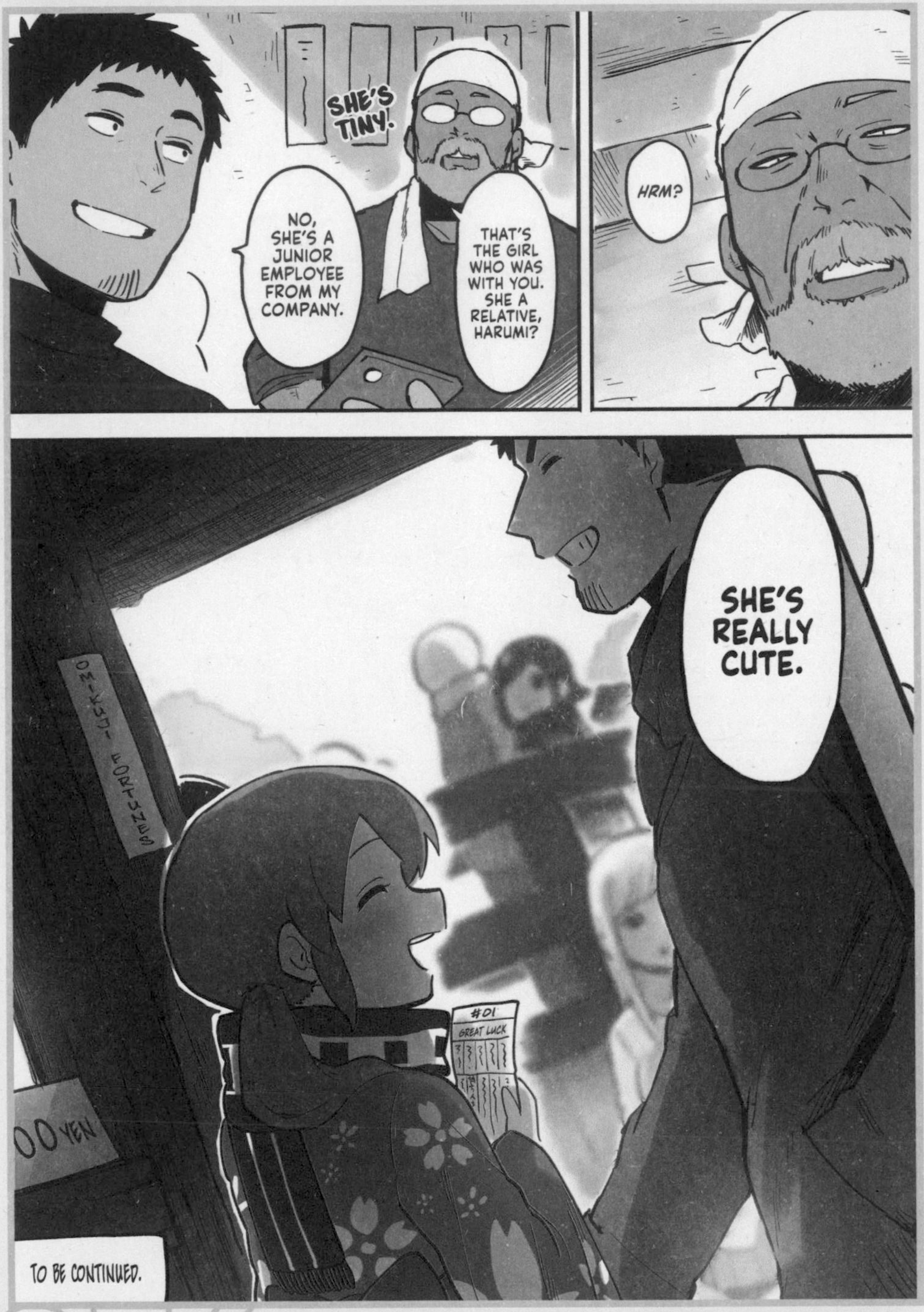
HRM?
THAT'S THE GIRL WHO WAS WITH YOU. SHE A RELATIVE, HARUMI?
SHE'S TINY!
NO, SHE'S A JUNIOR EMPLOYEE FROM MY COMPANY.
SHE'S REALLY CUTE.
OMIKUJI FORTUNES
#01
GREAT LUCK
00 YEN
TO BE CONTINUED.

Fortune: The one you're waiting for...

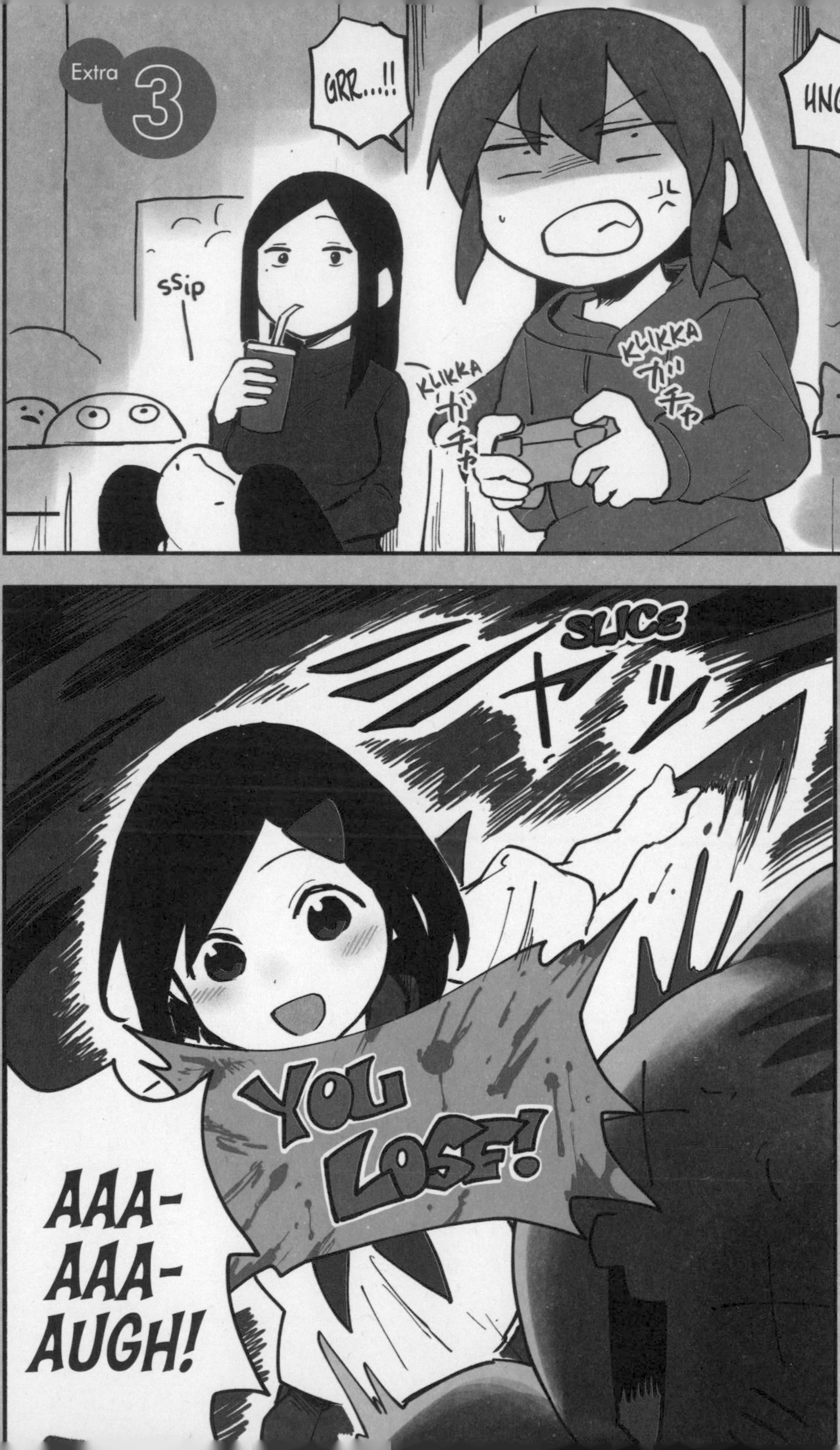
Extra 3
UNGH!
KLIKKA ガチャ
GRR...!!
KLIKKA ガチャ
sSip
SLICE
YOU LOSE!
AAA-AAA-AUGH!

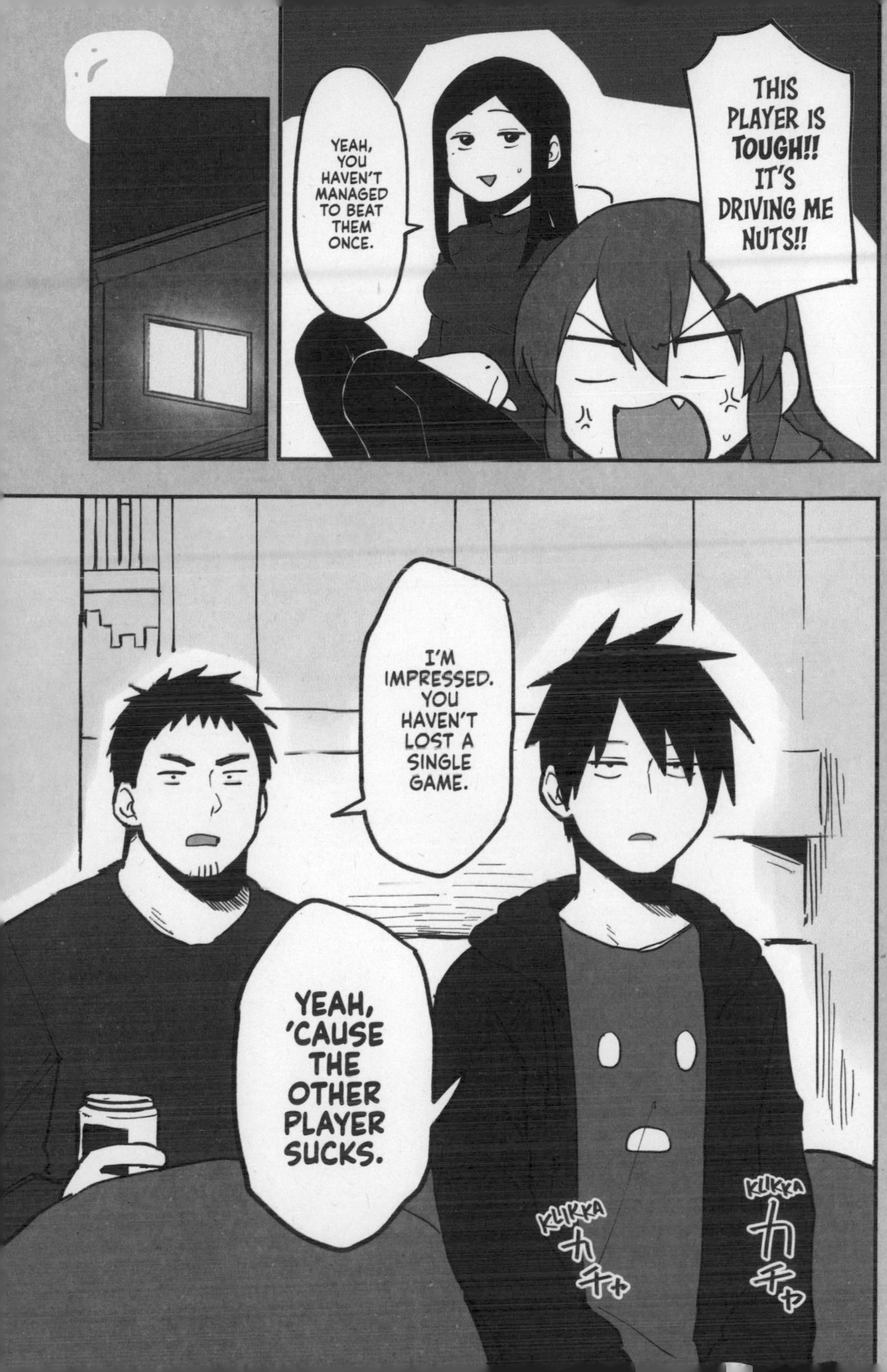
THIS PLAYER IS TOUGH!! IT'S DRIVING ME NUTS!!
YEAH, YOU HAVEN'T MANAGED TO BEAT THEM ONCE.
I'M IMPRESSED. YOU HAVEN'T LOST A SINGLE GAME.
KLIKKA カチャ
YEAH, 'CAUSE THE OTHER PLAYER SUCKS.
KLIKKA カチャ

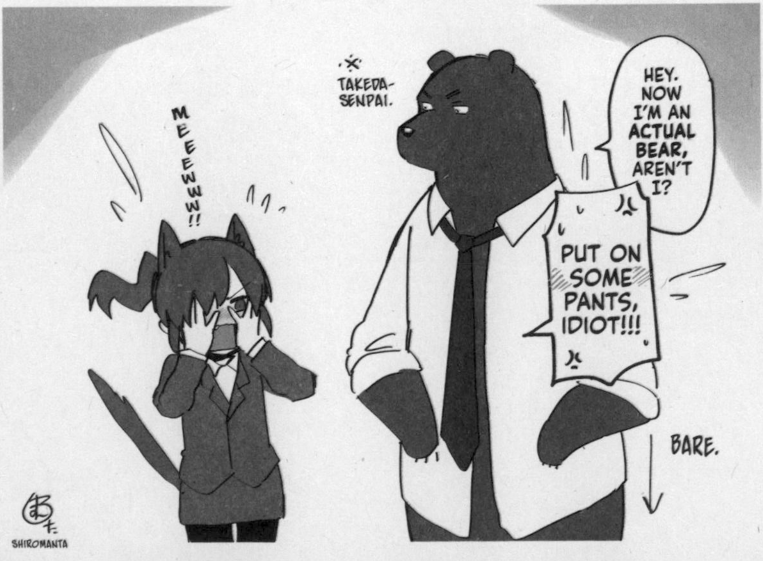
HEY. NOW I'M AN ACTUAL BEAR, AREN'T I?
TAKEDA-SENPAI.
PUT ON SOME PANTS, IDIOT!!!
MEEEWWW!!
BARE.
SHIROMANTA

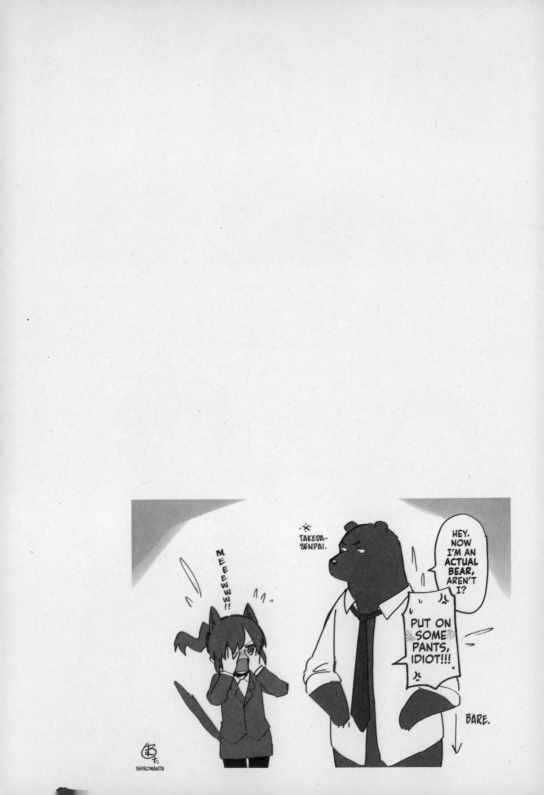

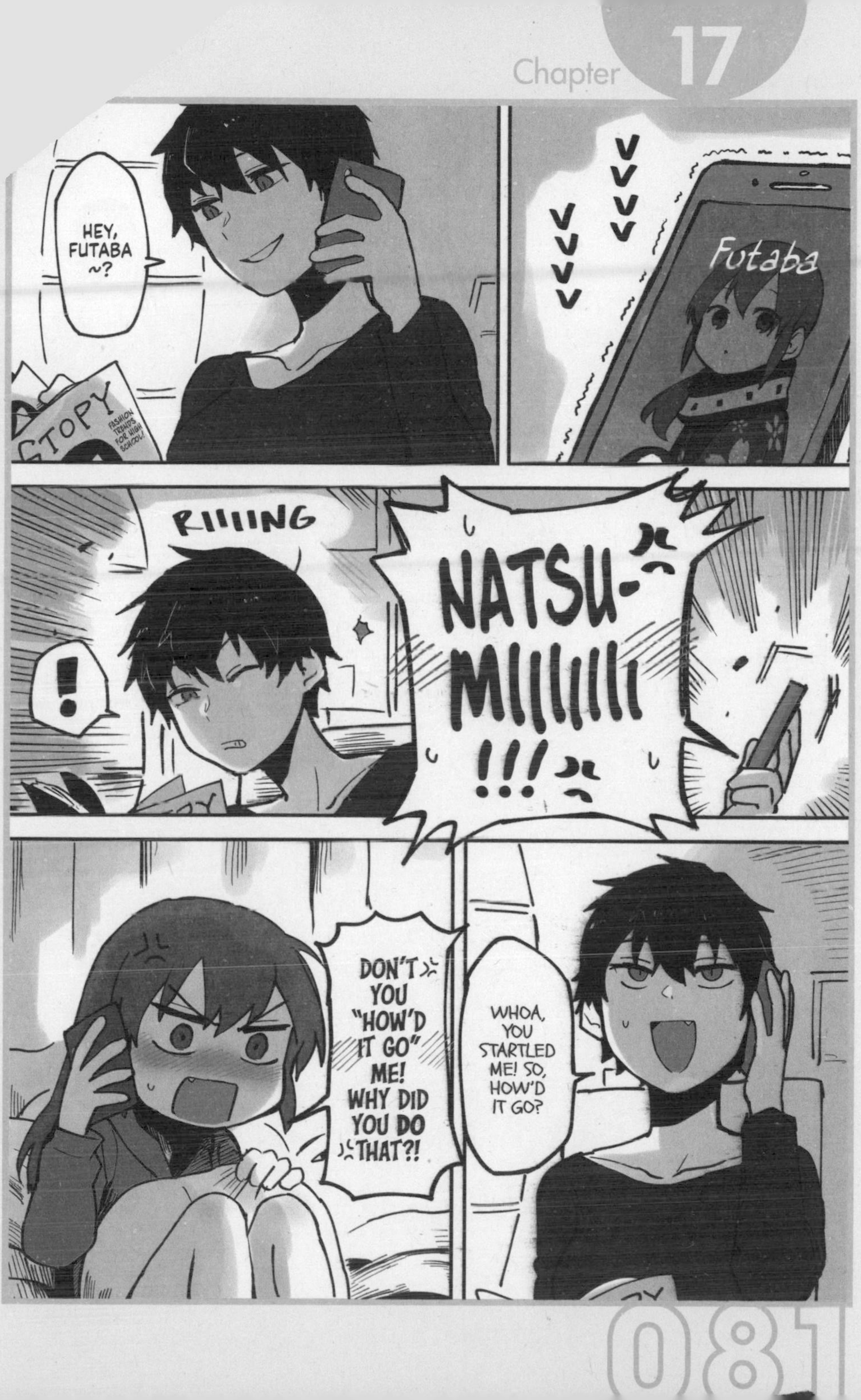
VVVV
VVVV
Futaba
HEY, FUTABA ~?
STOPY
FASHION TRENDS FOR HIGH SCHOOL!
NATSU-MIIIIII!!!
RIIIING
!
WHOA, YOU STARTLED ME! SO, HOW'D IT GO?
DON'T YOU "HOW'D IT GO" ME! WHY DID YOU DO THAT?!

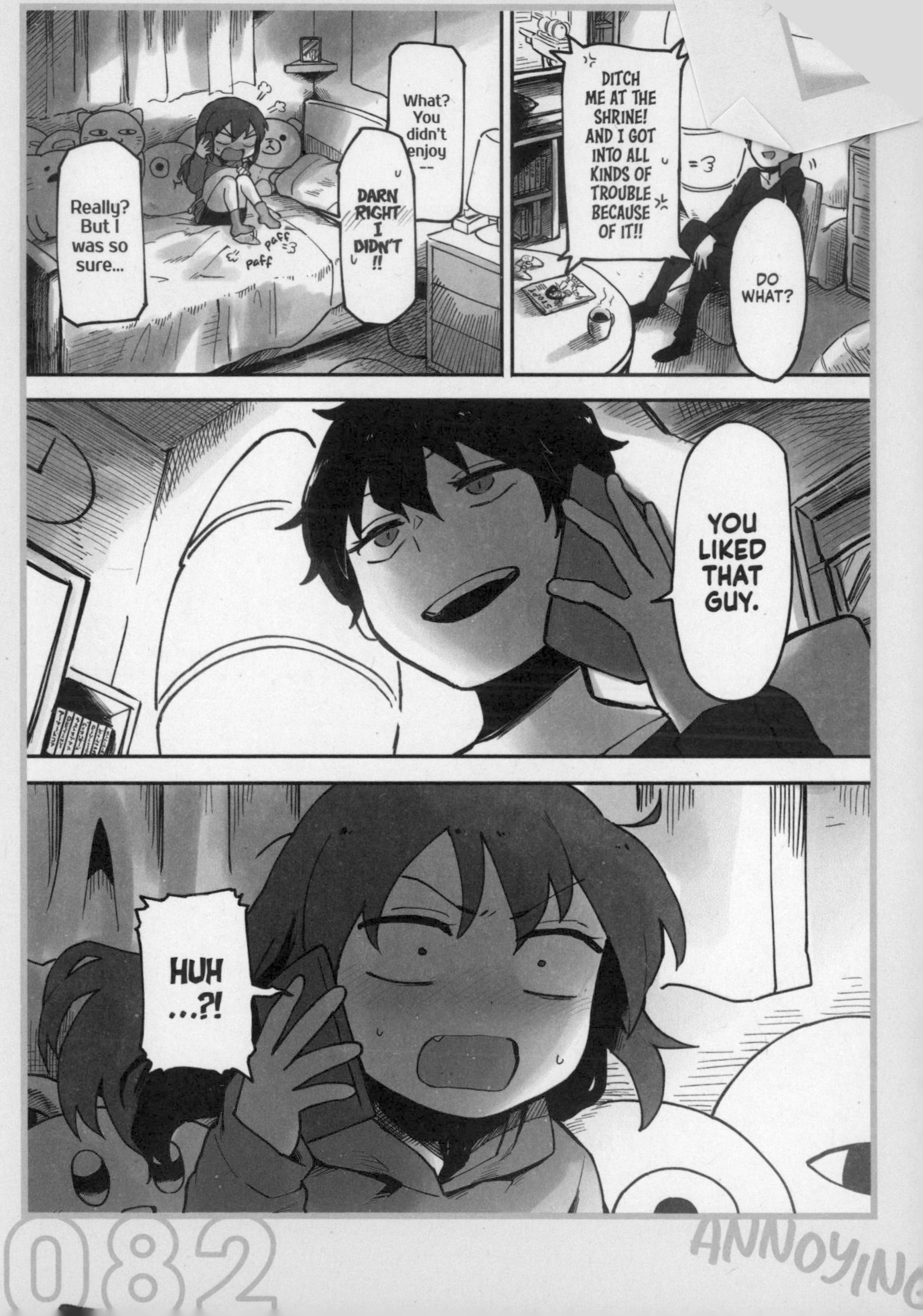
DITCH ME AT THE SHRINE! AND I GOT INTO ALL KINDS OF TROUBLE BECAUSE OF IT!!
DO WHAT?
What? You didn't enjoy --
DARN RIGHT I DIDN'T !!
paff
paff
Really? But I was so sure...
YOU LIKED THAT GUY.
HUH ...?!

082

ANNOYING

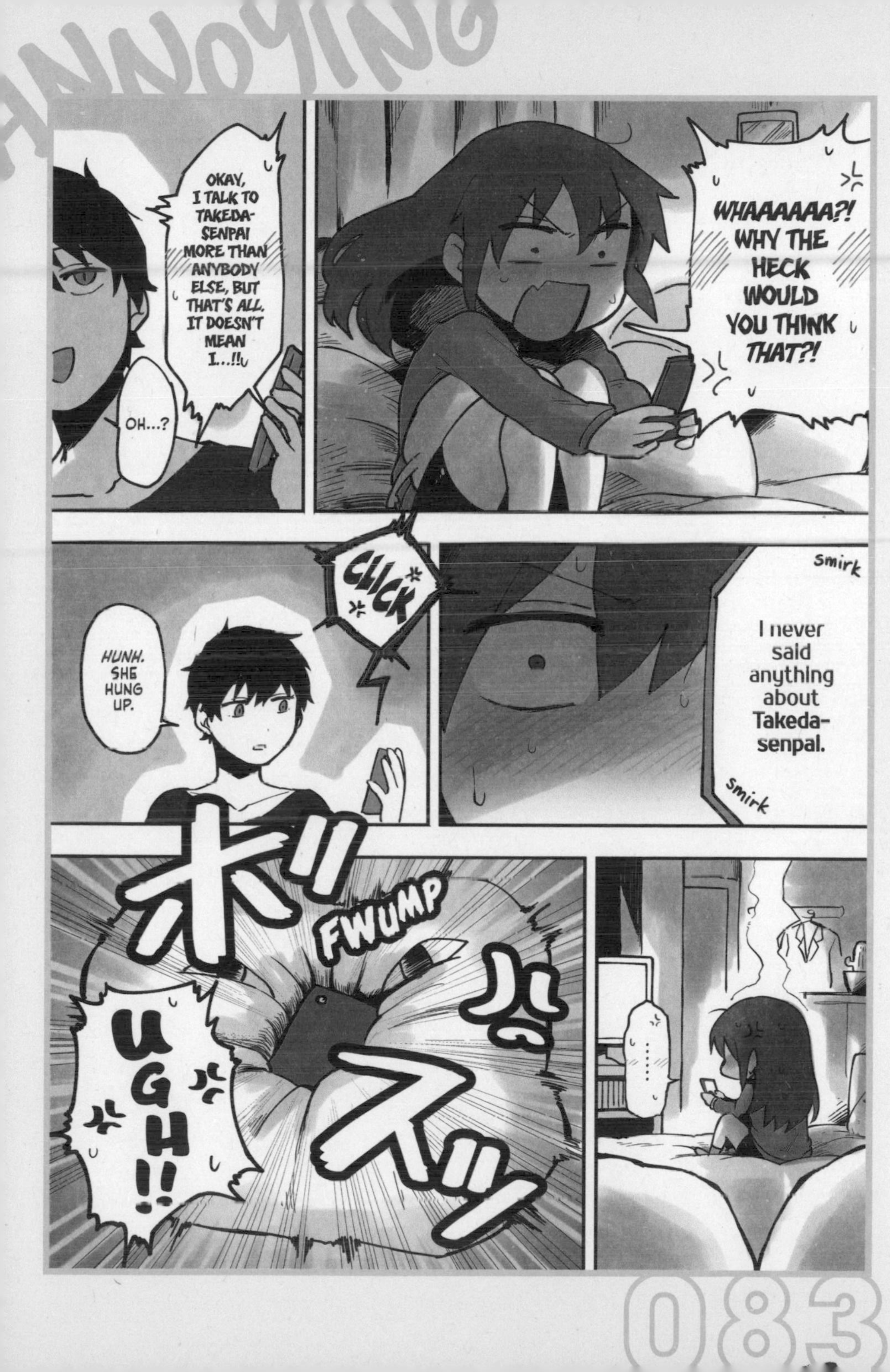
WHAAAAAA?! WHY THE HECK WOULD YOU THINK THAT?!
OKAY, I TALK TO TAKEDA-SENPAI MORE THAN ANYBODY ELSE, BUT THAT'S ALL. IT DOESN'T MEAN I...!!
OH...?
smirk
I never said anything about Takeda-senpai.
smirk
CLICK
HUNH. SHE HUNG UP.
......
ボスッ
FWUMP
UGH!!

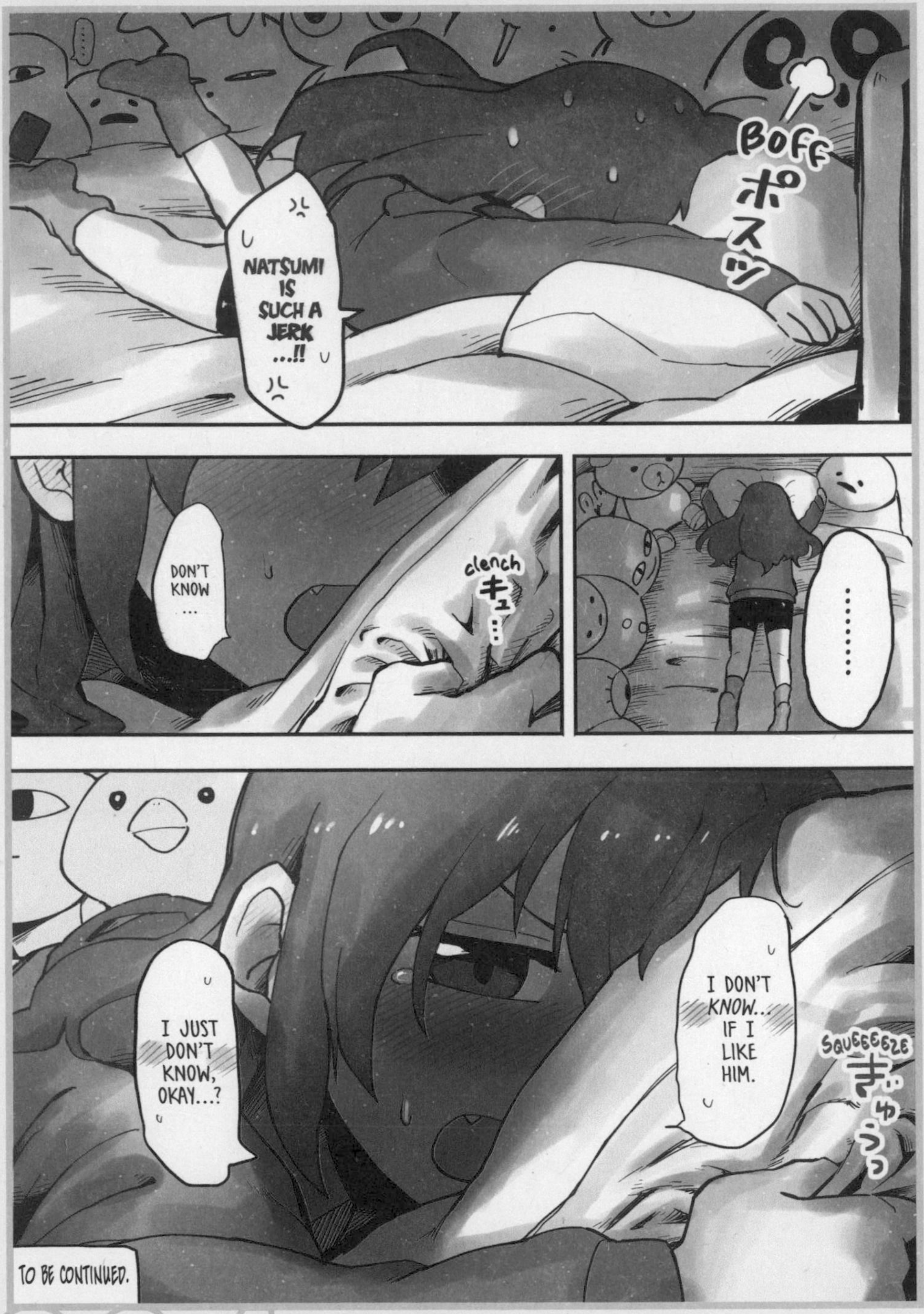

BOFF
ポスッ
…
NATSUMI IS SUCH A JERK …!!
……
clench
キュ…
DON'T KNOW …
SQUEEEEZE
ぎゅうっ
I DON'T KNOW… IF I LIKE HIM.
I JUST DON'T KNOW, OKAY…?
TO BE CONTINUED.

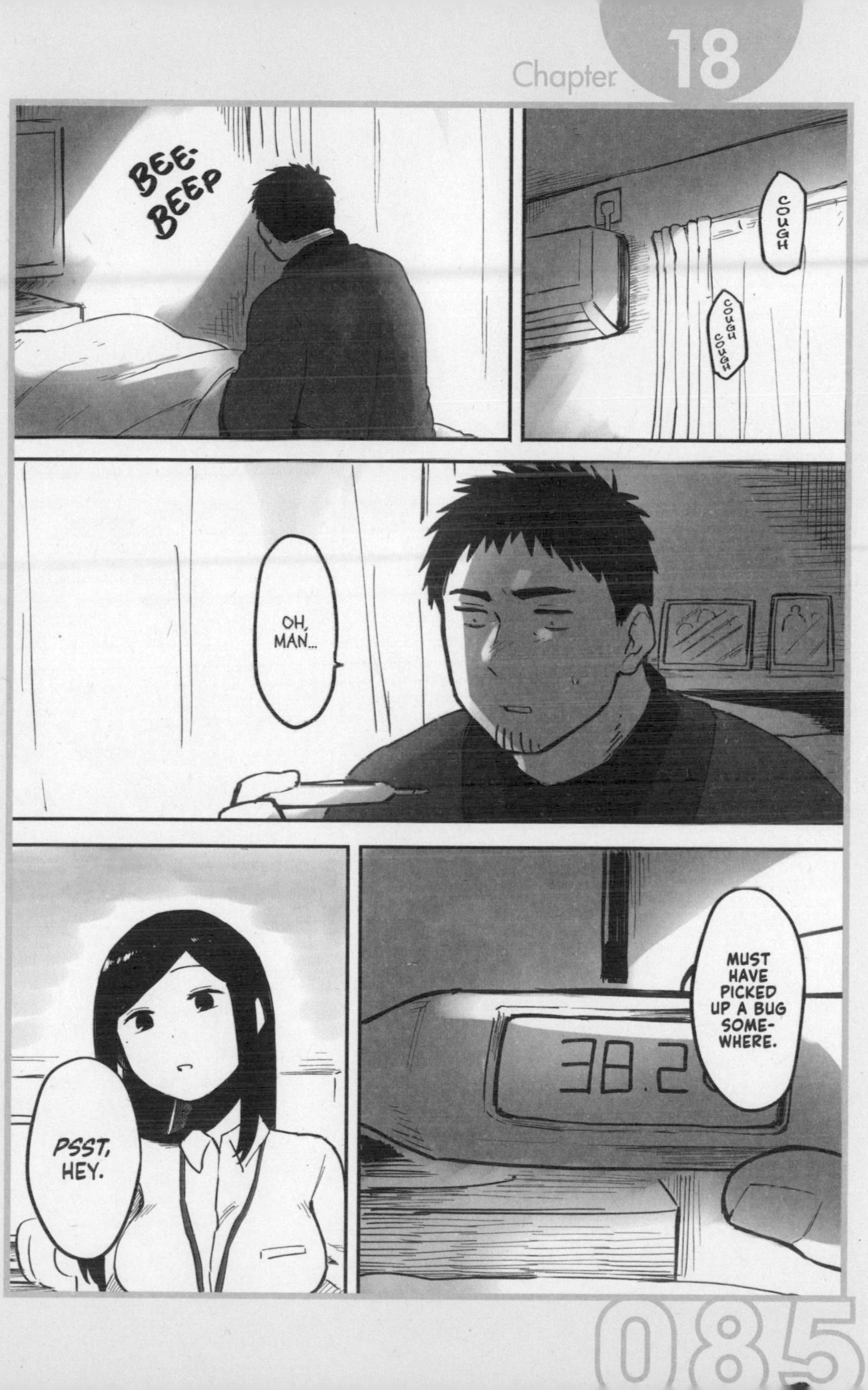
COUGH
COUGH COUGH
BEE-BEEP
OH, MAN...
MUST HAVE PICKED UP A BUG SOMEWHERE.
38.2
PSST, HEY.

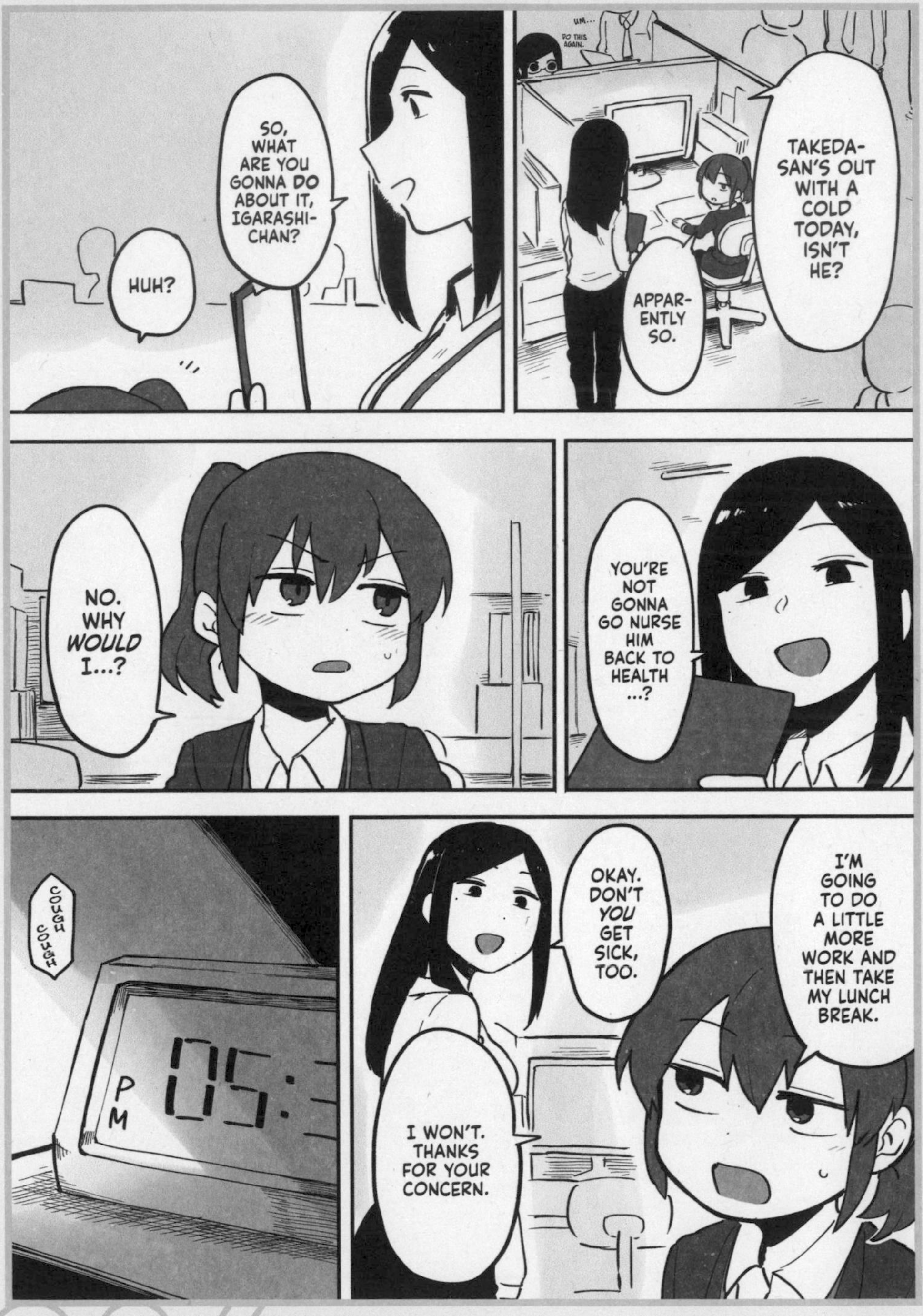
UM...
DO THIS AGAIN.
TAKEDA-SAN'S OUT WITH A COLD TODAY, ISN'T HE?
APPARENTLY SO.
SO, WHAT ARE YOU GONNA DO ABOUT IT, IGARASHI-CHAN?
HUH?
YOU'RE NOT GONNA GO NURSE HIM BACK TO HEALTH ...?
NO. WHY *WOULD* I...?
I'M GOING TO DO A LITTLE MORE WORK AND THEN TAKE MY LUNCH BREAK.
OKAY. DON'T *YOU* GET SICK, TOO.
I WON'T. THANKS FOR YOUR CONCERN.
COUGH COUGH
PM 05:

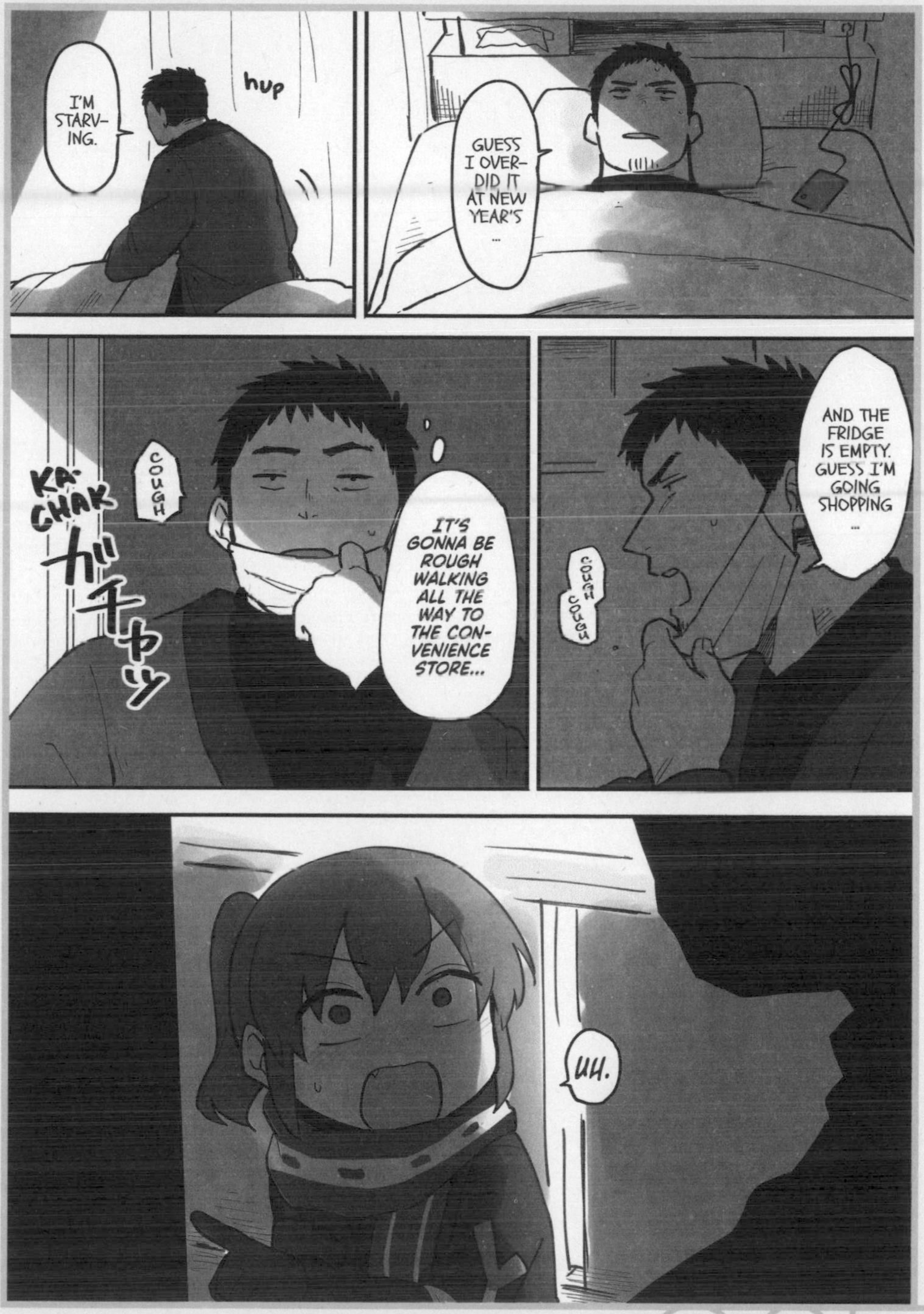
GUESS I OVERDID IT AT NEW YEAR'S...
hup
I'M STARVING.
AND THE FRIDGE IS EMPTY. GUESS I'M GOING SHOPPING...
COUGH COUGH
IT'S GONNA BE ROUGH WALKING ALL THE WAY TO THE CONVENIENCE STORE...
COUGH
KA-CHAK ガチャッ
UH.

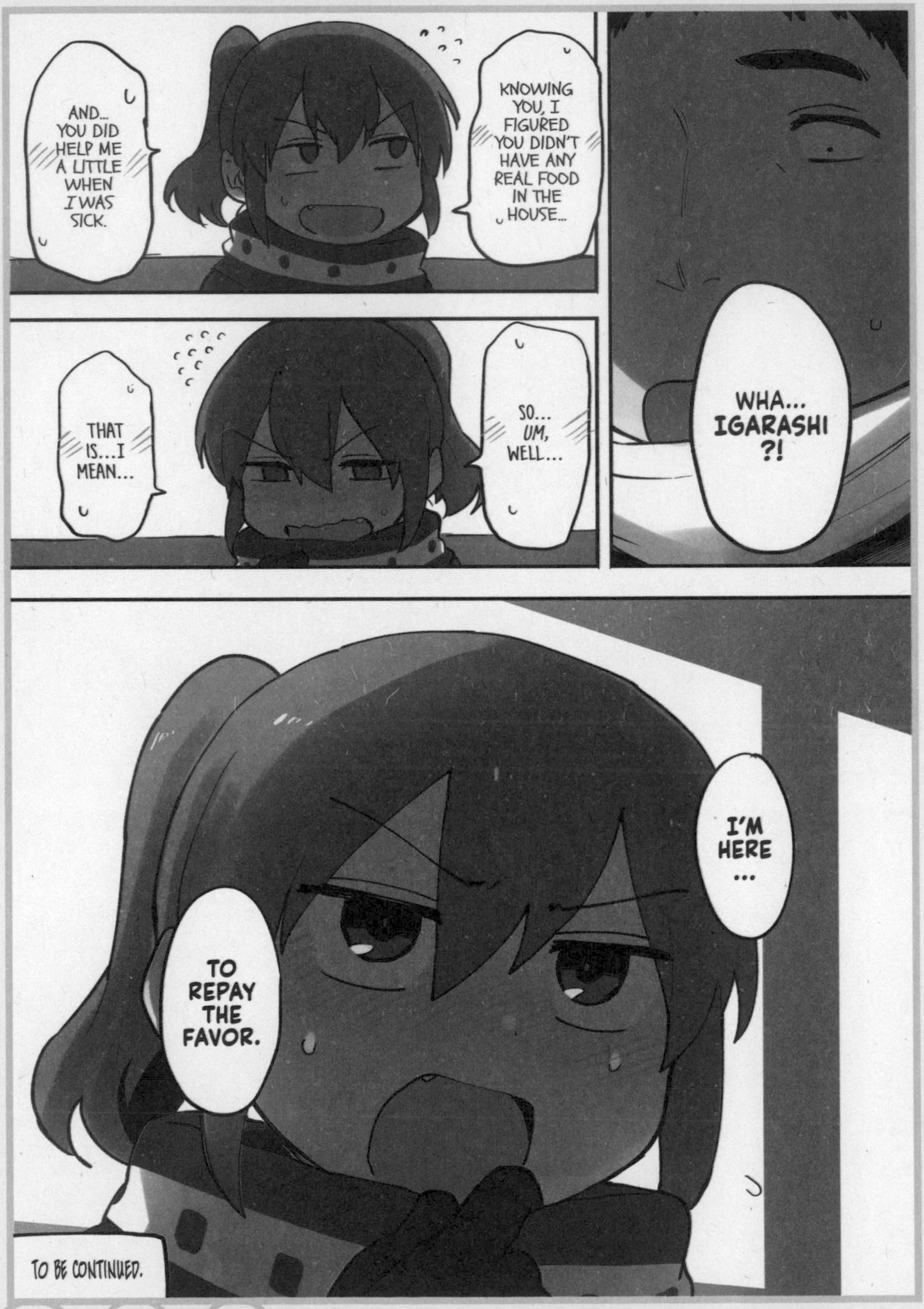
WHA... IGARASHI?!
KNOWING YOU, I FIGURED YOU DIDN'T HAVE ANY REAL FOOD IN THE HOUSE...
AND... YOU DID HELP ME A LITTLE WHEN I WAS SICK.
SO... UM, WELL...
THAT IS...I MEAN...
I'M HERE...
TO REPAY THE FAVOR.
TO BE CONTINUED.

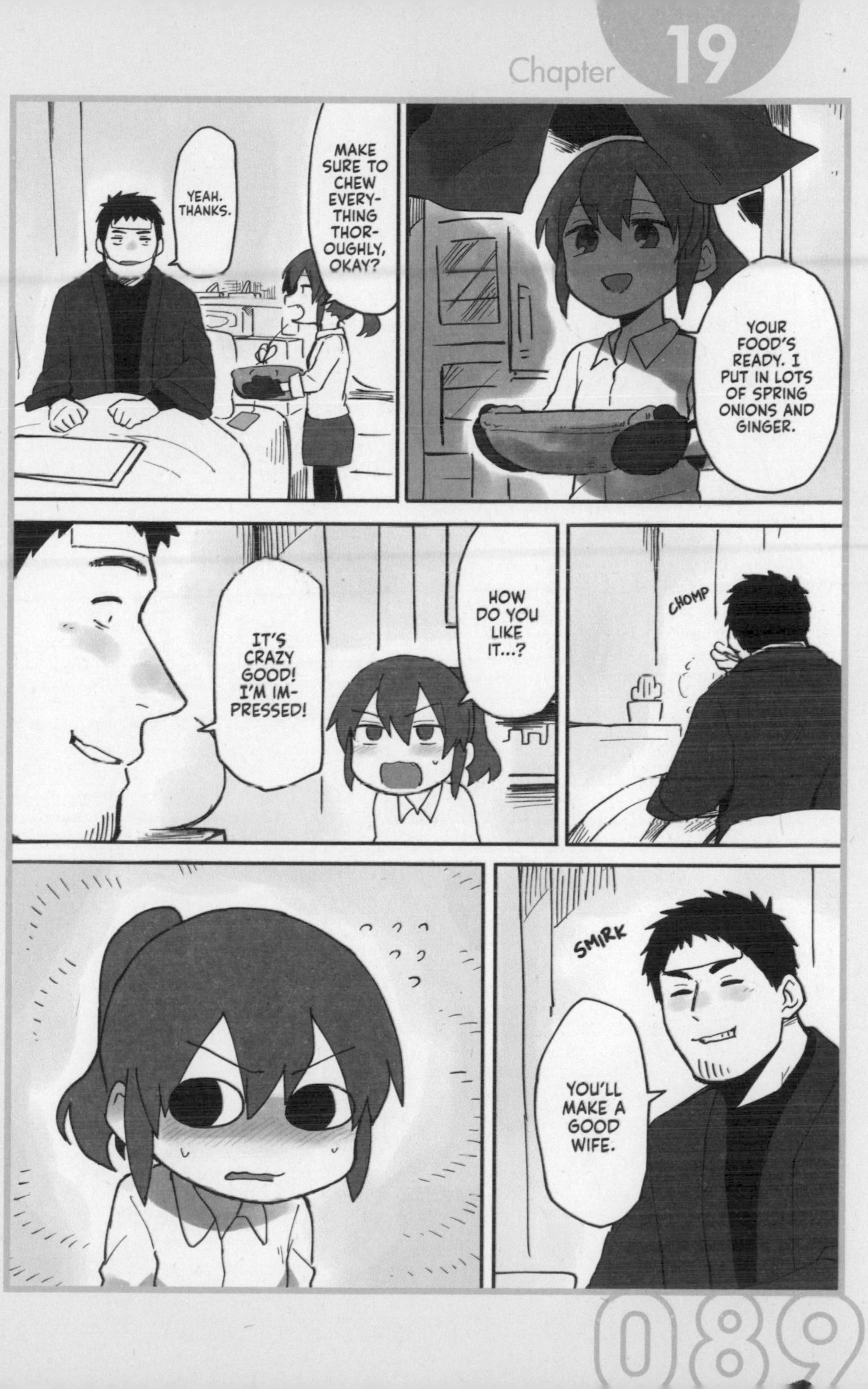
YOUR FOOD'S READY. I PUT IN LOTS OF SPRING ONIONS AND GINGER.
MAKE SURE TO CHEW EVERYTHING THOROUGHLY, OKAY?
YEAH. THANKS.
CHOMP
HOW DO YOU LIKE IT...?
IT'S CRAZY GOOD! I'M IMPRESSED!
SMIRK
YOU'LL MAKE A GOOD WIFE.

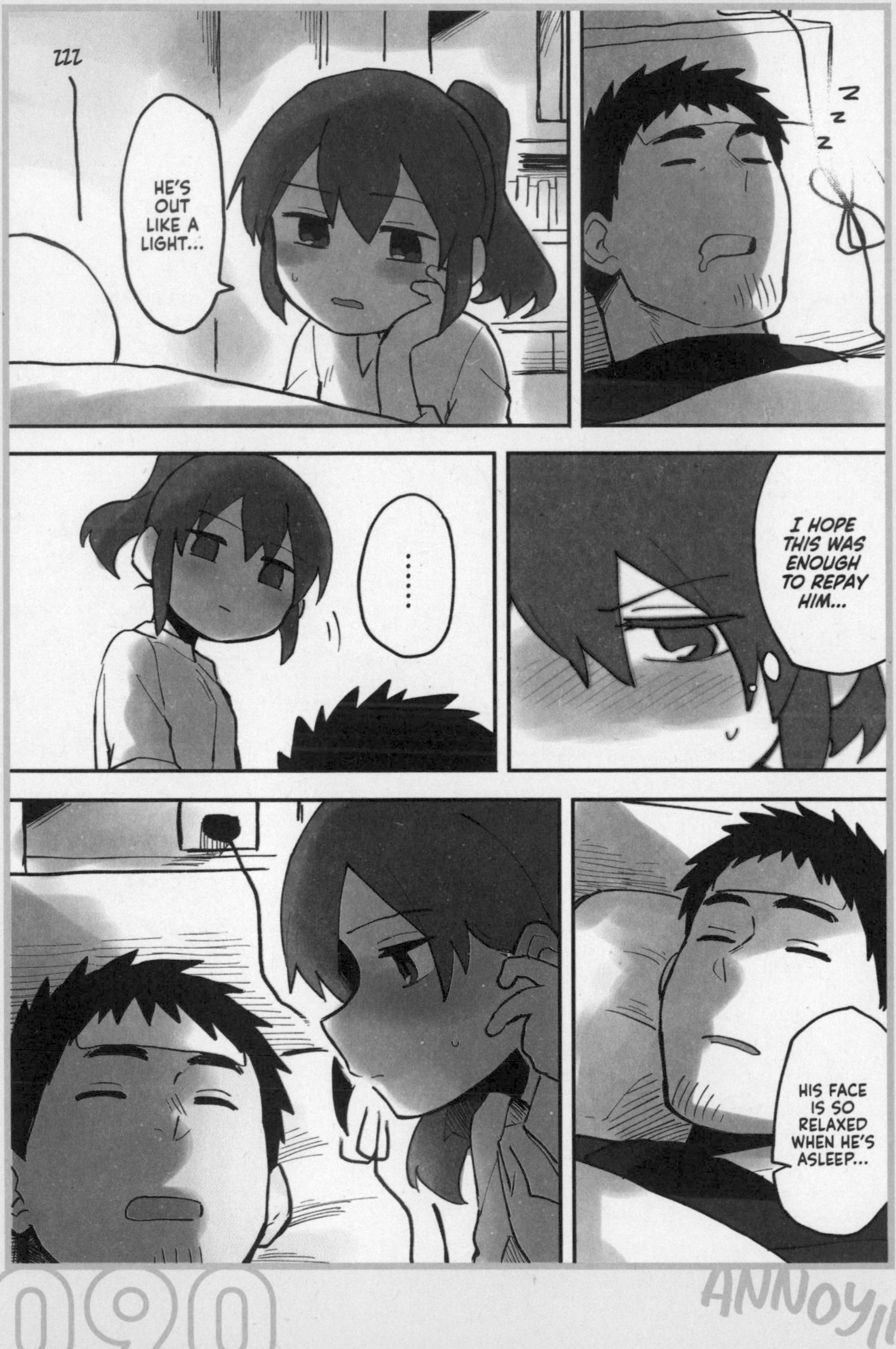
Z
Z
Z
zzz
HE'S OUT LIKE A LIGHT...
I HOPE THIS WAS ENOUGH TO REPAY HIM...
......
HIS FACE IS SO RELAXED WHEN HE'S ASLEEP...

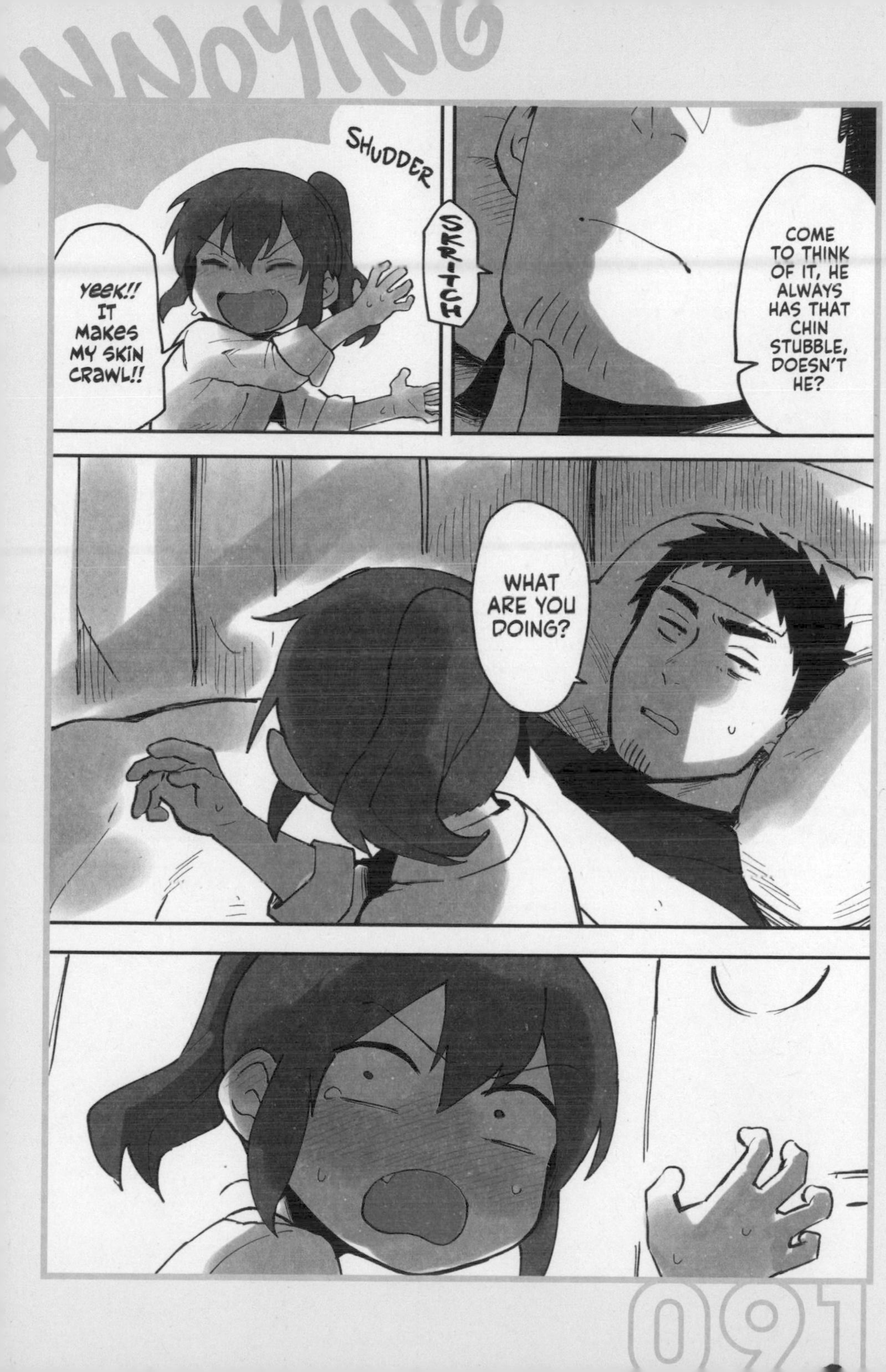
COME TO THINK OF IT, HE ALWAYS HAS THAT CHIN STUBBLE, DOESN'T HE?
SKRITCH
SHUDDER
YEEK!! IT MAKES MY SKIN CRAWL!!
WHAT ARE YOU DOING?

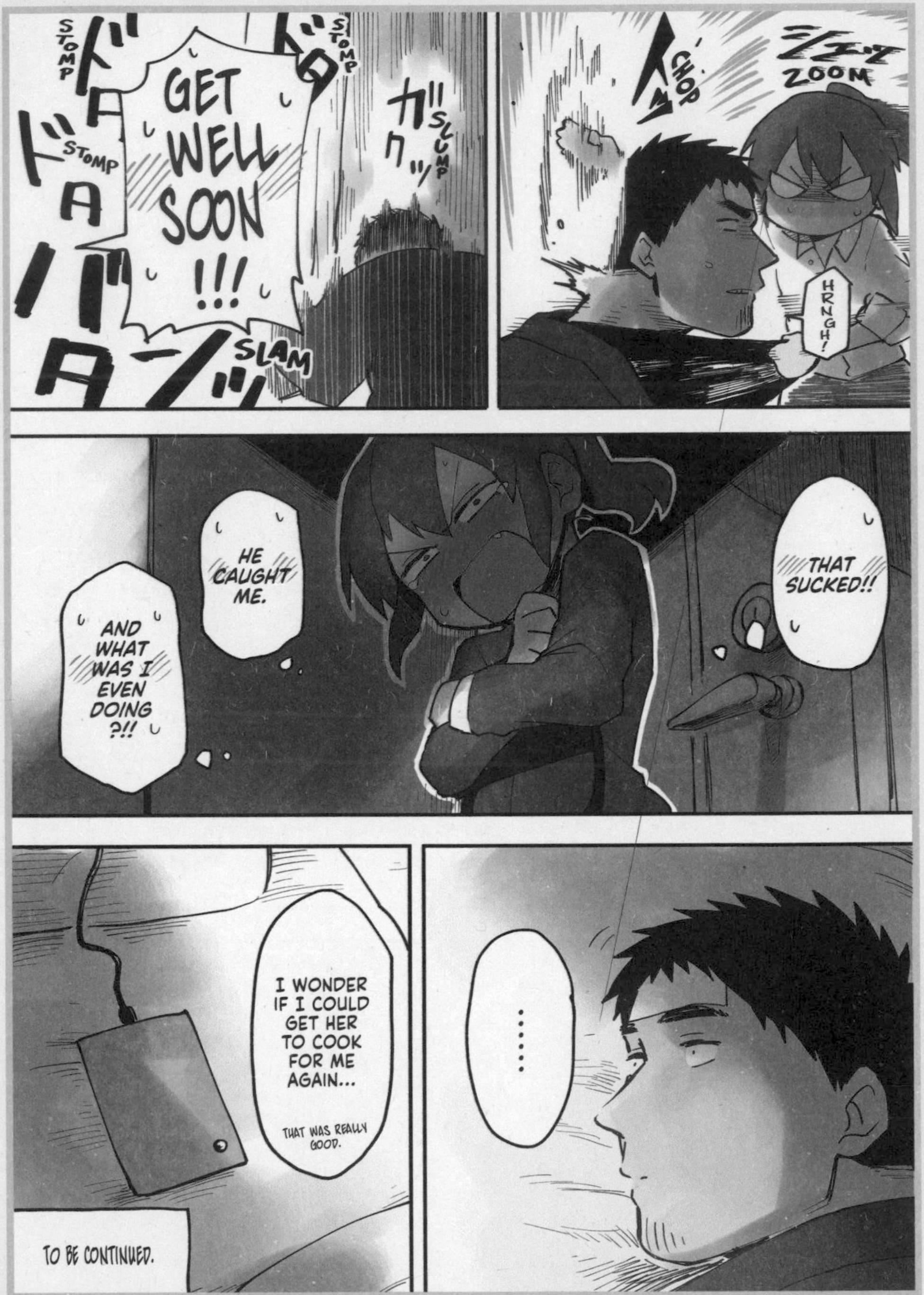
CHOP
ZOOM
HRNGH!
STOMP
STOMP
STOMP
GET WELL SOON!!!
SLUMP
SLAM
THAT SUCKED!!
HE CAUGHT ME.
AND WHAT WAS I EVEN DOING?!!
......
I WONDER IF I COULD GET HER TO COOK FOR ME AGAIN...
THAT WAS REALLY GOOD.
TO BE CONTINUED.

Chapter 20

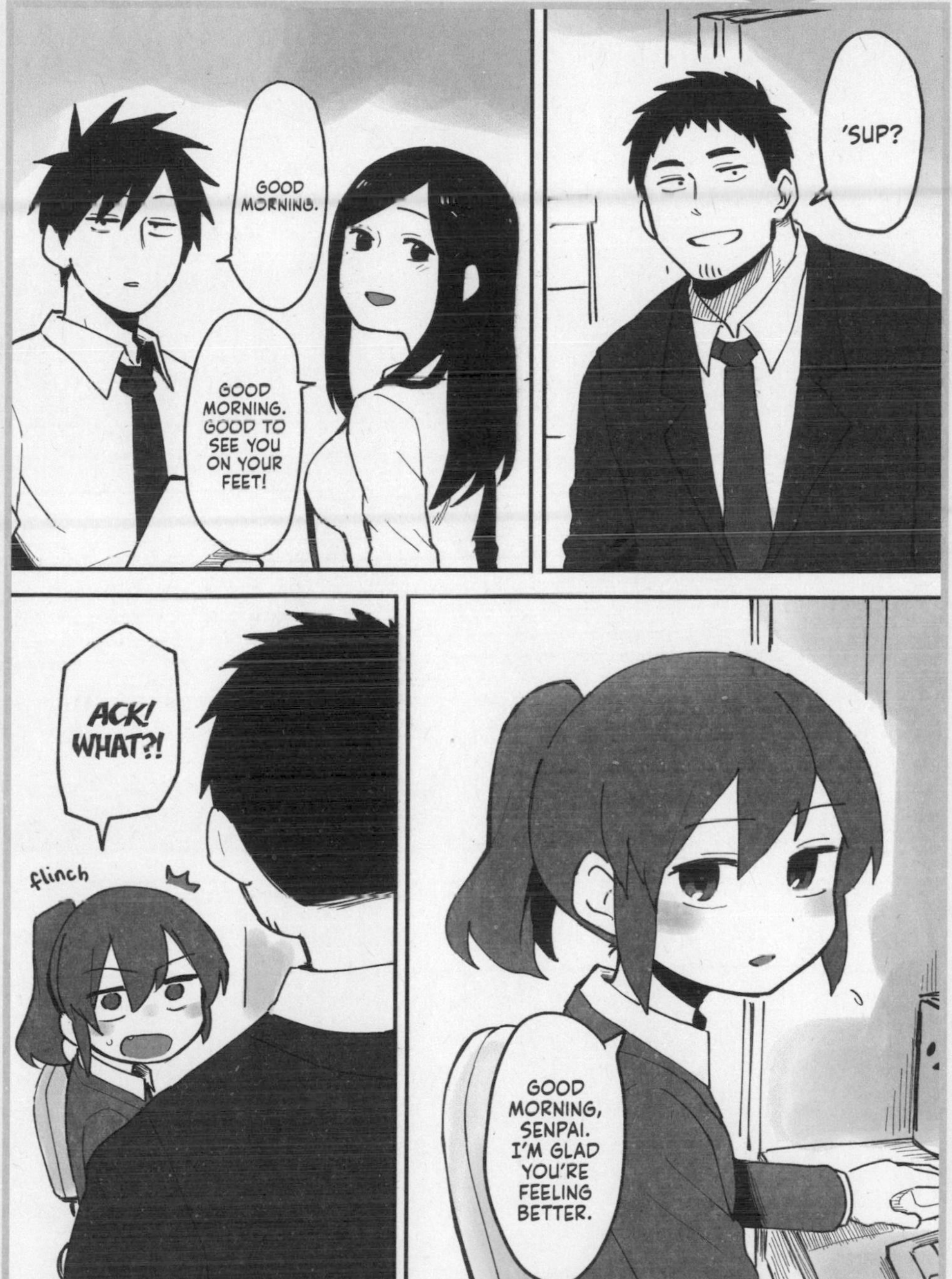
'SUP?
GOOD MORNING.
GOOD MORNING. GOOD TO SEE YOU ON YOUR FEET!
GOOD MORNING, SENPAI. I'M GLAD YOU'RE FEELING BETTER.
ACK! WHAT?!
flinch

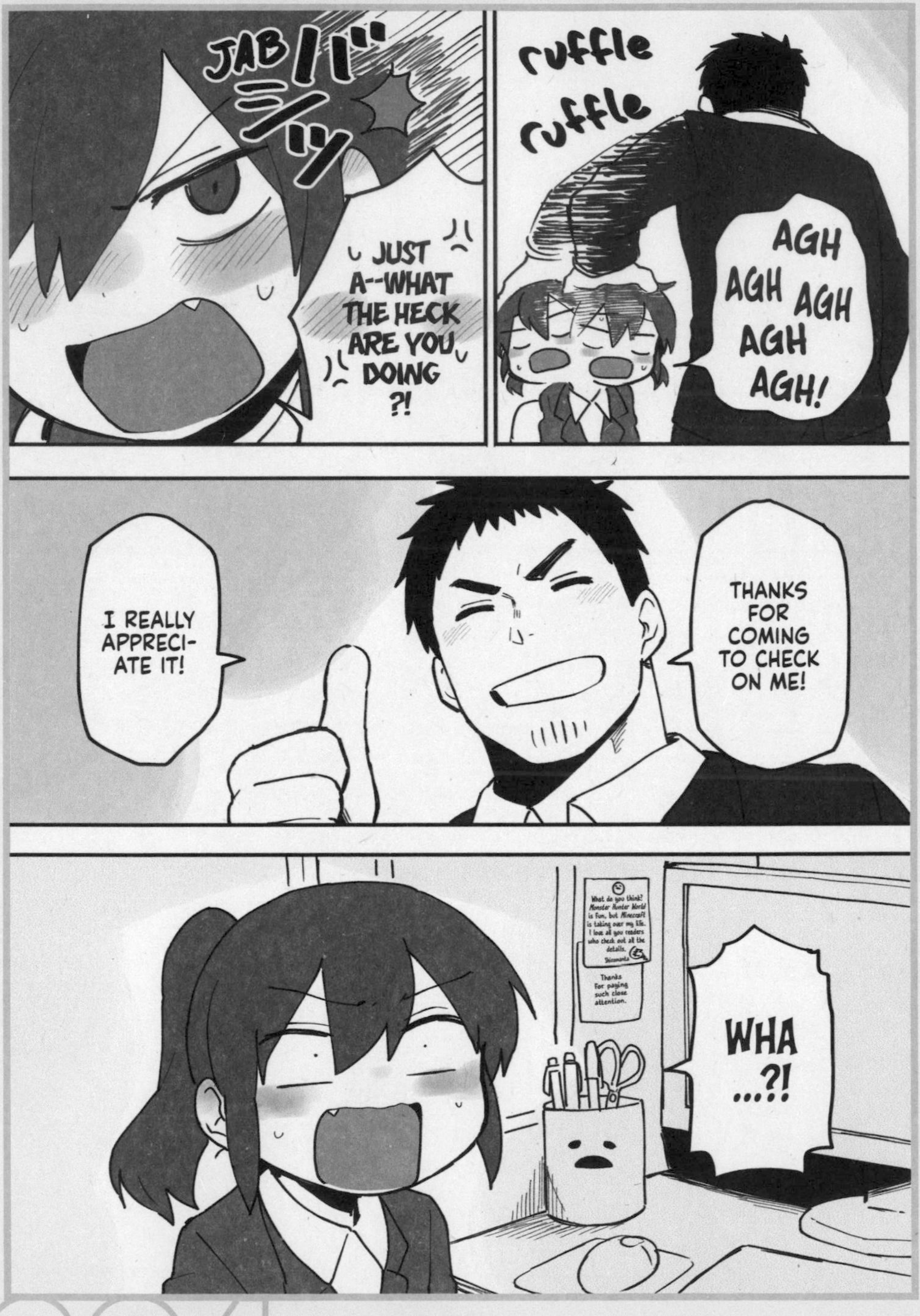
ruffle
ruffle
AGH AGH AGH AGH AGH!
JAB
JUST A--WHAT THE HECK ARE YOU DOING ?!
THANKS FOR COMING TO CHECK ON ME!
I REALLY APPRECI- ATE IT!
What do you think? Monster Hunter World is fun, but Minecraft is taking over my life. I love all you readers who check out all the details.
Thanks for paying such close attention.
WHA ...?!

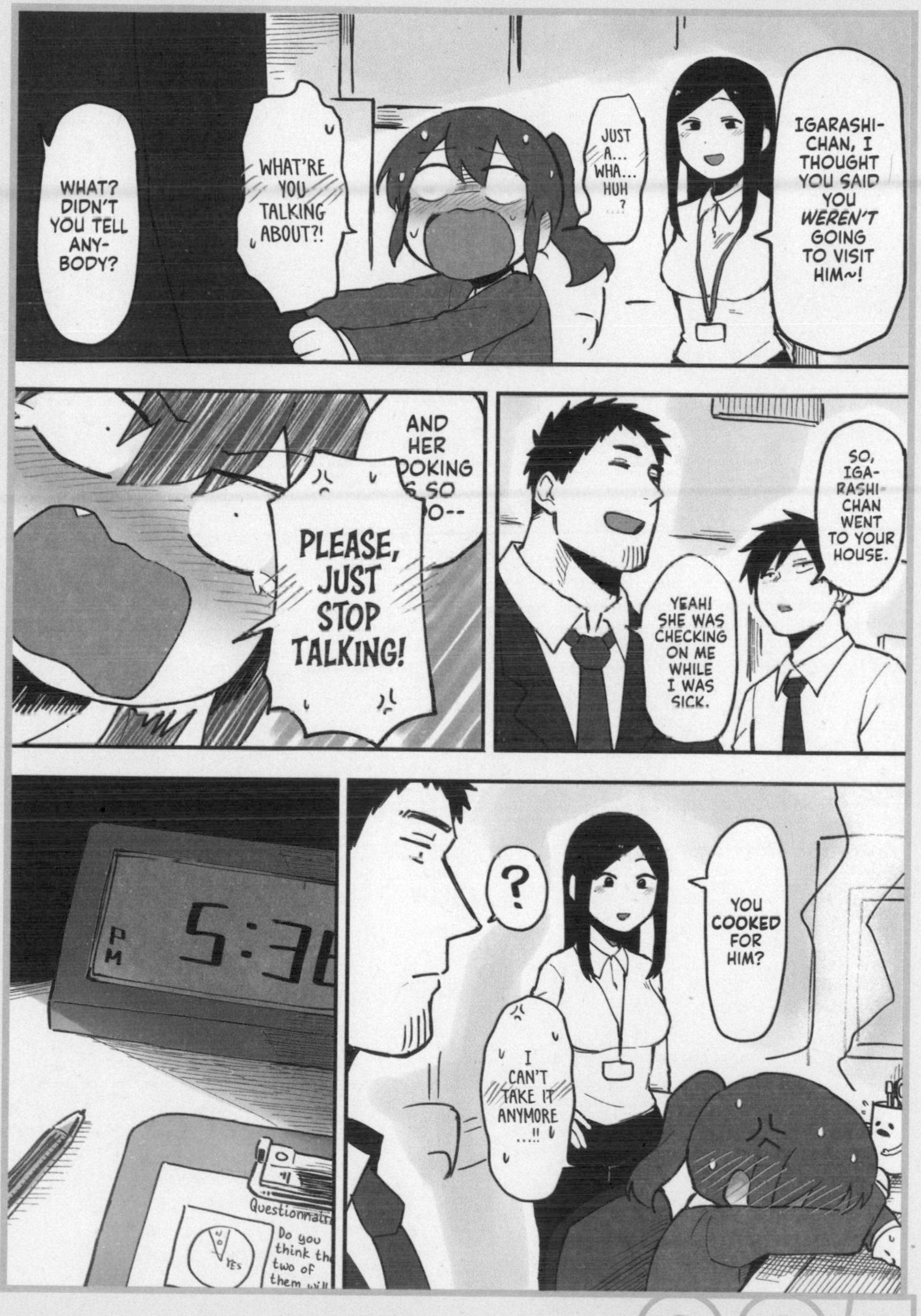
IGARASHI-CHAN, I THOUGHT YOU SAID YOU *WEREN'T* GOING TO VISIT HIM~!
JUST A... WHA... HUH?
WHAT'RE YOU TALKING ABOUT?!
WHAT? DIDN'T YOU TELL ANYBODY?
SO, IGA-RASHI-CHAN WENT TO YOUR HOUSE.
YEAH! SHE WAS CHECKING ON ME WHILE I WAS SICK.
AND HER
OOKING S SO O--
PLEASE, JUST STOP TALKING!
YOU COOKED FOR HIM?
?
I CAN'T TAKE IT ANYMORE ...!!
PM
NO
YES

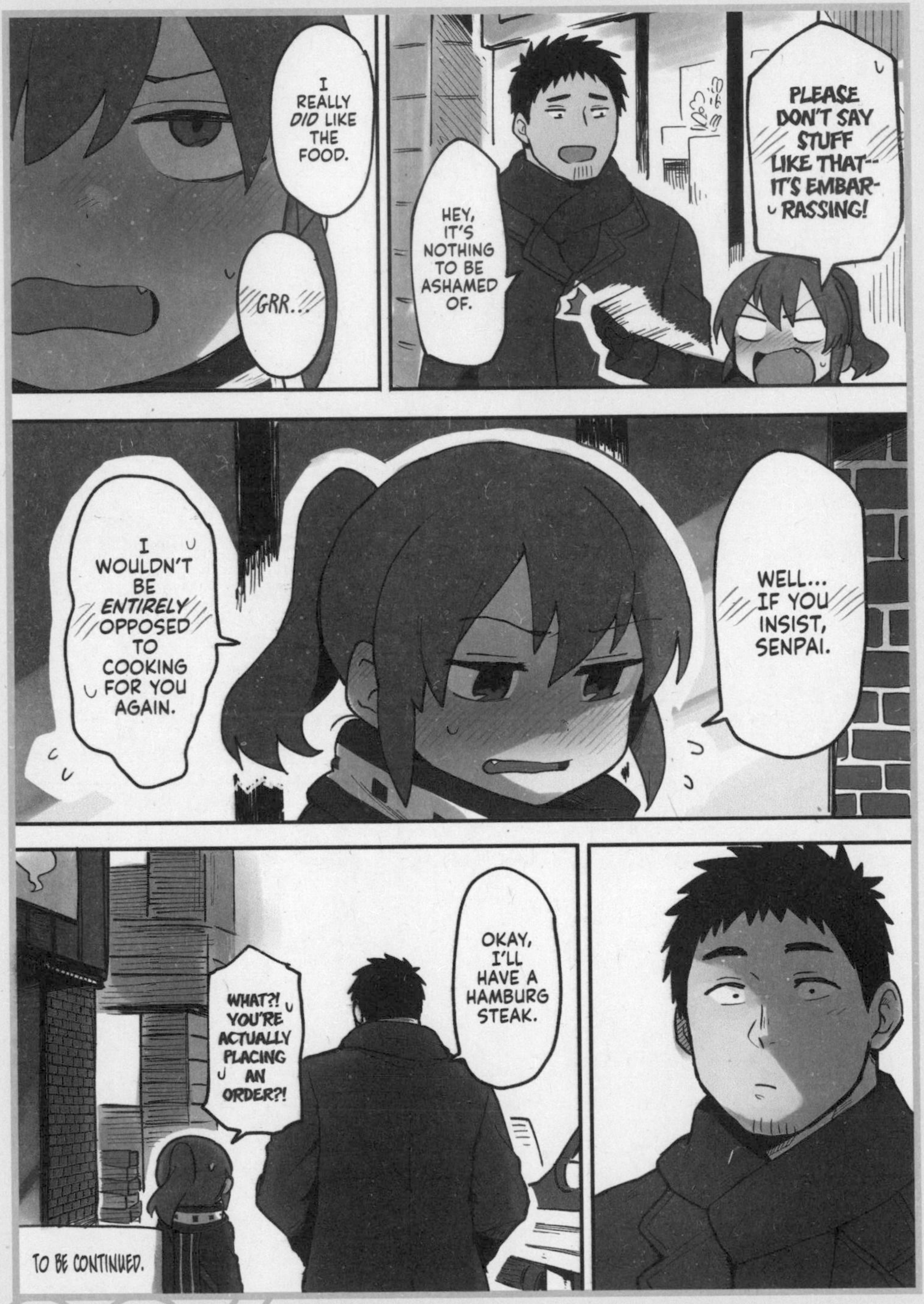
PLEASE DON'T SAY STUFF LIKE THAT-- IT'S EMBARRASSING!
HEY, IT'S NOTHING TO BE ASHAMED OF.
I REALLY DID LIKE THE FOOD.
GRR...
WELL... IF YOU INSIST, SENPAI.
I WOULDN'T BE ENTIRELY OPPOSED TO COOKING FOR YOU AGAIN.
OKAY, I'LL HAVE A HAMBURG STEAK.
WHAT?! YOU'RE ACTUALLY PLACING AN ORDER?!
TO BE CONTINUED.

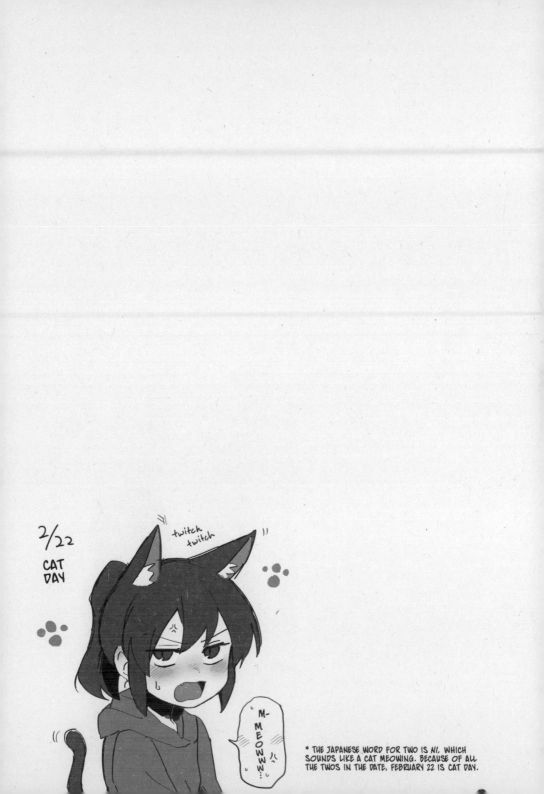

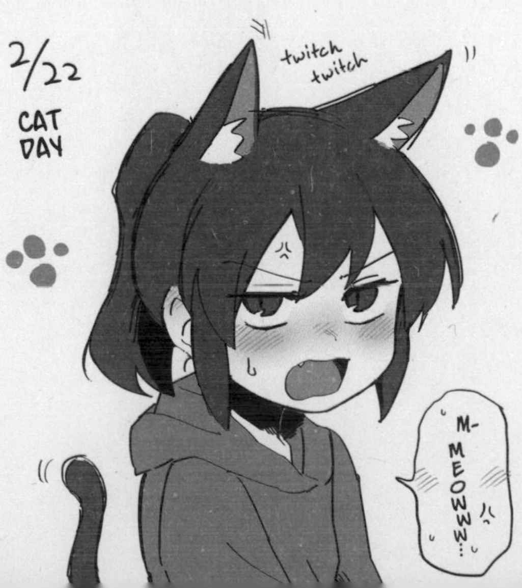
2/22
CAT DAY
twitch twitch
M-MEOWWW...

* THE JAPANESE WORD FOR TWO IS *NI*, WHICH SOUNDS LIKE A CAT MEOWING. BECAUSE OF ALL THE TWOS IN THE DATE, FEBRUARY 22 IS CAT DAY.

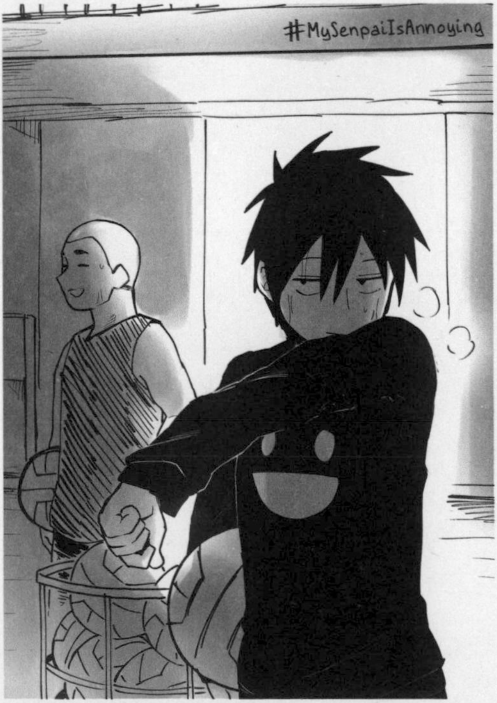
#MySenpaiIsAnnoying

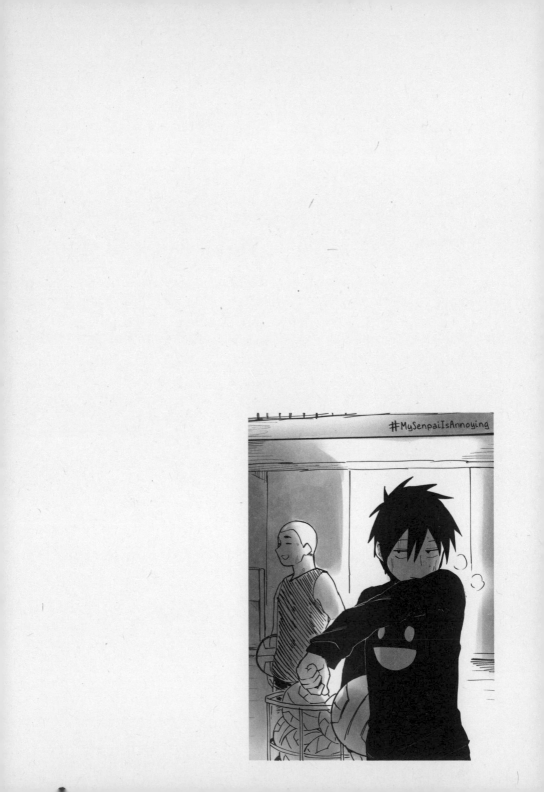

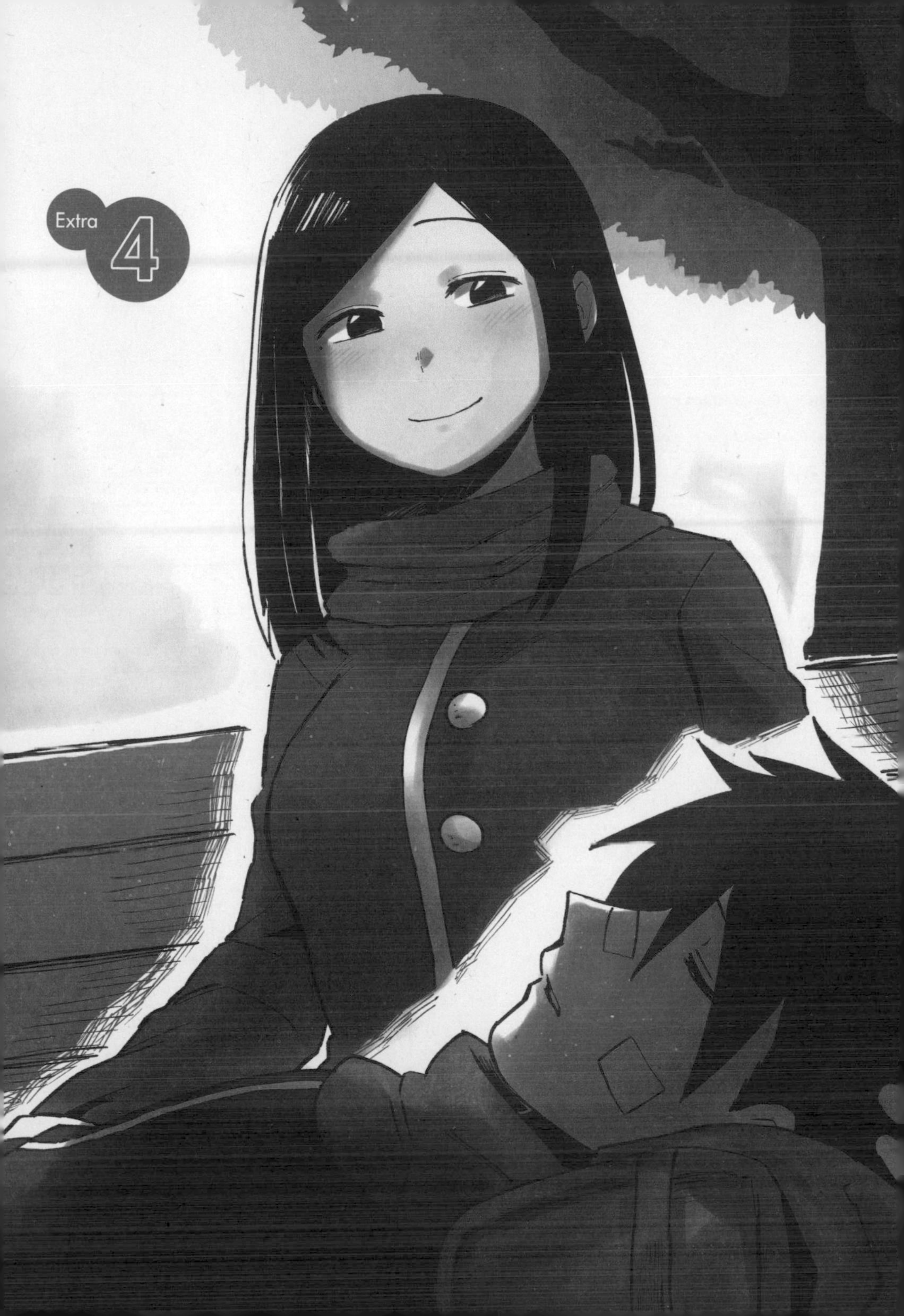
Extra 4

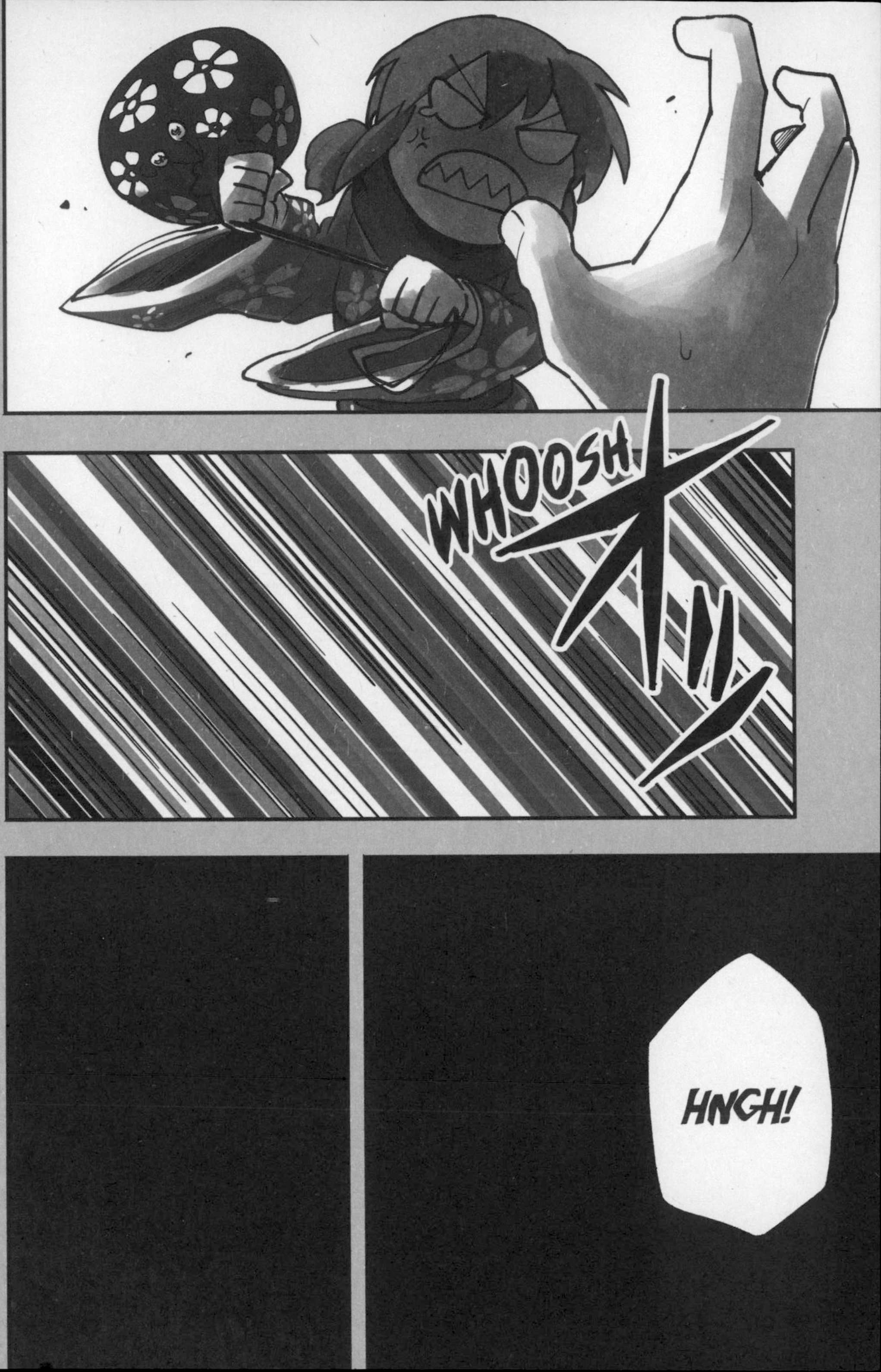
WHOOSH
HNGH!

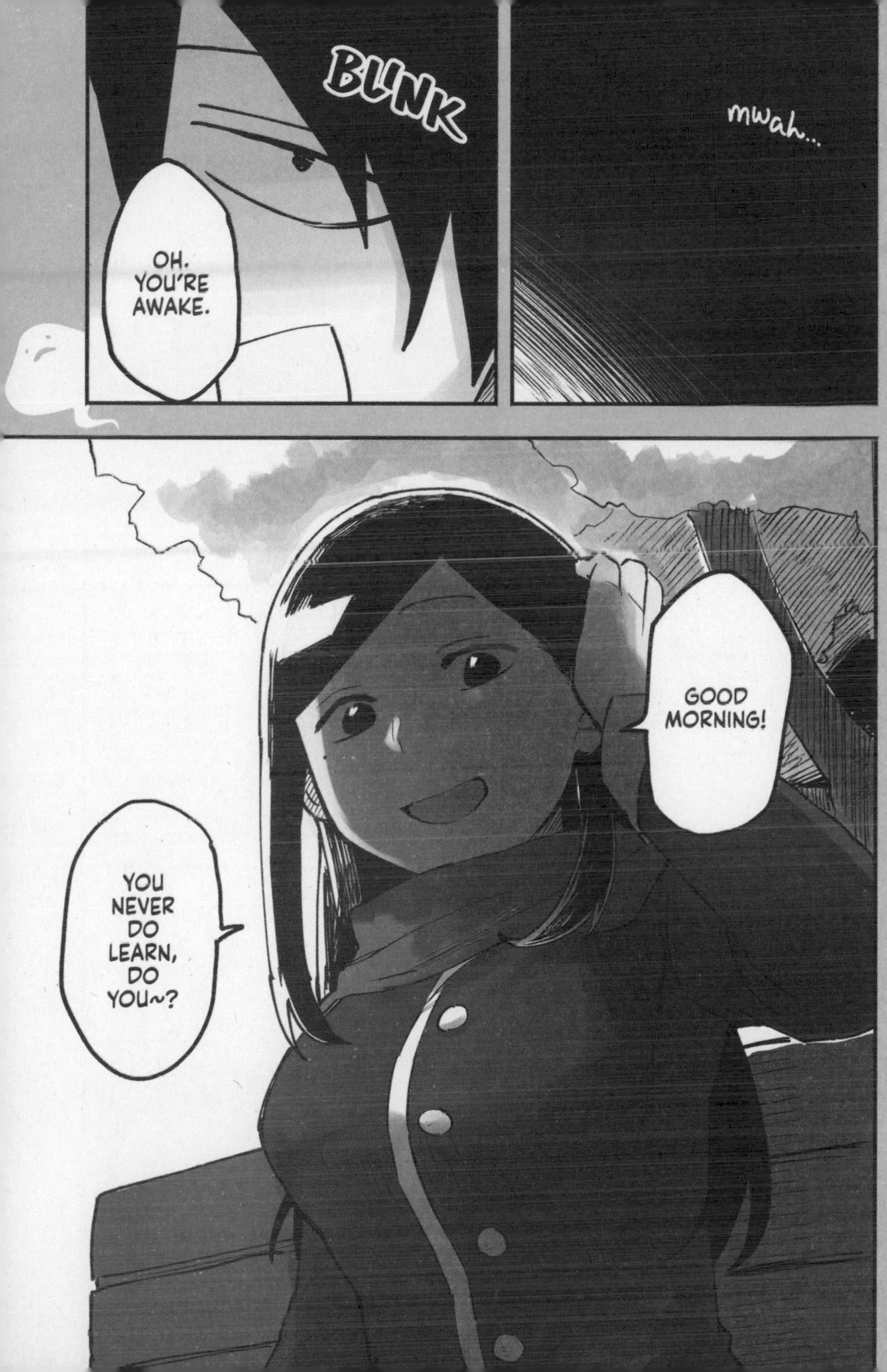
mwah...
BLINK
OH. YOU'RE AWAKE.
GOOD MORNING!
YOU NEVER DO LEARN, DO YOU~?

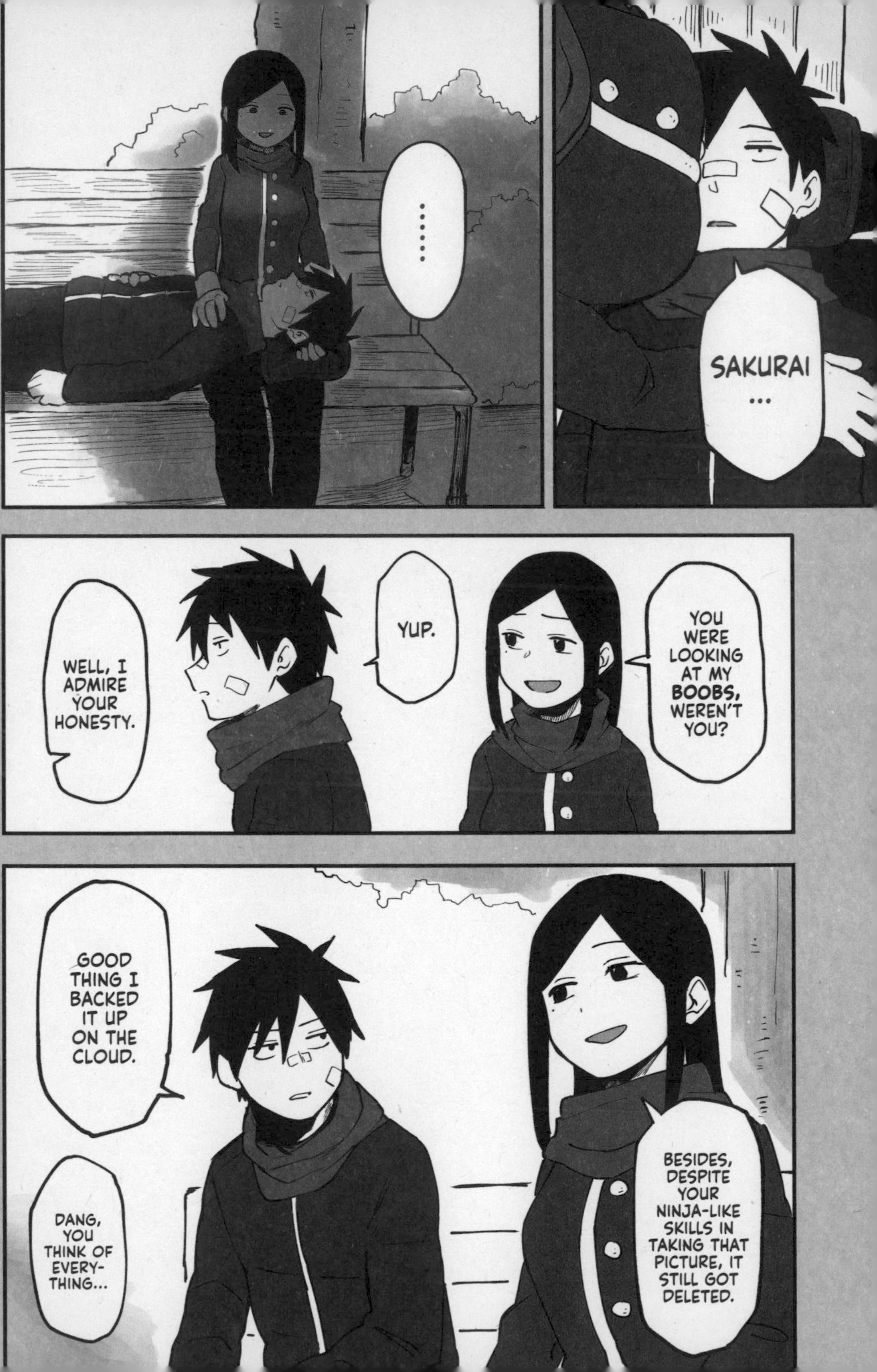
SAKURAI ...
......
YOU WERE LOOKING AT MY BOOBS, WEREN'T YOU?
YUP.
WELL, I ADMIRE YOUR HONESTY.
BESIDES, DESPITE YOUR NINJA-LIKE SKILLS IN TAKING THAT PICTURE, IT STILL GOT DELETED.
GOOD THING I BACKED IT UP ON THE CLOUD.
DANG, YOU THINK OF EVERYTHING...

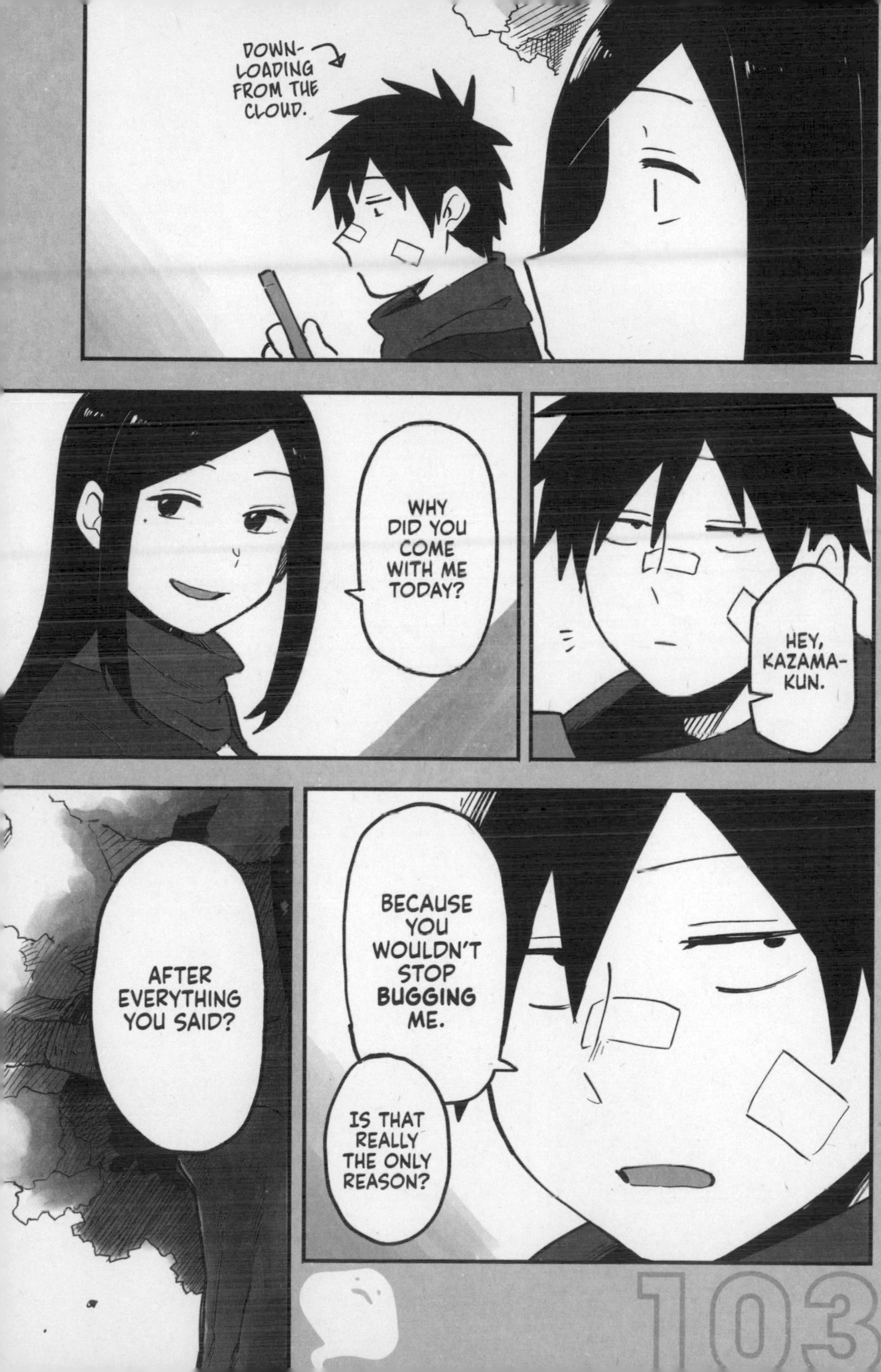
DOWN-LOADING FROM THE CLOUD.
HEY, KAZAMA-KUN.
WHY DID YOU COME WITH ME TODAY?
BECAUSE YOU WOULDN'T STOP BUGGING ME.
IS THAT REALLY THE ONLY REASON?
AFTER EVERYTHING YOU SAID?

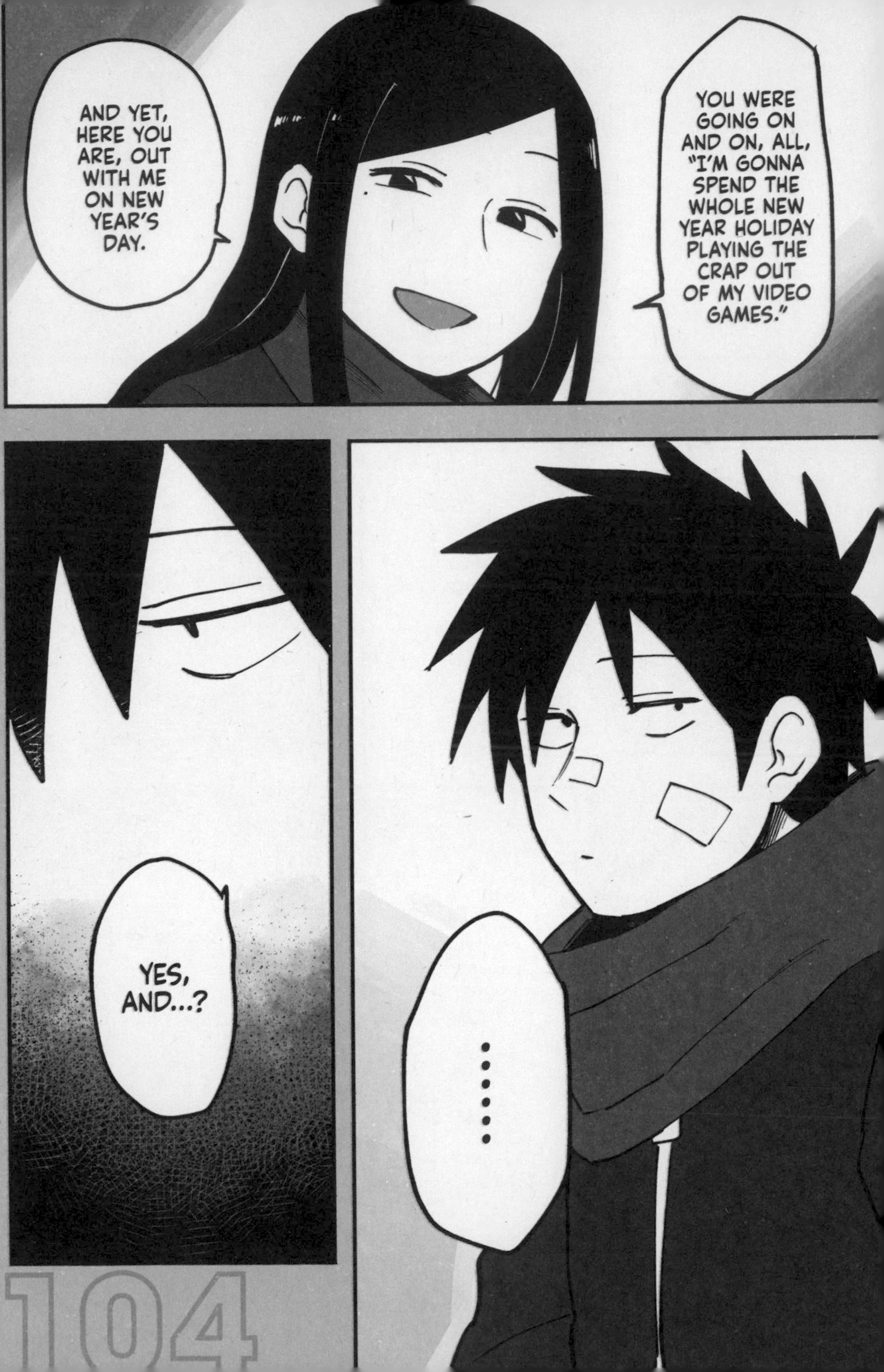
YOU WERE GOING ON AND ON, ALL, "I'M GONNA SPEND THE WHOLE NEW YEAR HOLIDAY PLAYING THE CRAP OUT OF MY VIDEO GAMES."
AND YET, HERE YOU ARE, OUT WITH ME ON NEW YEAR'S DAY.
......
YES, AND...?

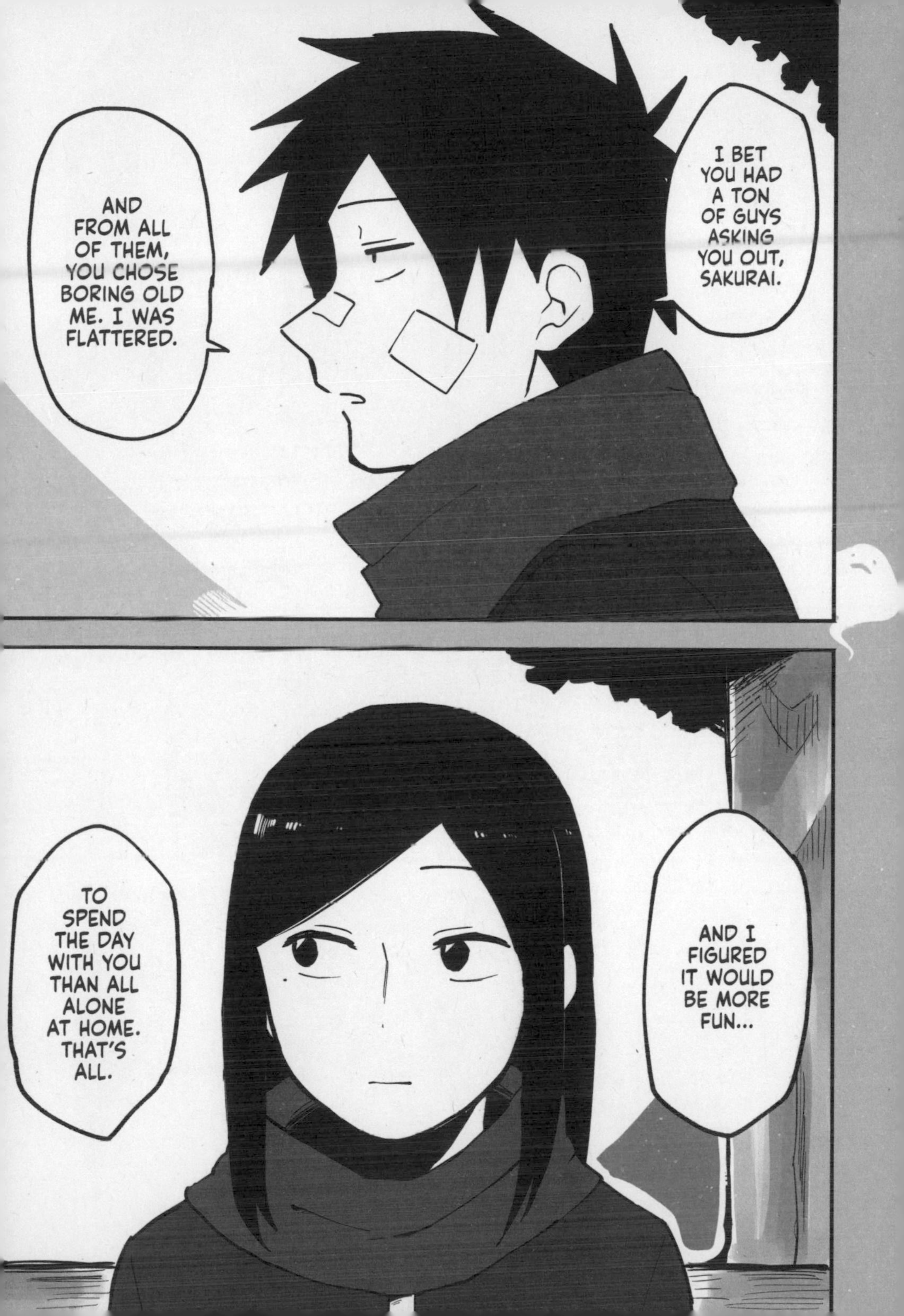
I BET YOU HAD A TON OF GUYS ASKING YOU OUT, SAKURAI.
AND FROM ALL OF THEM, YOU CHOSE BORING OLD ME. I WAS FLATTERED.
AND I FIGURED IT WOULD BE MORE FUN...
TO SPEND THE DAY WITH YOU THAN ALL ALONE AT HOME. THAT'S ALL.

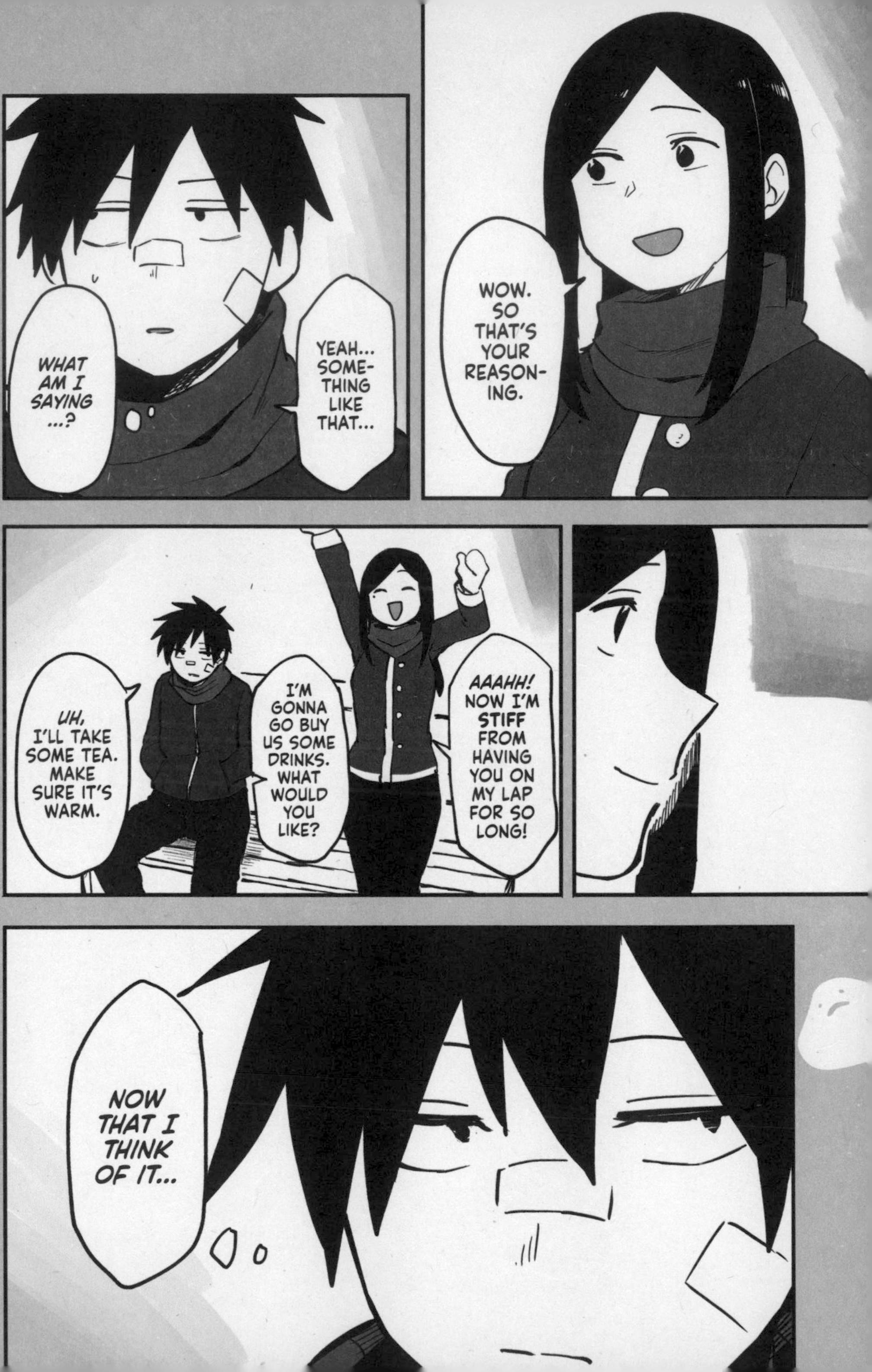
WOW. SO THAT'S YOUR REASON-ING.
YEAH... SOME-THING LIKE THAT...
WHAT AM I SAYING ...?
AAAHH! NOW I'M STIFF FROM HAVING YOU ON MY LAP FOR SO LONG!
I'M GONNA GO BUY US SOME DRINKS. WHAT WOULD YOU LIKE?
UH, I'LL TAKE SOME TEA. MAKE SURE IT'S WARM.
NOW THAT I THINK OF IT...

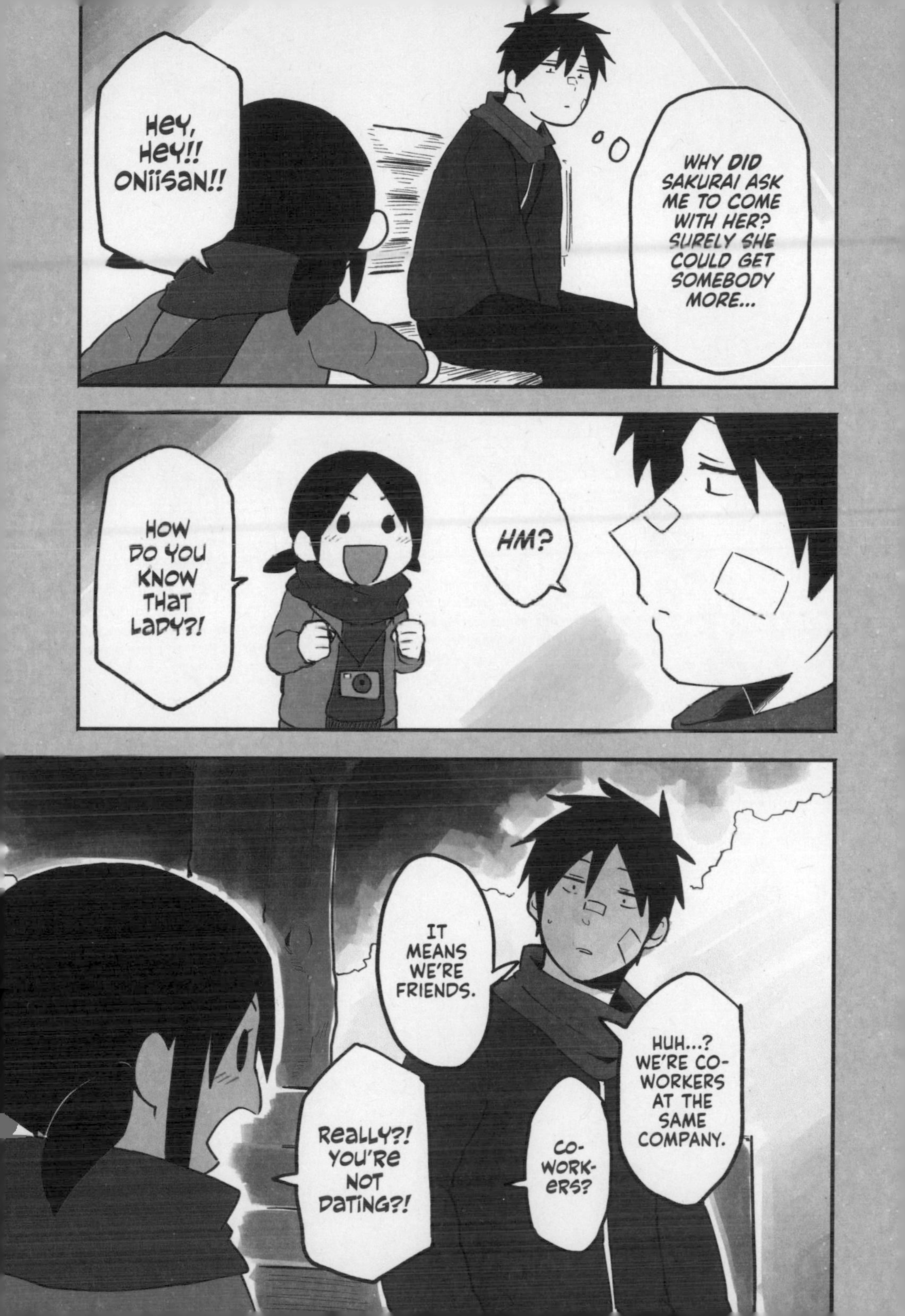
WHY DID SAKURAI ASK ME TO COME WITH HER? SURELY SHE COULD GET SOMEBODY MORE...
HEY, HEY!! ONIISAN!!
HM?
HOW DO YOU KNOW THAT LADY?!
HUH...? WE'RE CO-WORKERS AT THE SAME COMPANY.
CO-WORK-ERS?
IT MEANS WE'RE FRIENDS.
REALLY?! YOU'RE NOT DATING?!

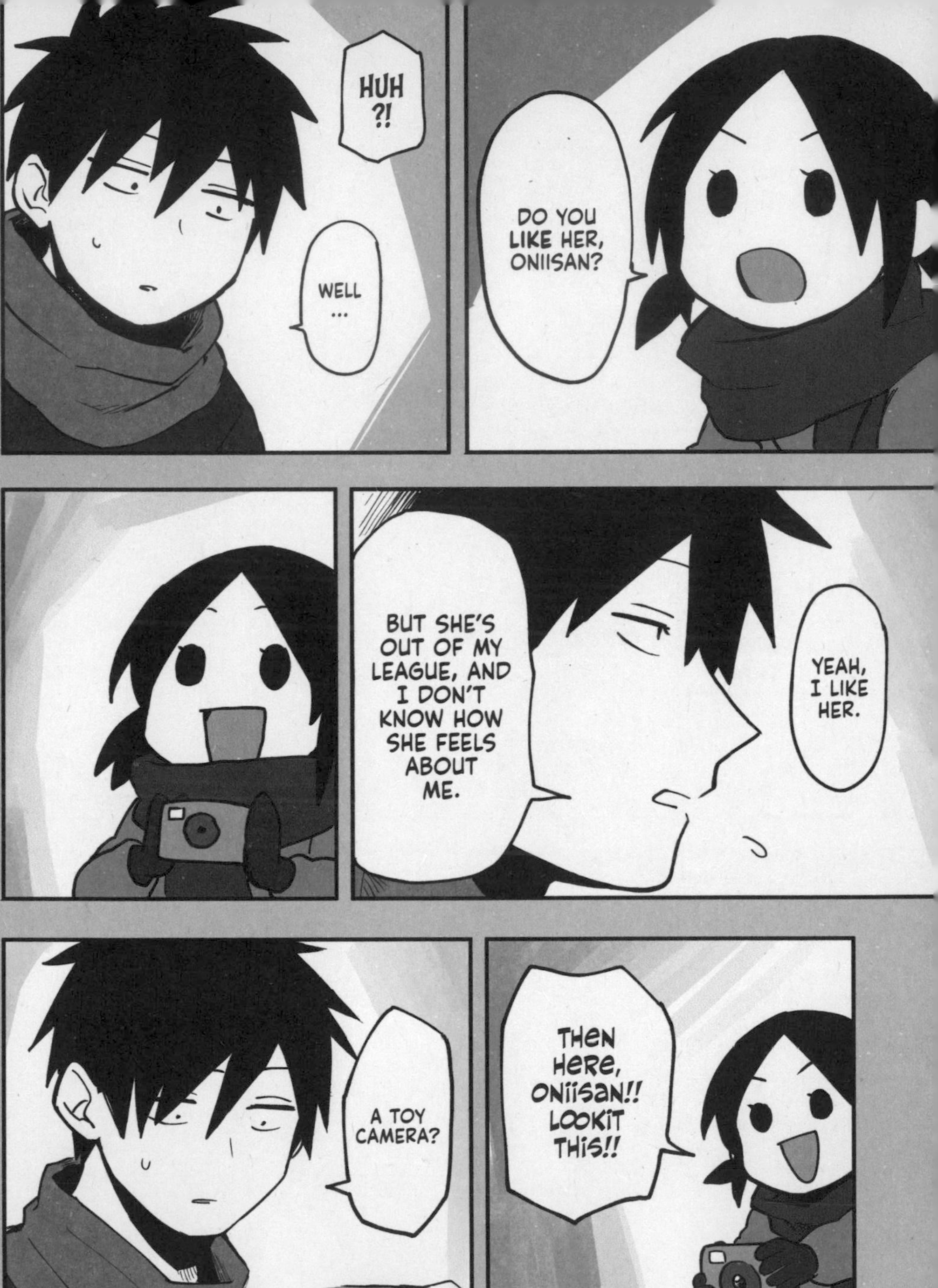
DO YOU LIKE HER, ONIISAN?
HUH ?!
WELL ...
YEAH, I LIKE HER.
BUT SHE'S OUT OF MY LEAGUE, AND I DON'T KNOW HOW SHE FEELS ABOUT ME.
THEN HERE, ONIISAN!! LOOKIT THIS!!
A TOY CAMERA?

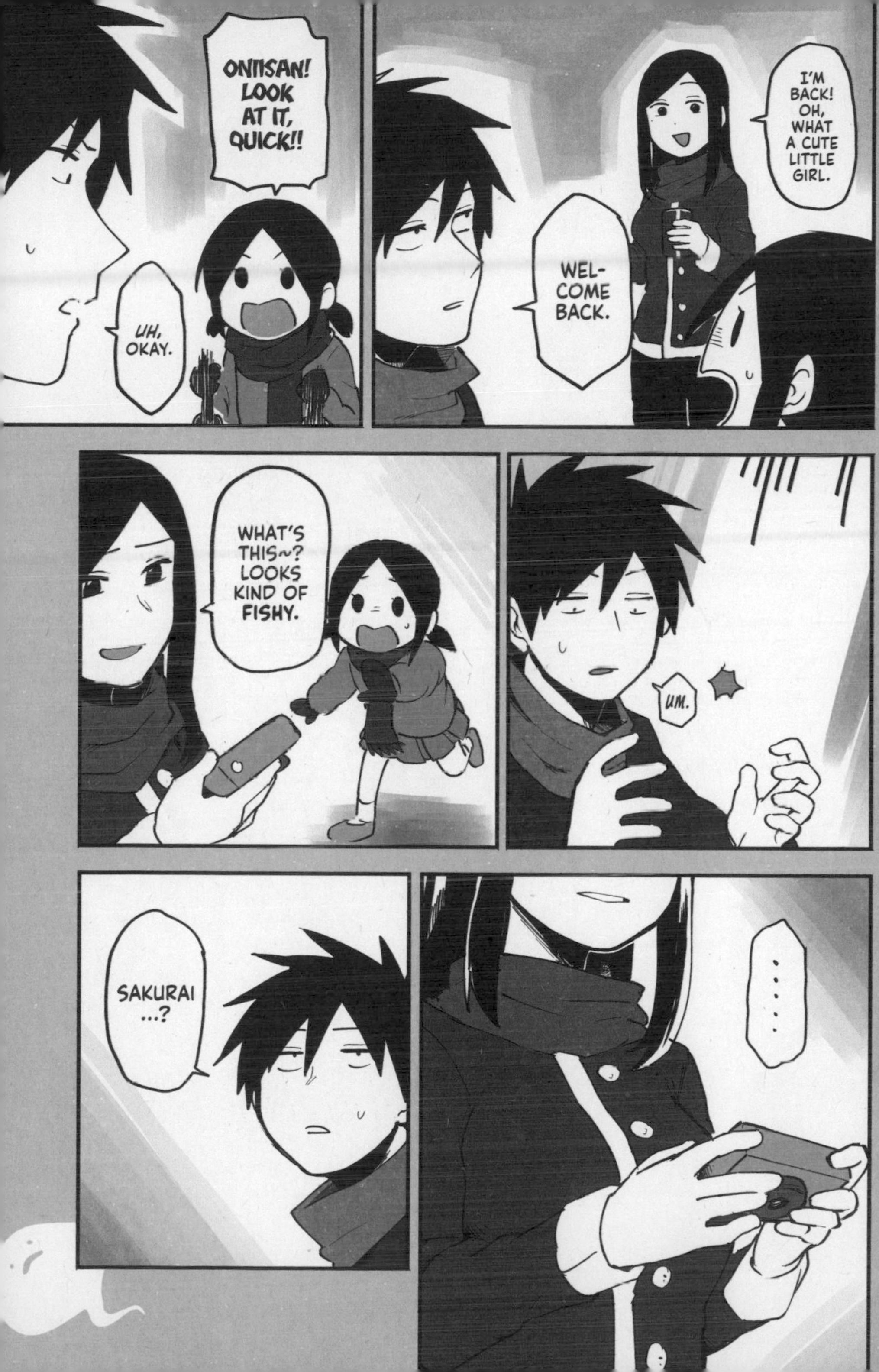
I'M BACK! OH, WHAT A CUTE LITTLE GIRL.
WEL-COME BACK.
ONIISAN! LOOK AT IT, QUICK!!
UH, OKAY.
UM.
WHAT'S THIS~? LOOKS KIND OF FISHY.
......
SAKURAI ...?

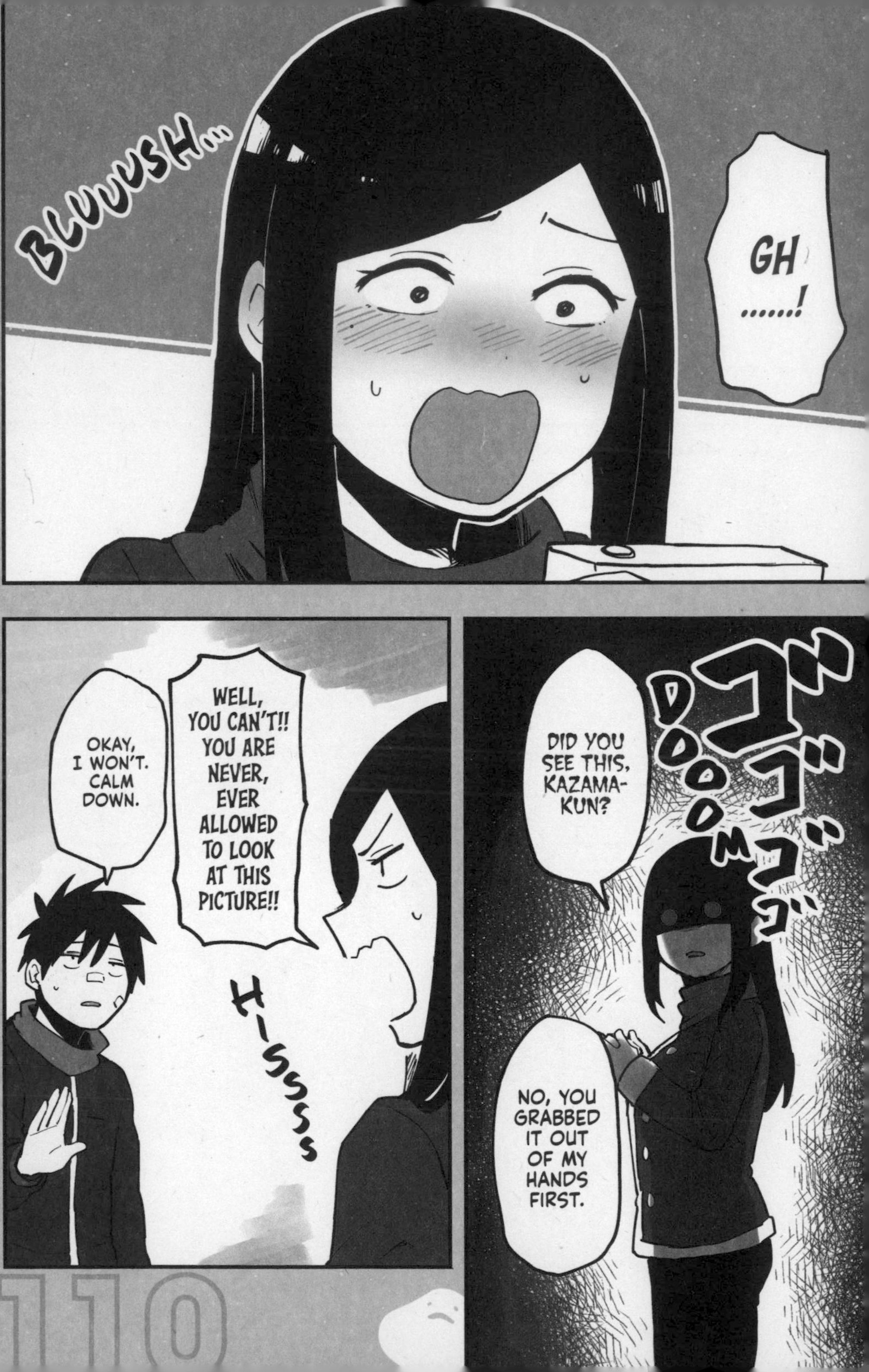
GH ......!
BLUUUSH...
DID YOU SEE THIS, KAZAMA-KUN?
ゴゴゴ
DOOOOM
NO, YOU GRABBED IT OUT OF MY HANDS FIRST.
WELL, YOU CAN'T!! YOU ARE NEVER, EVER ALLOWED TO LOOK AT THIS PICTURE!!
HISSSS
OKAY, I WON'T. CALM DOWN.

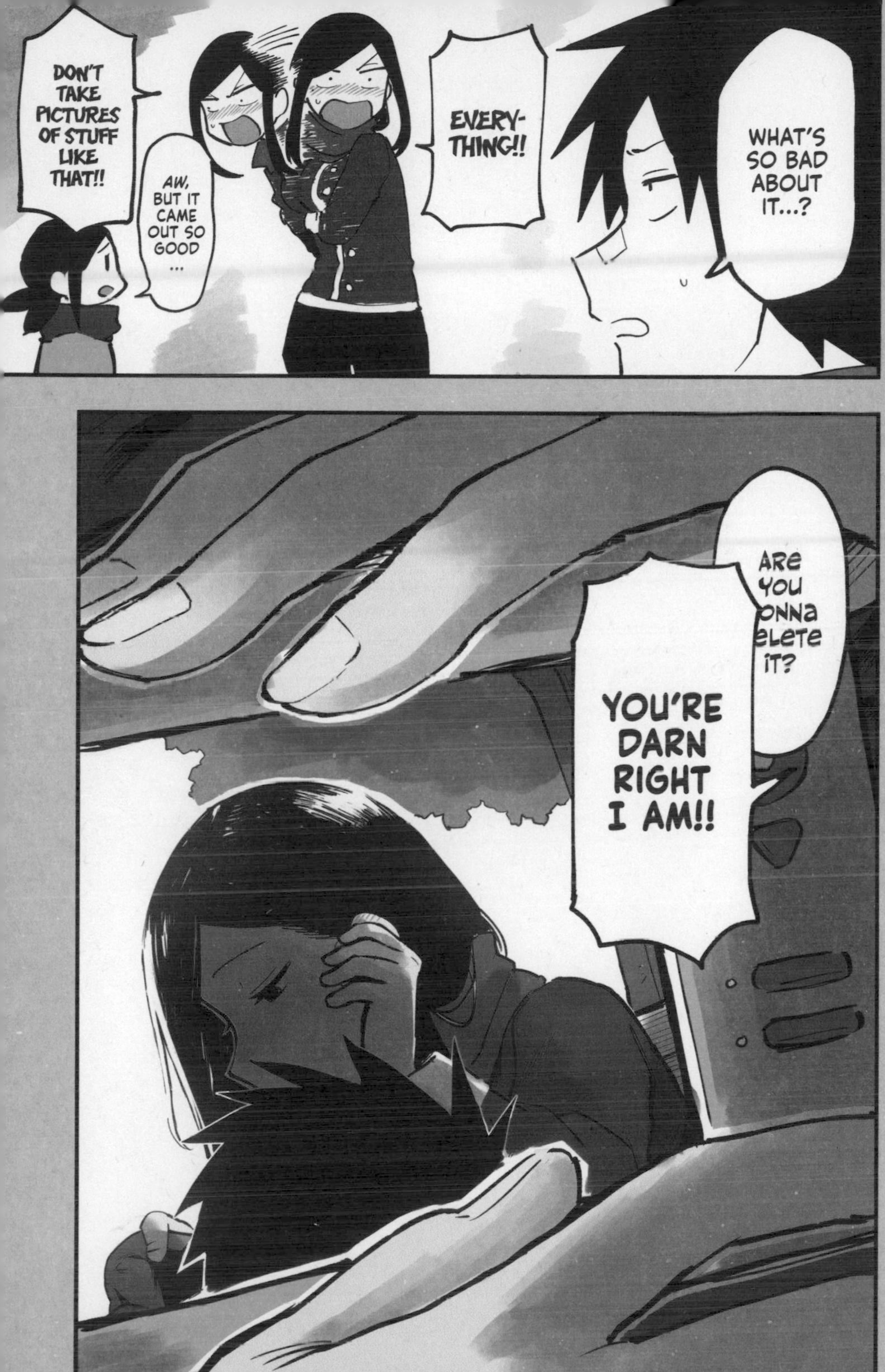
WHAT'S SO BAD ABOUT IT...?
EVERY-THING!!
DON'T TAKE PICTURES OF STUFF LIKE THAT!!
AW, BUT IT CAME OUT SO GOOD...
ARE YOU ONNA ELETE IT?
YOU'RE DARN RIGHT I AM!!

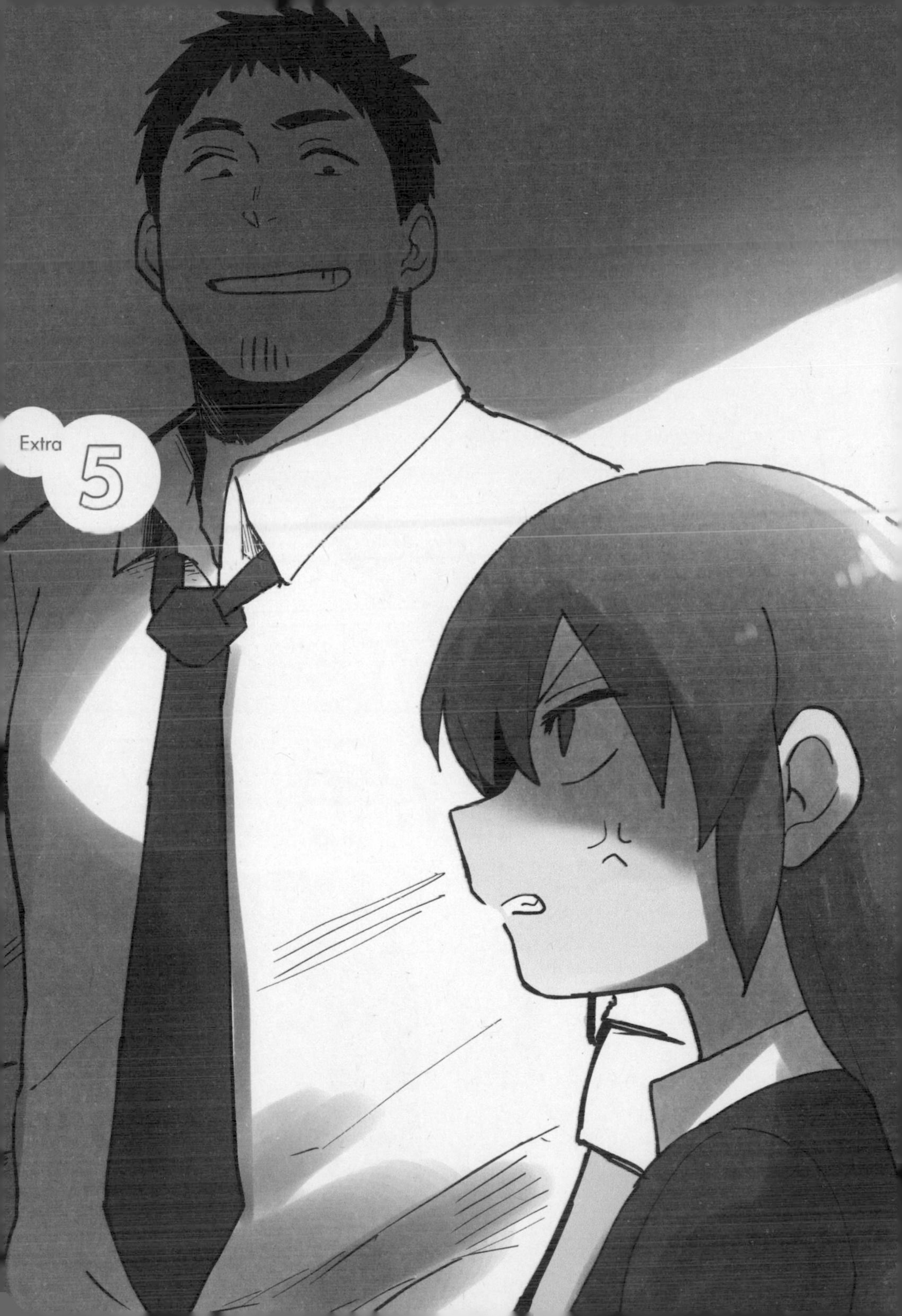
Extra
5

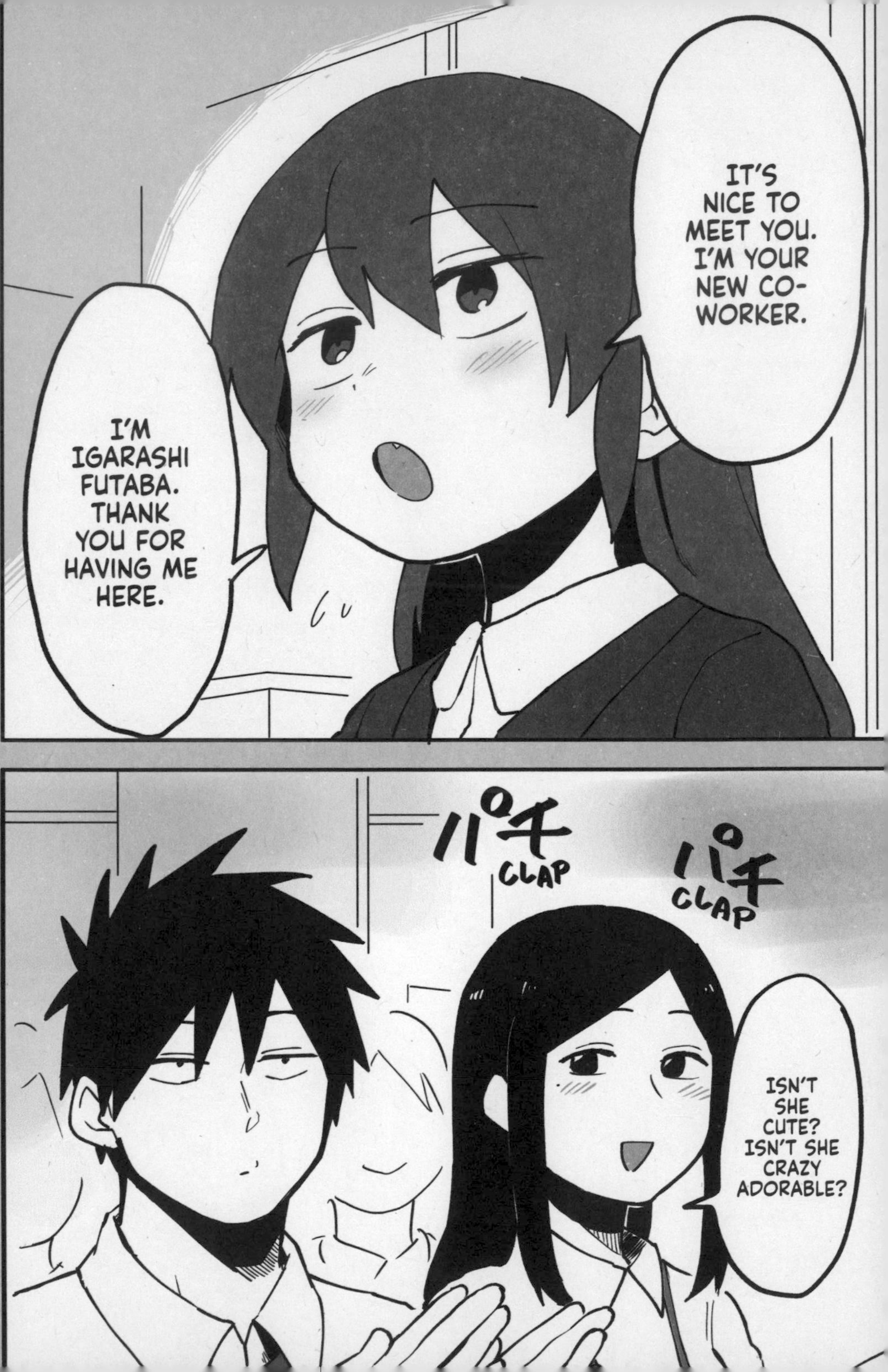
IT'S NICE TO MEET YOU. I'M YOUR NEW CO-WORKER.
I'M IGARASHI FUTABA. THANK YOU FOR HAVING ME HERE.
パチ CLAP
パチ CLAP
ISN'T SHE CUTE? ISN'T SHE CRAZY ADORABLE?

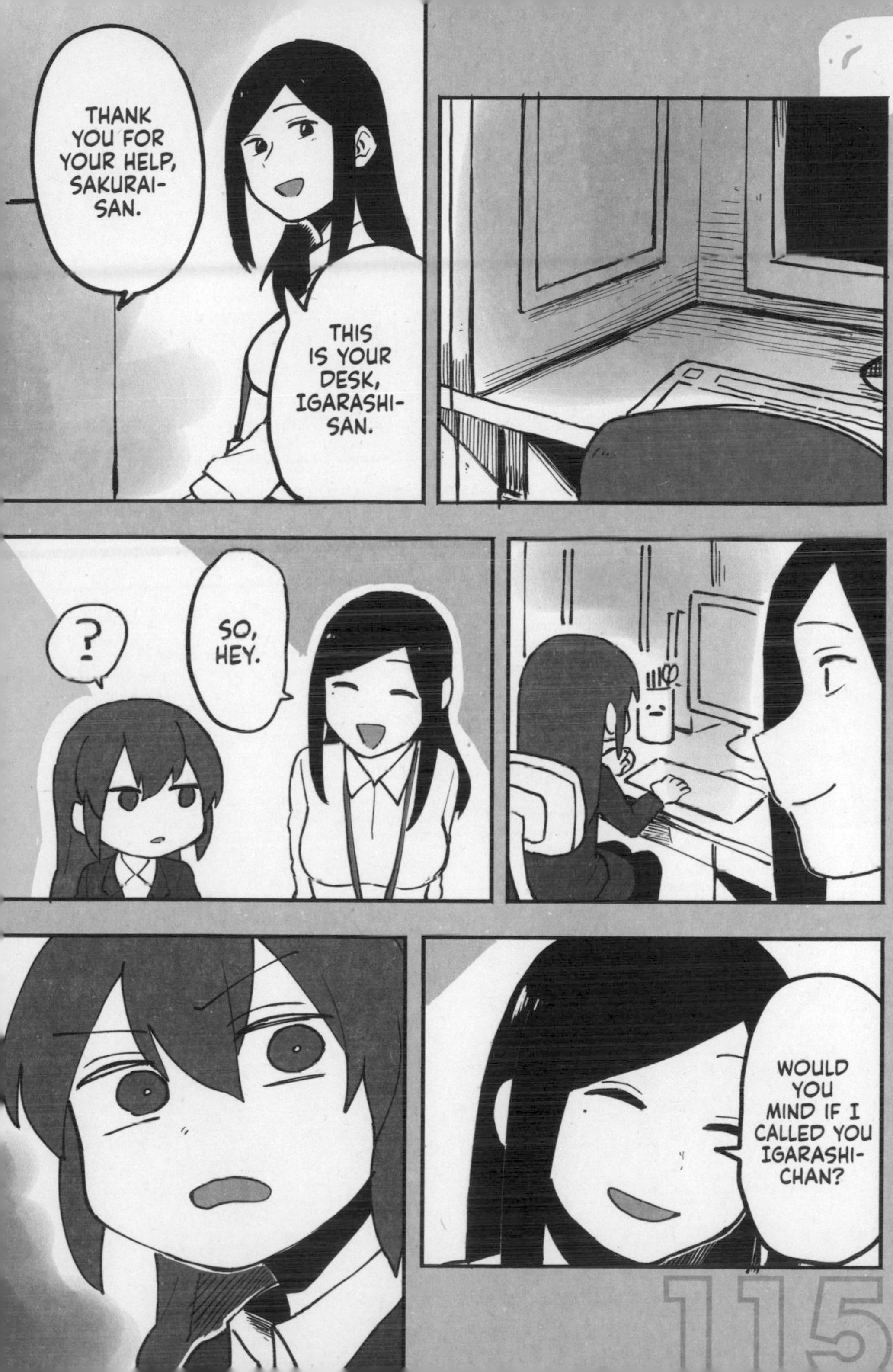
THIS IS YOUR DESK, IGARASHI-SAN.
THANK YOU FOR YOUR HELP, SAKURAI-SAN.
SO, HEY.
?
WOULD YOU MIND IF I CALLED YOU IGARASHI-CHAN?

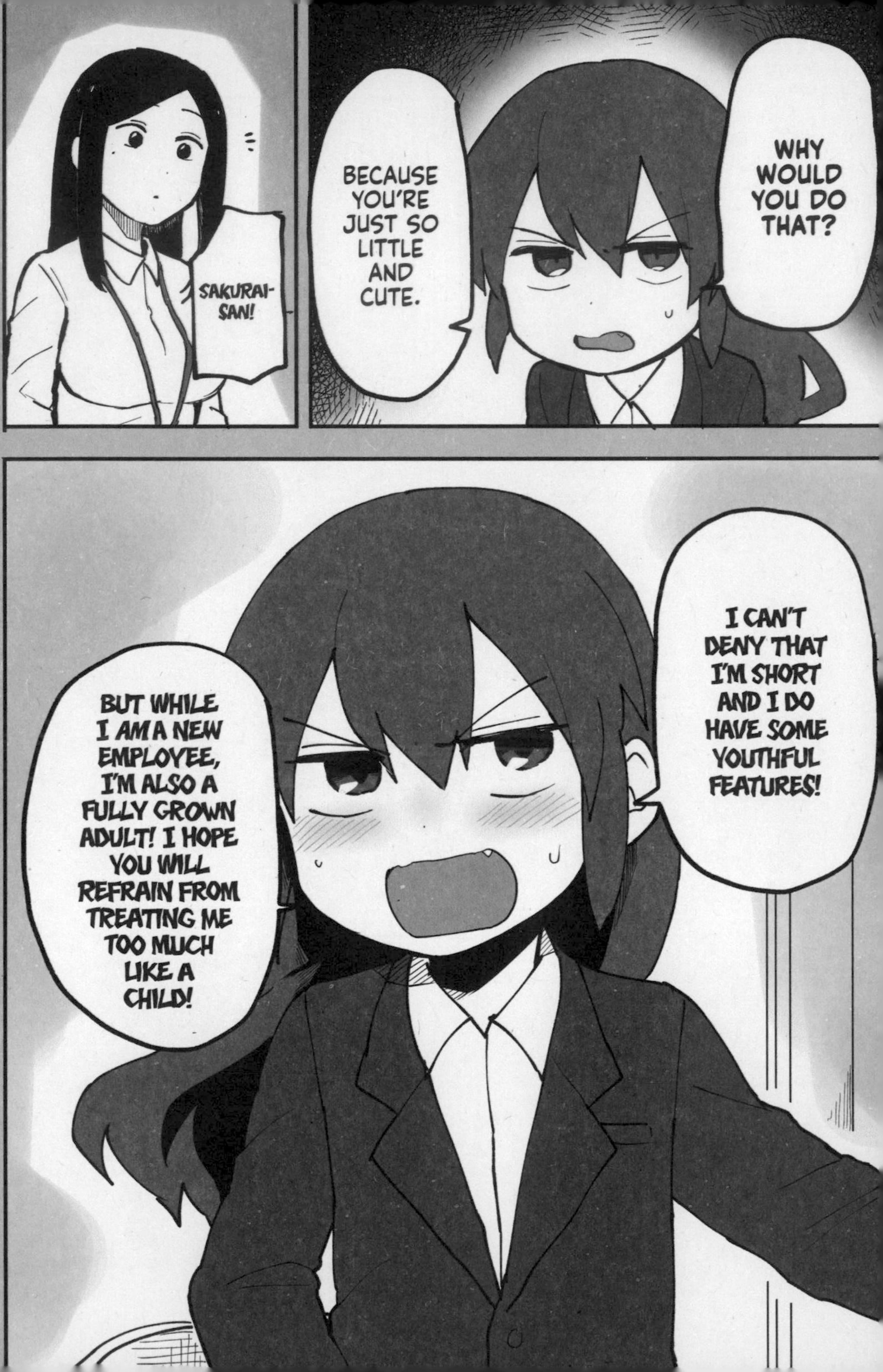
WHY WOULD YOU DO THAT?
BECAUSE YOU'RE JUST SO LITTLE AND CUTE.
SAKURAI-SAN!
I CAN'T DENY THAT I'M SHORT AND I DO HAVE SOME YOUTHFUL FEATURES!
BUT WHILE I AM A NEW EMPLOYEE, I'M ALSO A FULLY GROWN ADULT! I HOPE YOU WILL REFRAIN FROM TREATING ME TOO MUCH LIKE A CHILD!

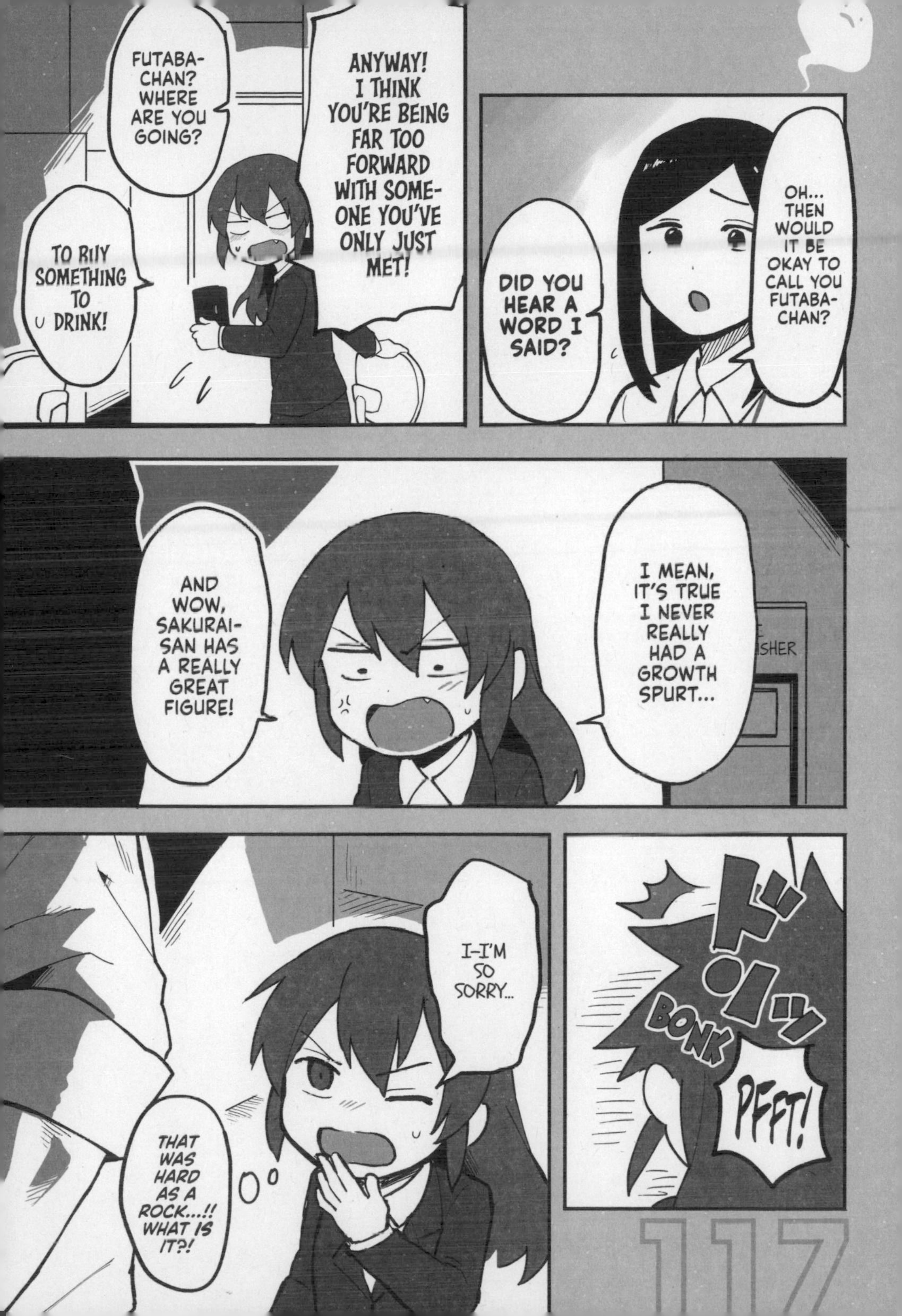
OH... THEN WOULD IT BE OKAY TO CALL YOU FUTABA-CHAN?
DID YOU HEAR A WORD I SAID?
ANYWAY! I THINK YOU'RE BEING FAR TOO FORWARD WITH SOMEONE YOU'VE ONLY JUST MET!
FUTABA-CHAN? WHERE ARE YOU GOING?
TO BUY SOMETHING TO DRINK!
I MEAN, IT'S TRUE I NEVER REALLY HAD A GROWTH SPURT...
AND WOW, SAKURAI-SAN HAS A REALLY GREAT FIGURE!
BONK
PFFT!
I-I'M SO SORRY...
THAT WAS HARD AS A ROCK...!! WHAT IS IT?!

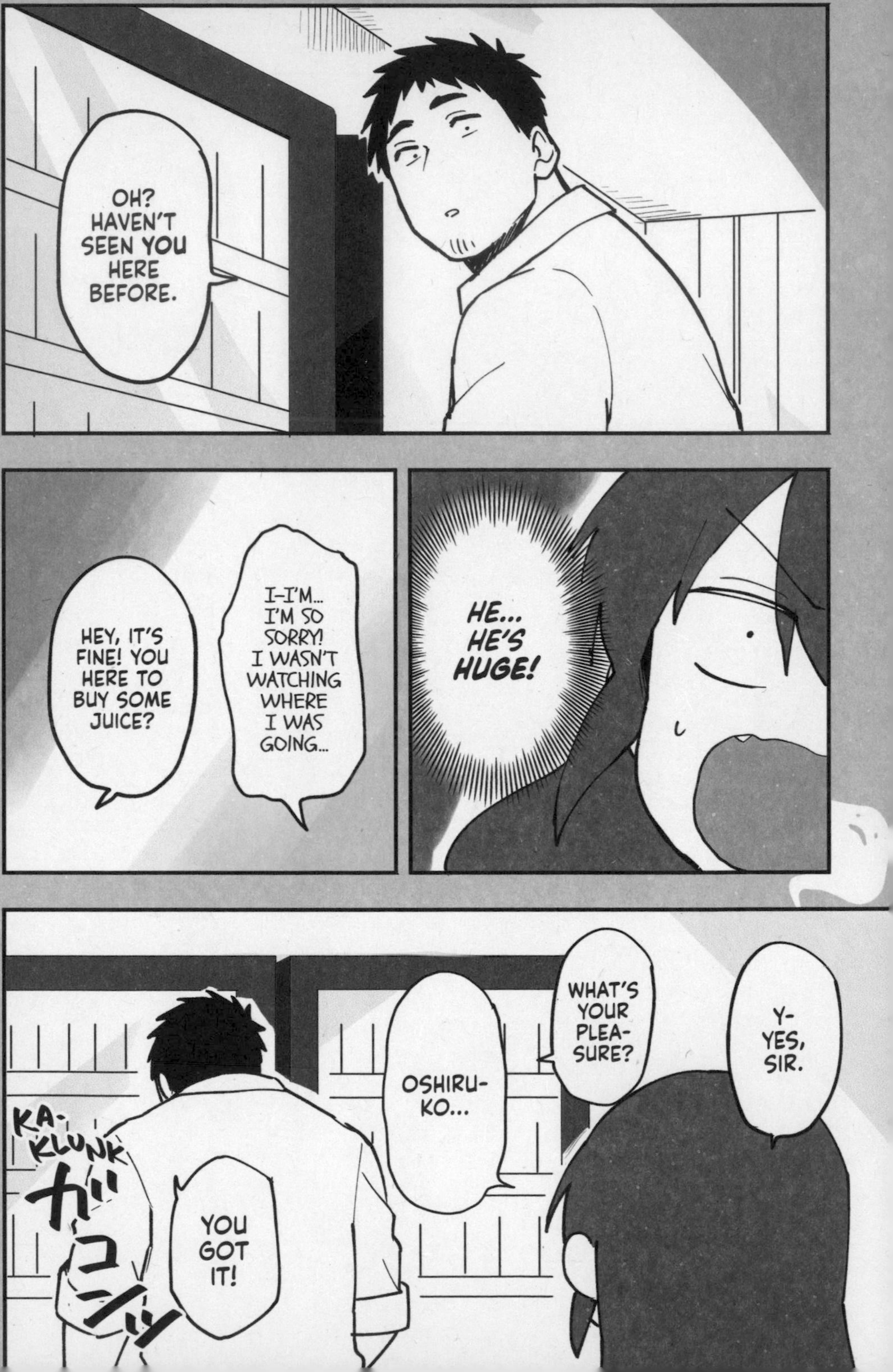
OH? HAVEN'T SEEN YOU HERE BEFORE.
HE... HE'S HUGE!
I-I'M... I'M SO SORRY! I WASN'T WATCHING WHERE I WAS GOING...
HEY, IT'S FINE! YOU HERE TO BUY SOME JUICE?
Y-YES, SIR.
WHAT'S YOUR PLEA-SURE?
OSHIRU-KO...
YOU GOT IT!
KA-KLUNK
ガコンッ

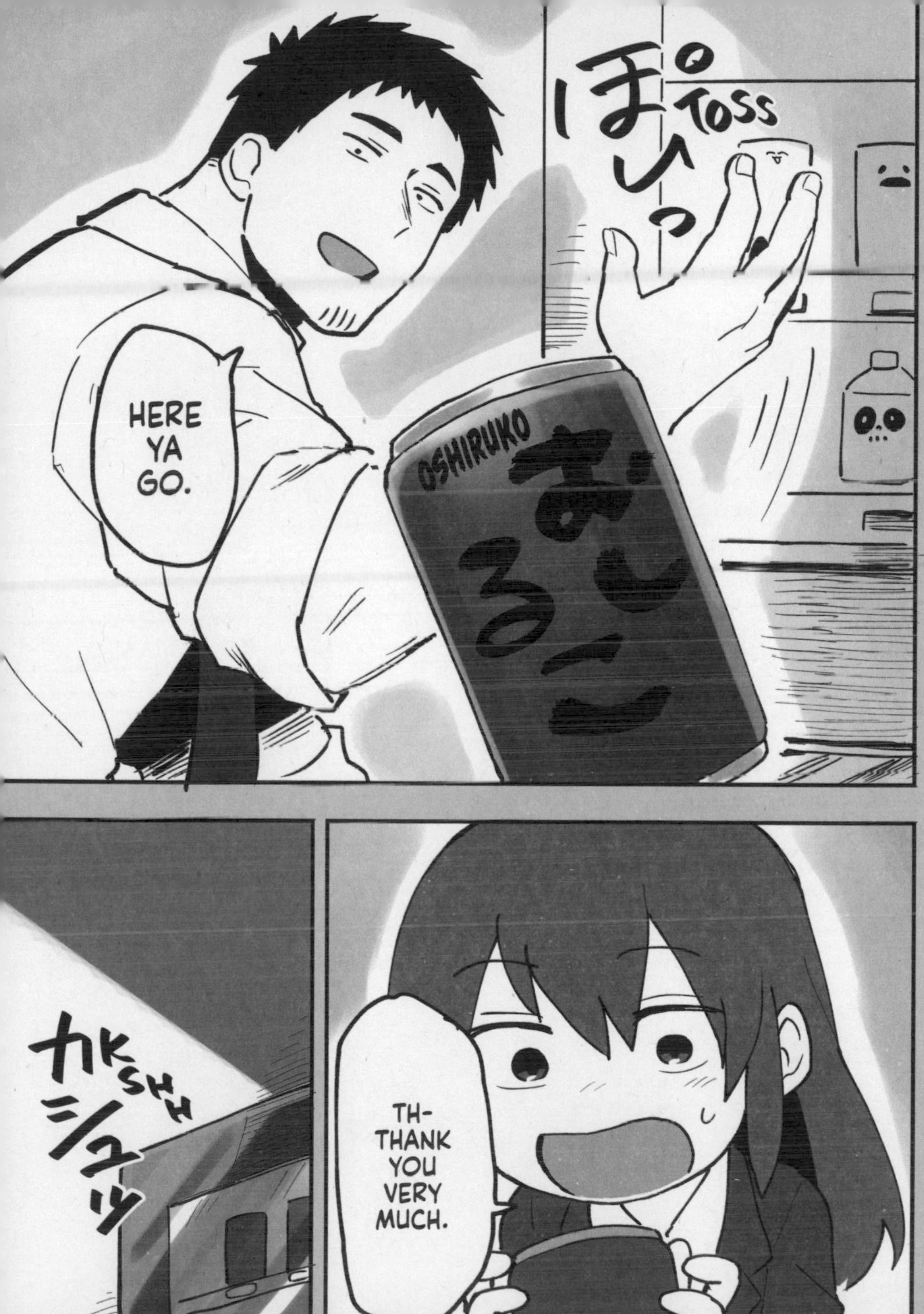
ぽいっ
TOSS
HERE YA GO.
OSHIRUKO
おしるこ
TH-THANK YOU VERY MUCH.
カシュッ
KSHH

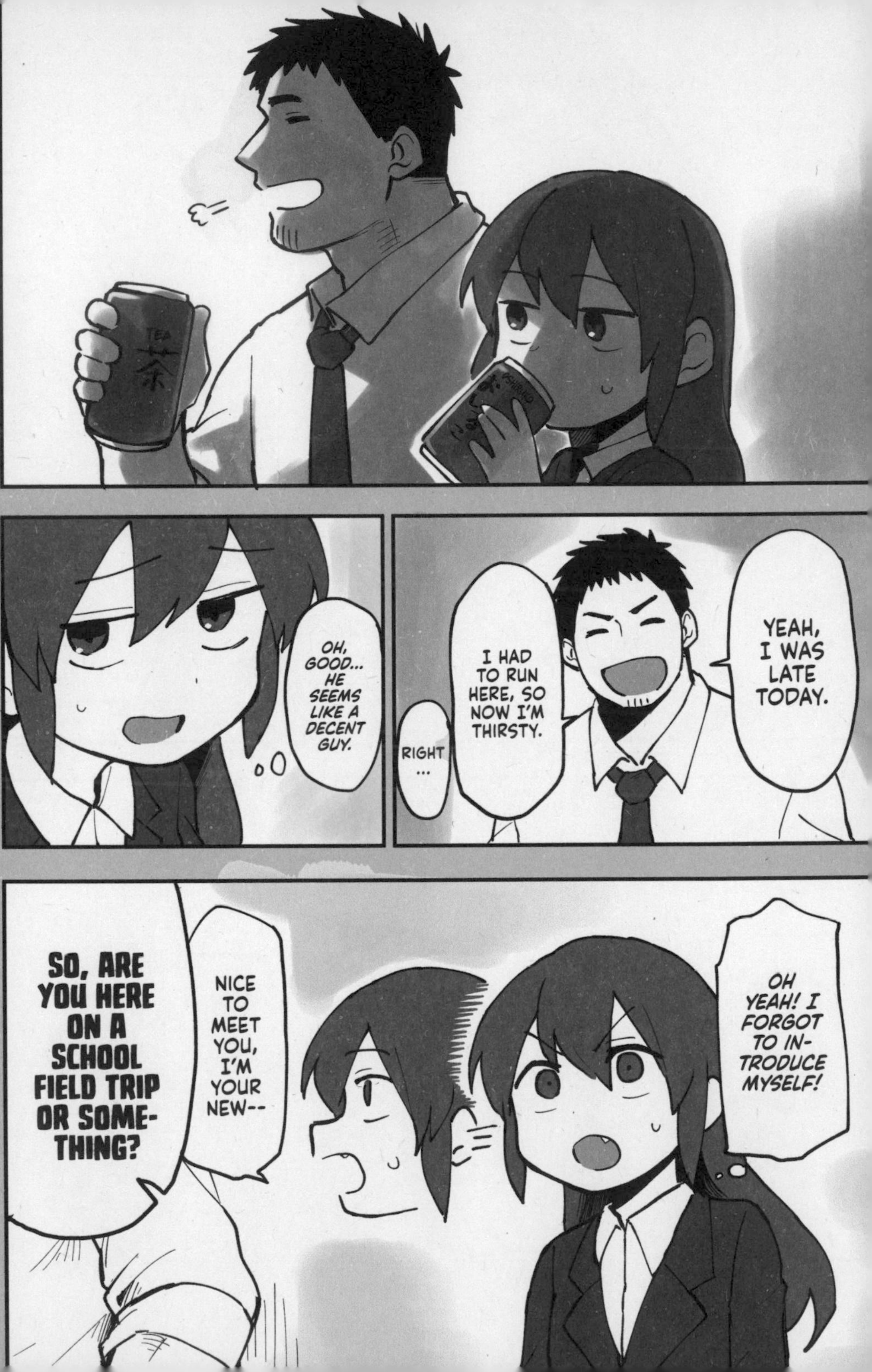
TEA
茶
YEAH, I WAS LATE TODAY.
I HAD TO RUN HERE, SO NOW I'M THIRSTY.
RIGHT...
OH, GOOD... HE SEEMS LIKE A DECENT GUY.
OH YEAH! I FORGOT TO IN-TRODUCE MYSELF!
NICE TO MEET YOU, I'M YOUR NEW--
SO, ARE YOU HERE ON A SCHOOL FIELD TRIP OR SOME-THING?

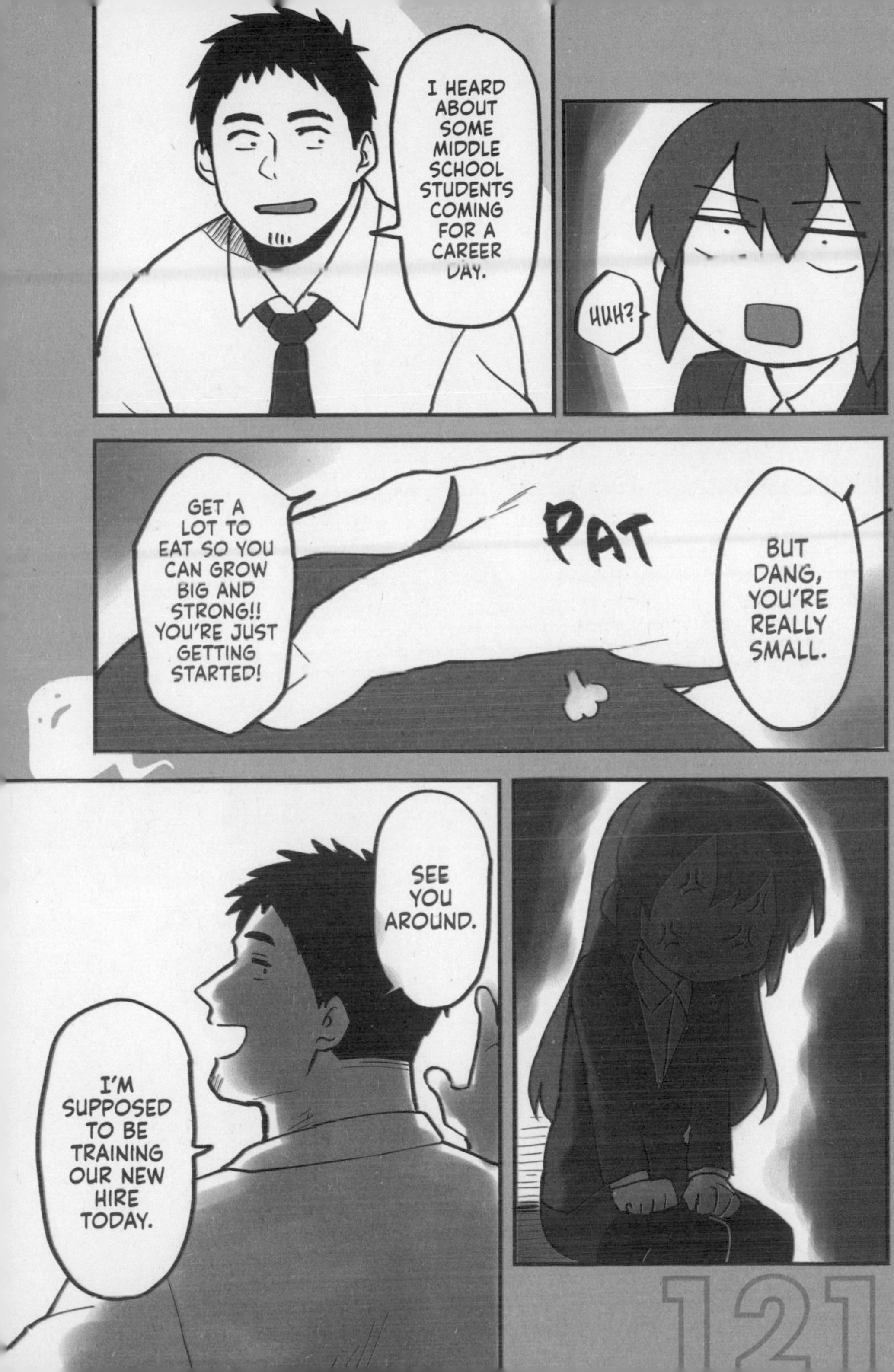
HUH?
I HEARD ABOUT SOME MIDDLE SCHOOL STUDENTS COMING FOR A CAREER DAY.
BUT DANG, YOU'RE REALLY SMALL.
PAT
GET A LOT TO EAT SO YOU CAN GROW BIG AND STRONG!! YOU'RE JUST GETTING STARTED!
SEE YOU AROUND.
I'M SUPPOSED TO BE TRAINING OUR NEW HIRE TODAY.

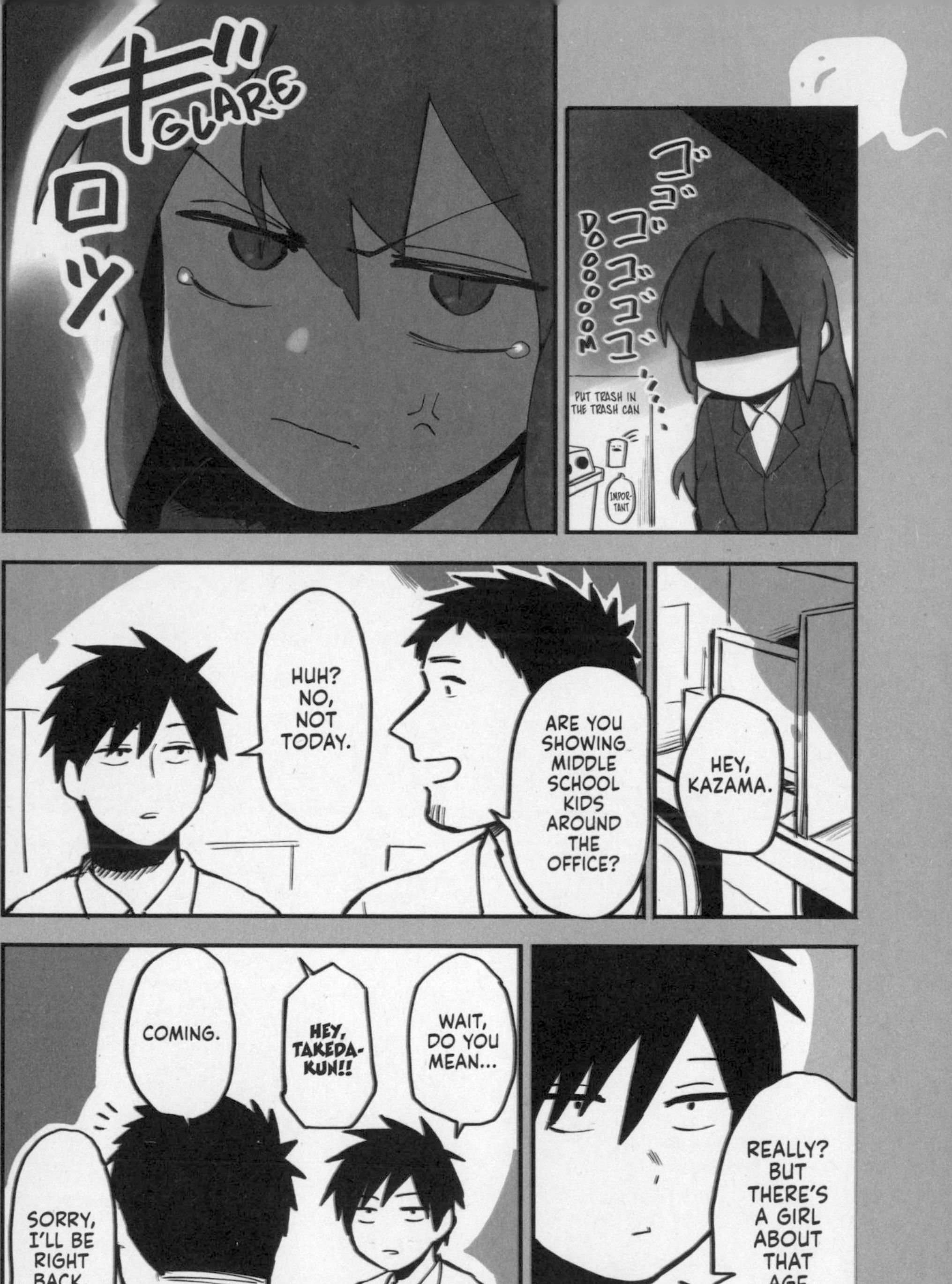
ゴゴゴゴゴゴ
DOOOOOOOM
PUT TRASH IN THE TRASH CAN
IMPOR-TANT
ギロッ
GLARE
HEY, KAZAMA.
ARE YOU SHOWING MIDDLE SCHOOL KIDS AROUND THE OFFICE?
HUH? NO, NOT TODAY.
REALLY? BUT THERE'S A GIRL ABOUT THAT AGE HERE.
WAIT, DO YOU MEAN...
HEY, TAKEDA-KUN!!
COMING.
SORRY, I'LL BE RIGHT BACK.

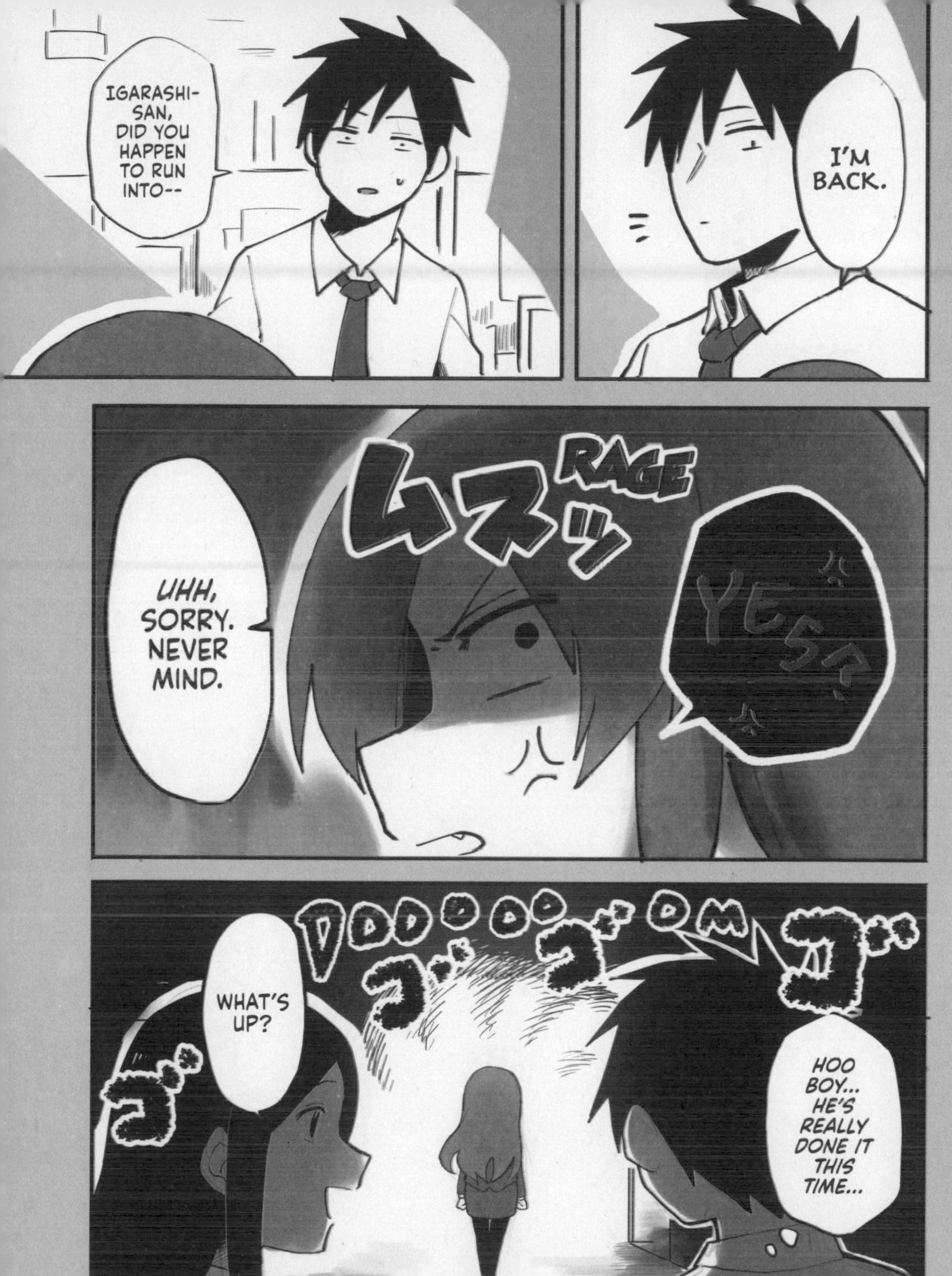
I'M BACK.
IGARASHI-SAN, DID YOU HAPPEN TO RUN INTO--
RAGE
YES?
UHH, SORRY. NEVER MIND.
DDDOOOOM
HOO BOY... HE'S REALLY DONE IT THIS TIME...
WHAT'S UP?

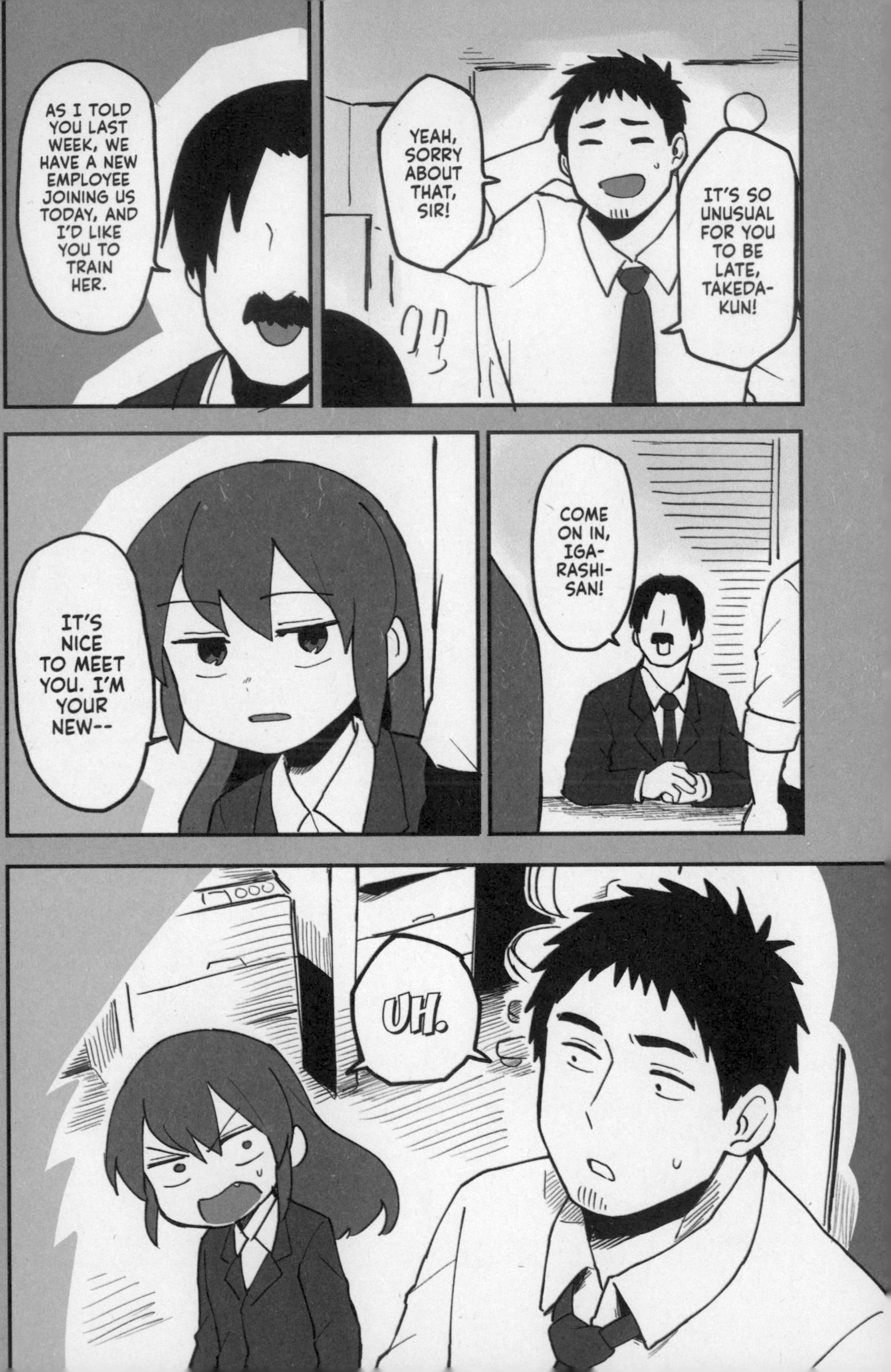
IT'S SO UNUSUAL FOR YOU TO BE LATE, TAKEDA-KUN!
YEAH, SORRY ABOUT THAT, SIR!
AS I TOLD YOU LAST WEEK, WE HAVE A NEW EMPLOYEE JOINING US TODAY, AND I'D LIKE YOU TO TRAIN HER.
COME ON IN, IGARASHI-SAN!
IT'S NICE TO MEET YOU. I'M YOUR NEW--
UH.

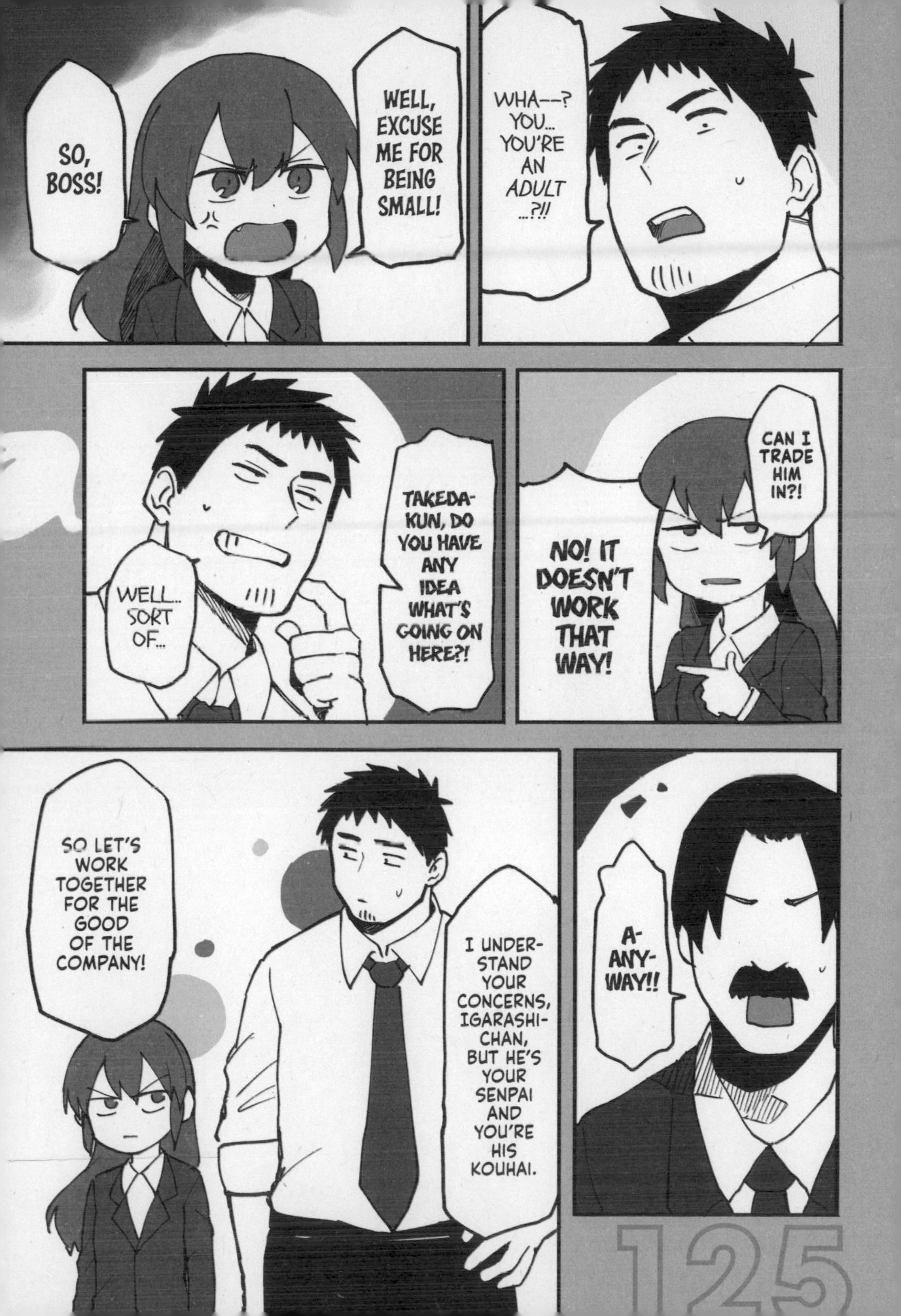
WHA--? YOU... YOU'RE AN *ADULT* ...?!!
WELL, EXCUSE ME FOR BEING SMALL!
SO, BOSS!
CAN I TRADE HIM IN?!
NO! IT DOESN'T WORK THAT WAY!
TAKEDA-KUN, DO YOU HAVE ANY IDEA WHAT'S GOING ON HERE?!
WELL... SORT OF...
A-ANY-WAY!!
I UNDER-STAND YOUR CONCERNS, IGARASHI-CHAN, BUT HE'S YOUR SENPAI AND YOU'RE HIS KOUHAI.
SO LET'S WORK TOGETHER FOR THE GOOD OF THE COMPANY!

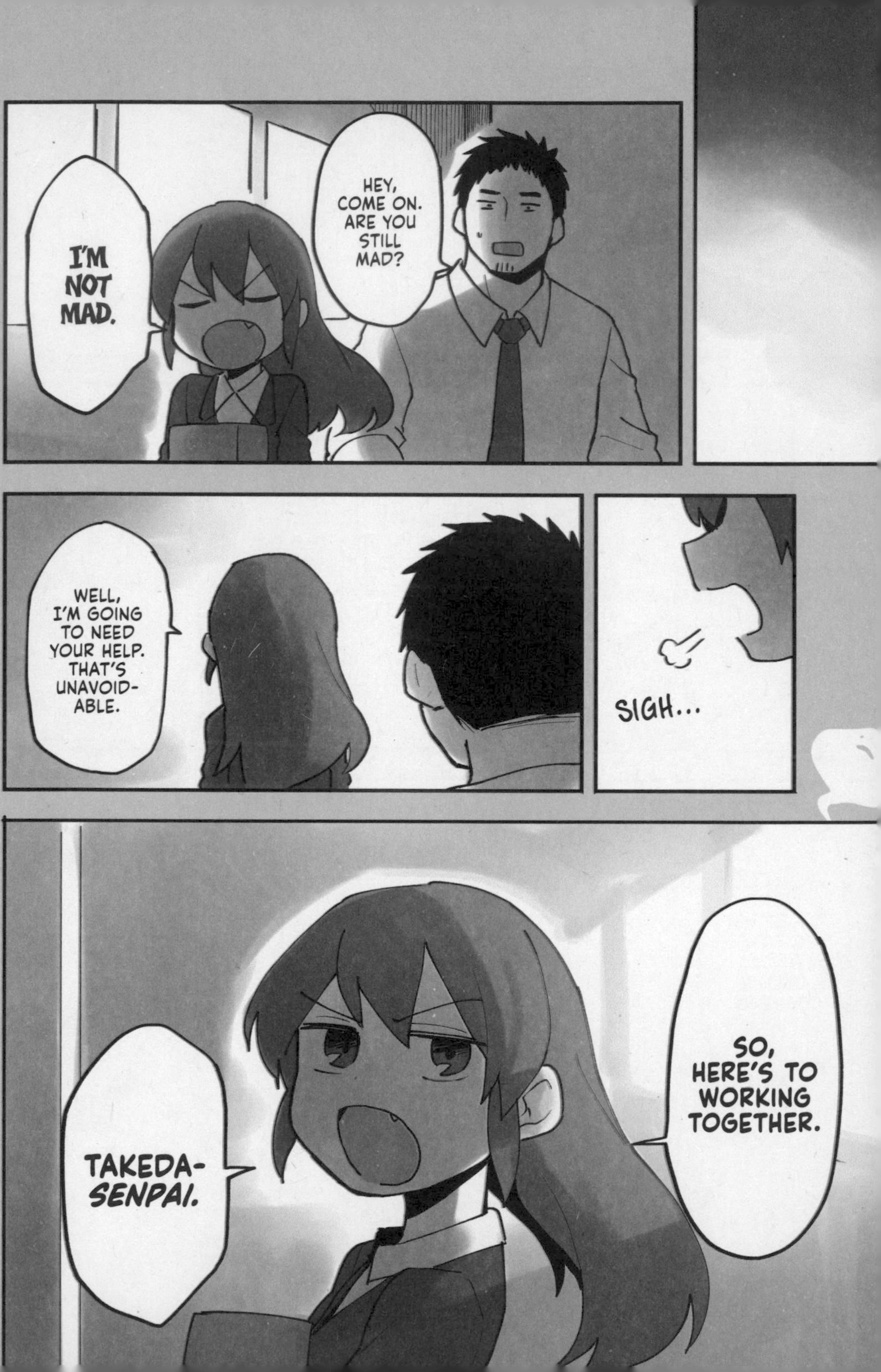
HEY, COME ON. ARE YOU STILL MAD?
I'M NOT MAD.
SIGH...
WELL, I'M GOING TO NEED YOUR HELP. THAT'S UNAVOIDABLE.
SO, HERE'S TO WORKING TOGETHER.
TAKEDA-SENPAI.

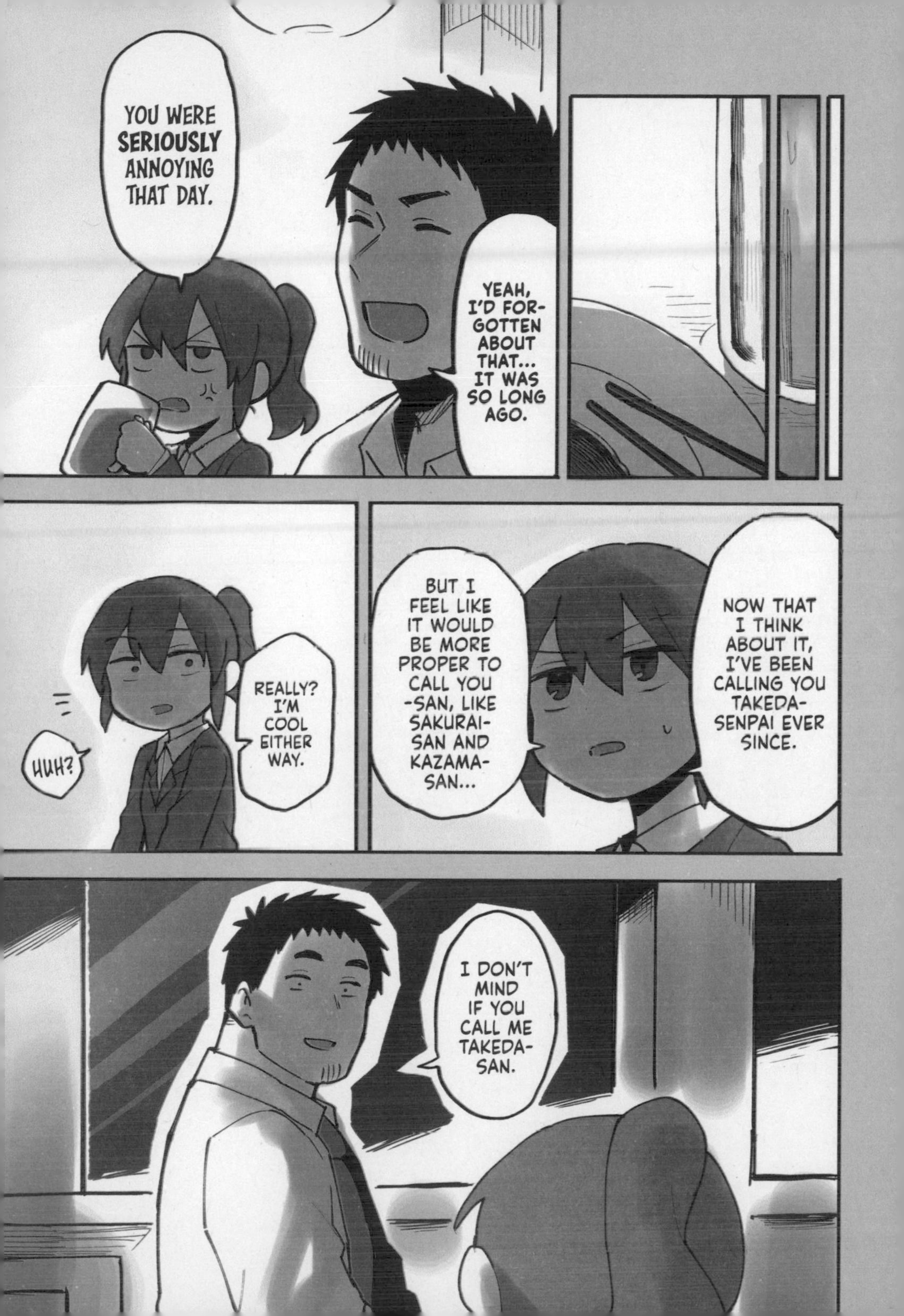
YOU WERE SERIOUSLY ANNOYING THAT DAY.
YEAH, I'D FOR-GOTTEN ABOUT THAT... IT WAS SO LONG AGO.
NOW THAT I THINK ABOUT IT, I'VE BEEN CALLING YOU TAKEDA-SENPAI EVER SINCE.
BUT I FEEL LIKE IT WOULD BE MORE PROPER TO CALL YOU -SAN, LIKE SAKURAI-SAN AND KAZAMA-SAN...
REALLY? I'M COOL EITHER WAY.
HUH?
I DON'T MIND IF YOU CALL ME TAKEDA-SAN.

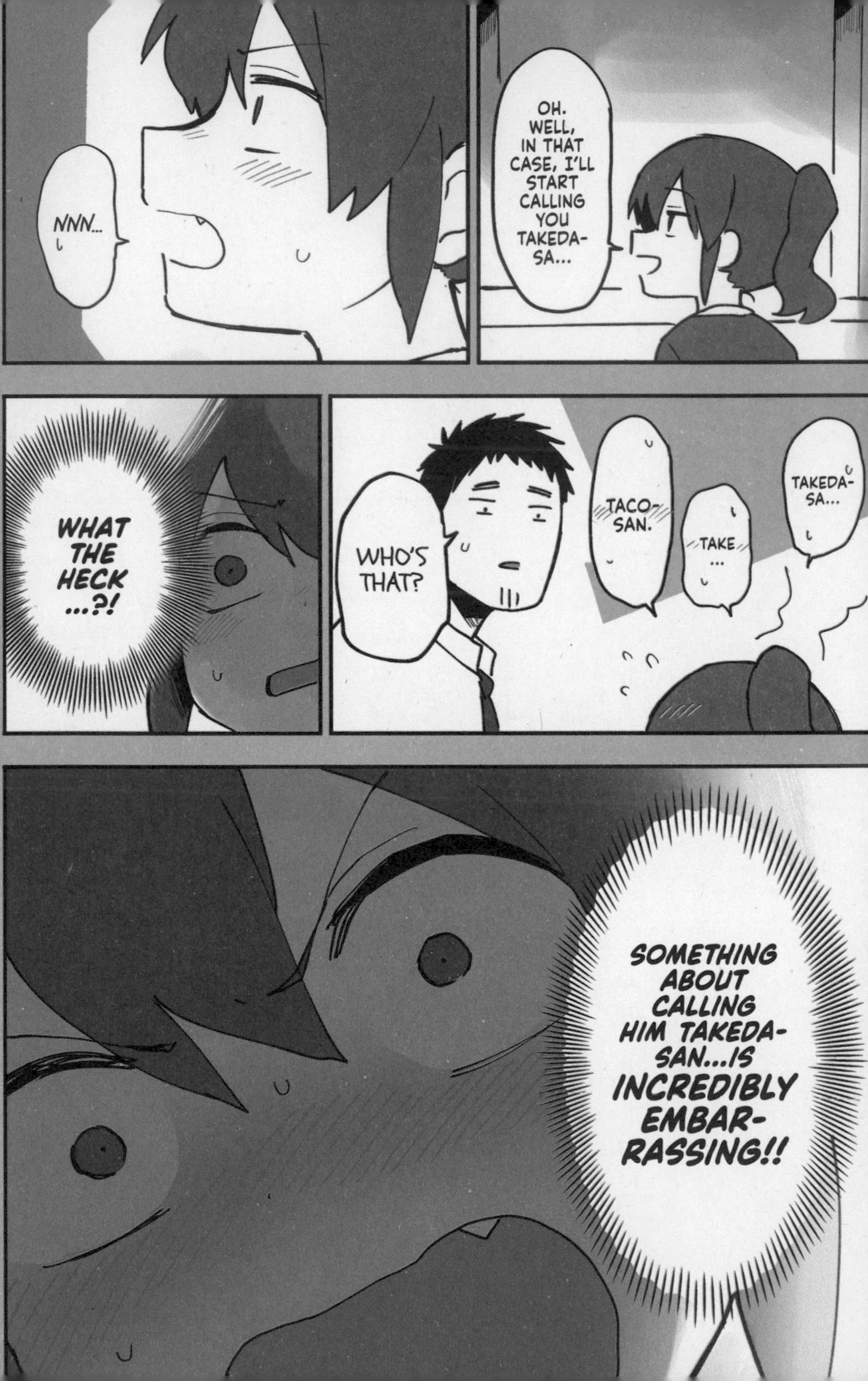
OH. WELL, IN THAT CASE, I'LL START CALLING YOU TAKEDA-SA...
NNN...
TAKEDA-SA...
TAKE...
TACO-SAN.
WHO'S THAT?
WHAT THE HECK...?!
SOMETHING ABOUT CALLING HIM TAKEDA-SAN...IS INCREDIBLY EMBARRASSING!!

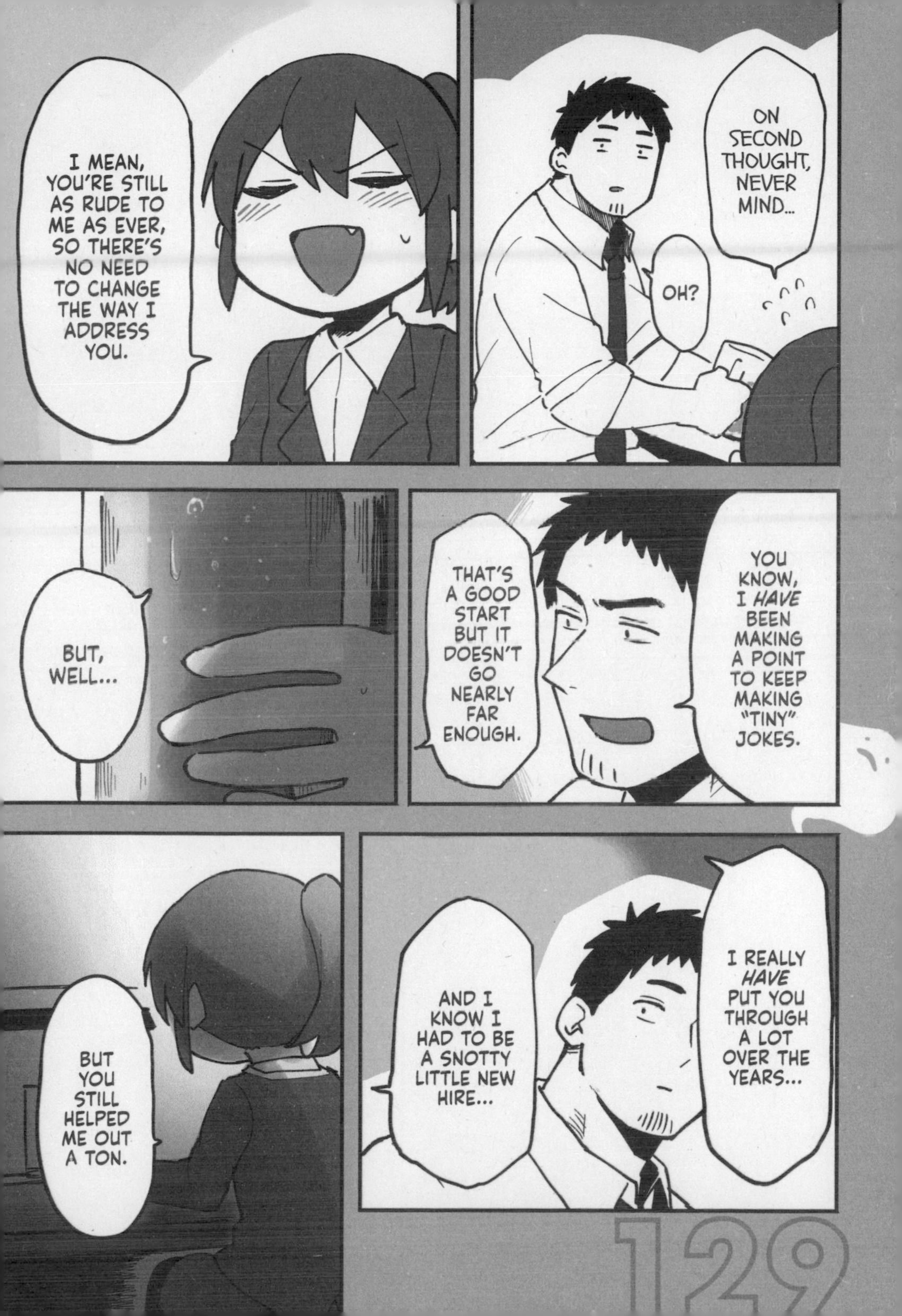
ON SECOND THOUGHT, NEVER MIND...
OH?
I MEAN, YOU'RE STILL AS RUDE TO ME AS EVER, SO THERE'S NO NEED TO CHANGE THE WAY I ADDRESS YOU.
YOU KNOW, I *HAVE* BEEN MAKING A POINT TO KEEP MAKING "TINY" JOKES.
THAT'S A GOOD START BUT IT DOESN'T GO NEARLY FAR ENOUGH.
BUT, WELL...
I REALLY *HAVE* PUT YOU THROUGH A LOT OVER THE YEARS...
AND I KNOW I HAD TO BE A SNOTTY LITTLE NEW HIRE...
BUT YOU STILL HELPED ME OUT A TON.

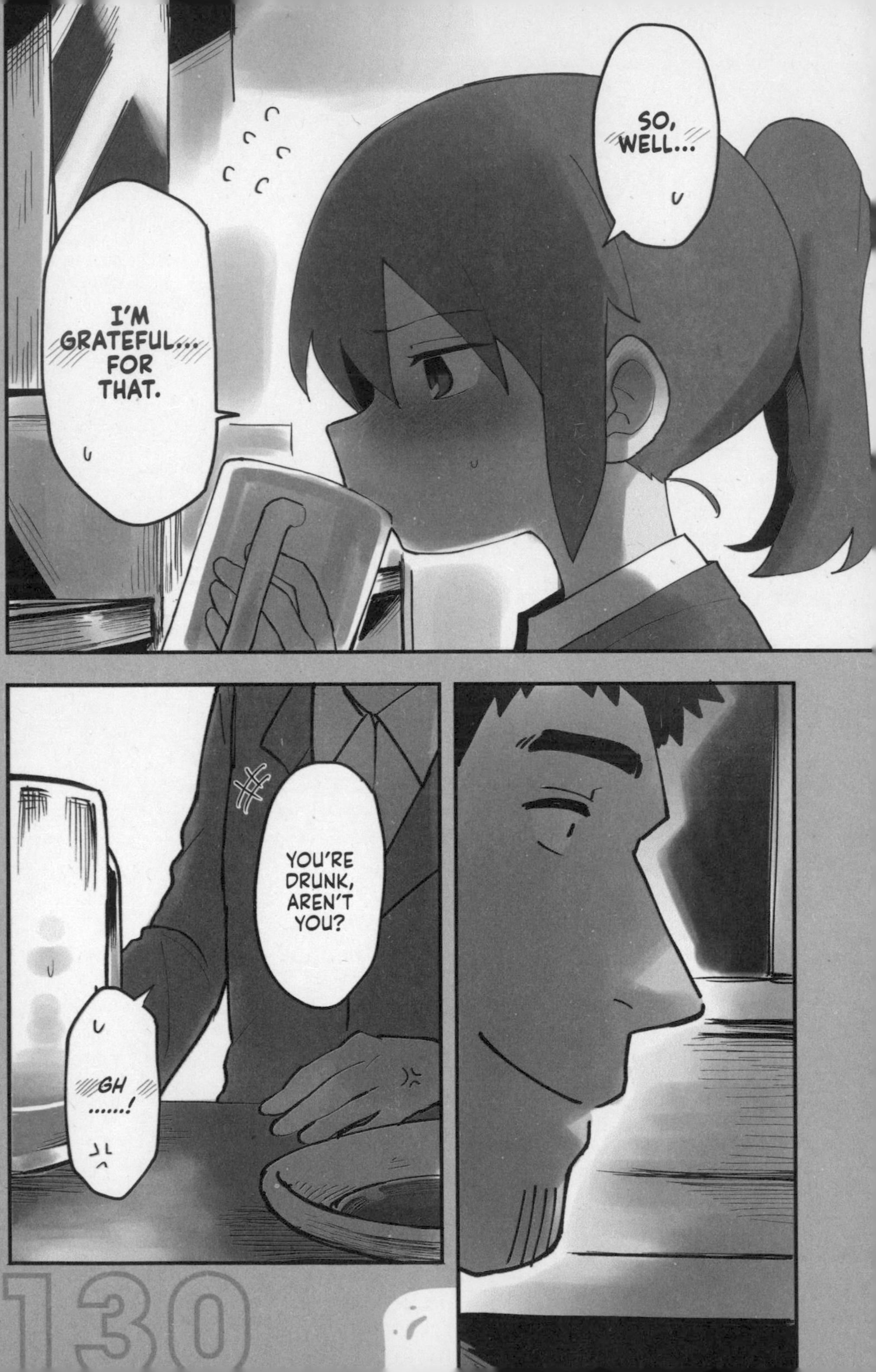
SO, WELL...
I'M GRATEFUL... FOR THAT.
YOU'RE DRUNK, AREN'T YOU?
GH ......!

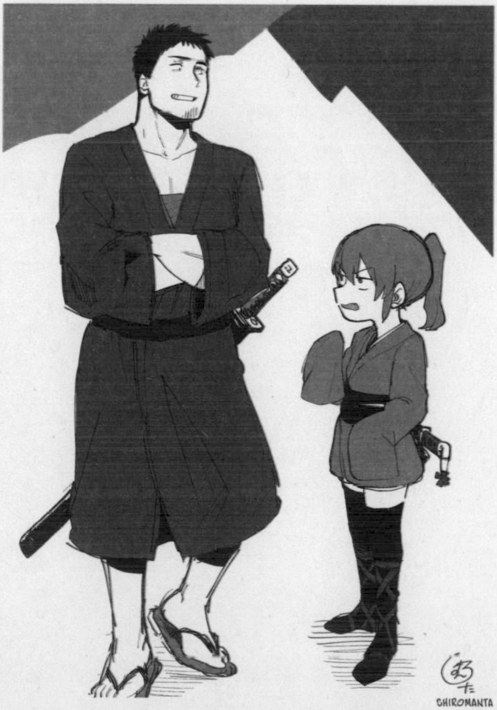
SHIROMANTA

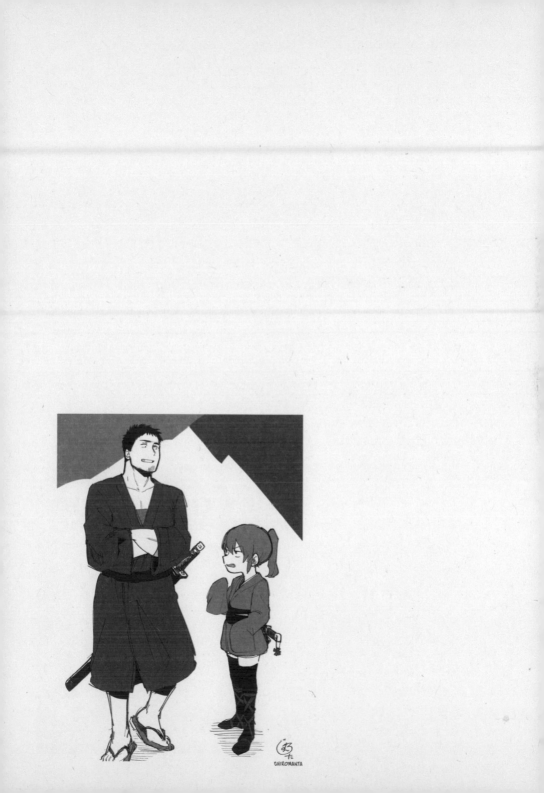

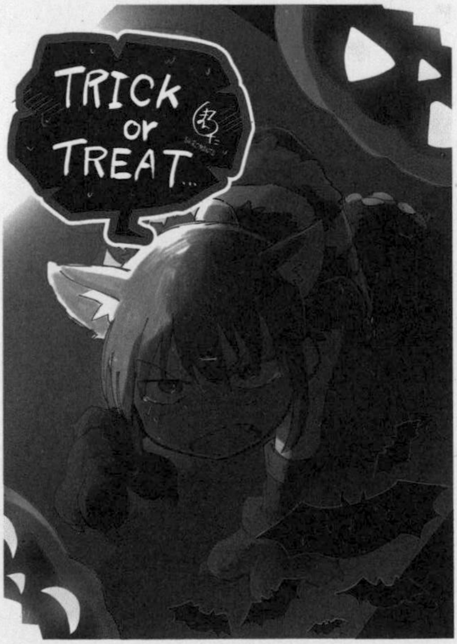
TRICK or TREAT...

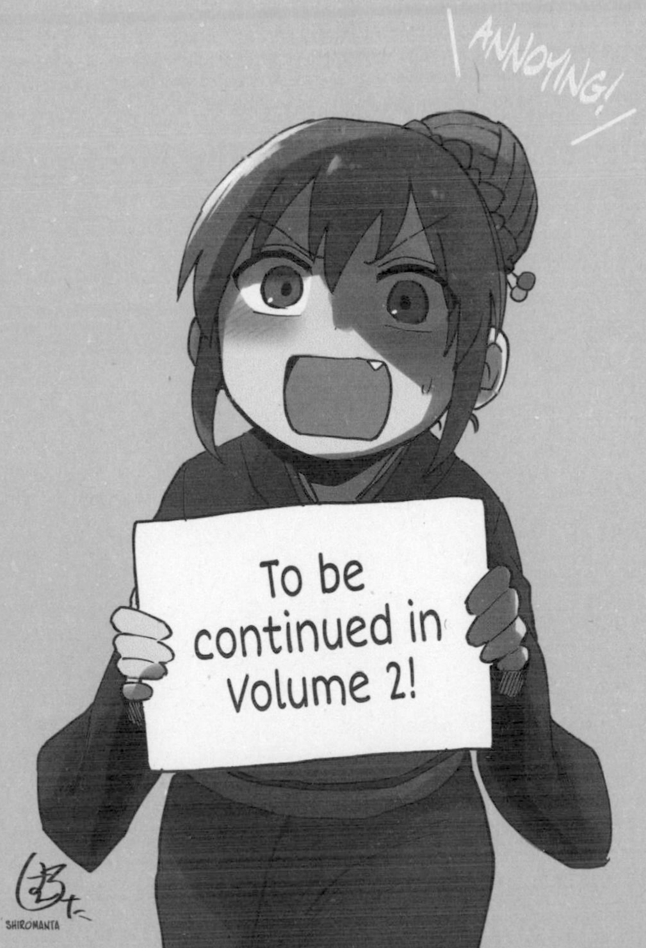
ANNOYING!
To be continued in Volume 2!
SHIROMANTA

Afterword

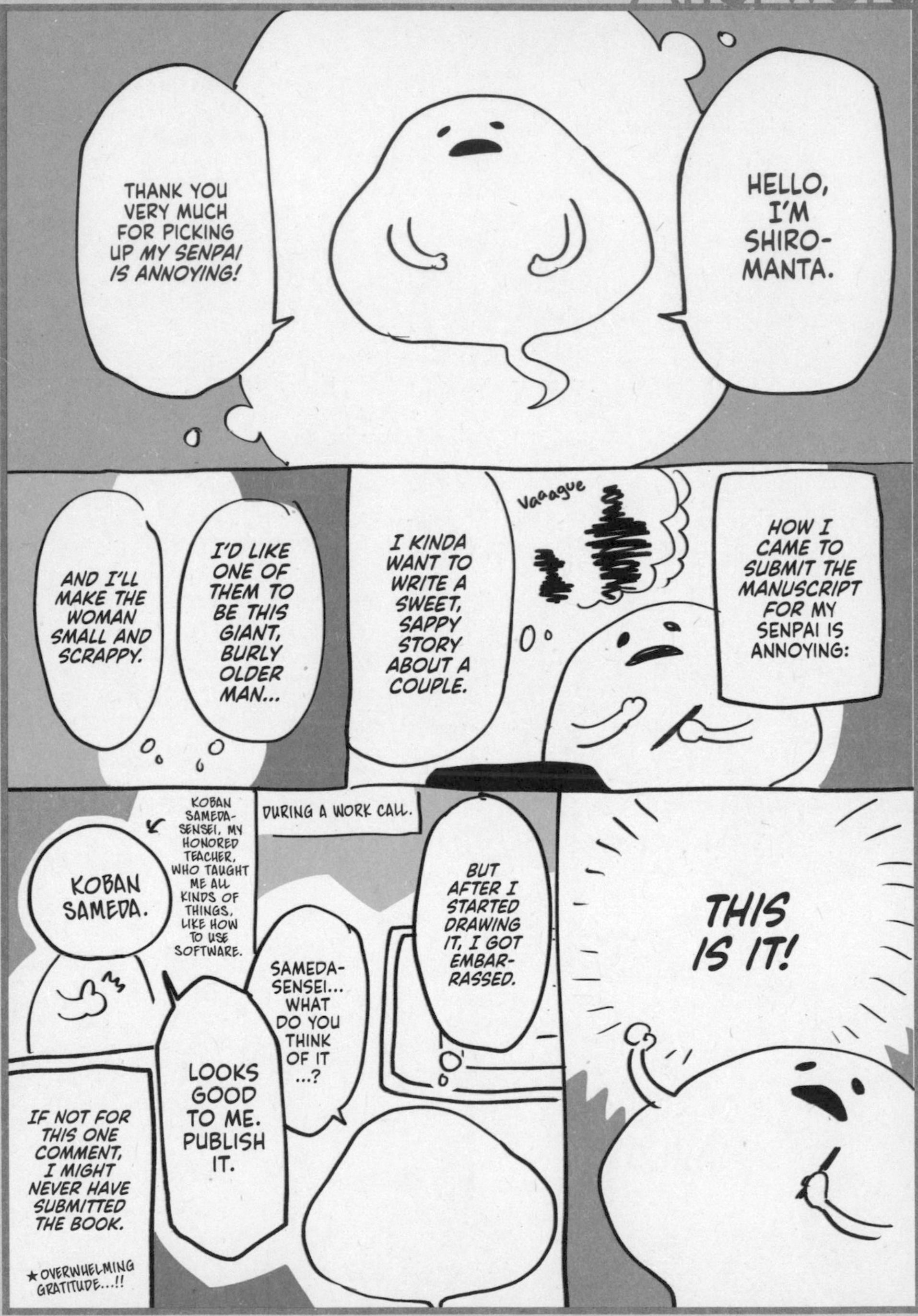

HELLO, I'M SHIROMANTA.
THANK YOU VERY MUCH FOR PICKING UP *MY SENPAI IS ANNOYING!*
HOW I CAME TO SUBMIT THE MANUSCRIPT FOR MY SENPAI IS ANNOYING:
Vaaague
I KINDA WANT TO WRITE A SWEET, SAPPY STORY ABOUT A COUPLE.
I'D LIKE ONE OF THEM TO BE THIS GIANT, BURLY OLDER MAN...
AND I'LL MAKE THE WOMAN SMALL AND SCRAPPY.
THIS IS IT!
DURING A WORK CALL.
BUT AFTER I STARTED DRAWING IT, I GOT EMBARRASSED.
SAMEDA-SENSEI... WHAT DO YOU THINK OF IT...?
LOOKS GOOD TO ME. PUBLISH IT.
KOBAN SAMEDA-SENSEI, MY HONORED TEACHER, WHO TAUGHT ME ALL KINDS OF THINGS, LIKE HOW TO USE SOFTWARE.
KOBAN SAMEDA.
IF NOT FOR THIS ONE COMMENT, I MIGHT NEVER HAVE SUBMITTED THE BOOK.
★OVERWHELMING GRATITUDE...!!

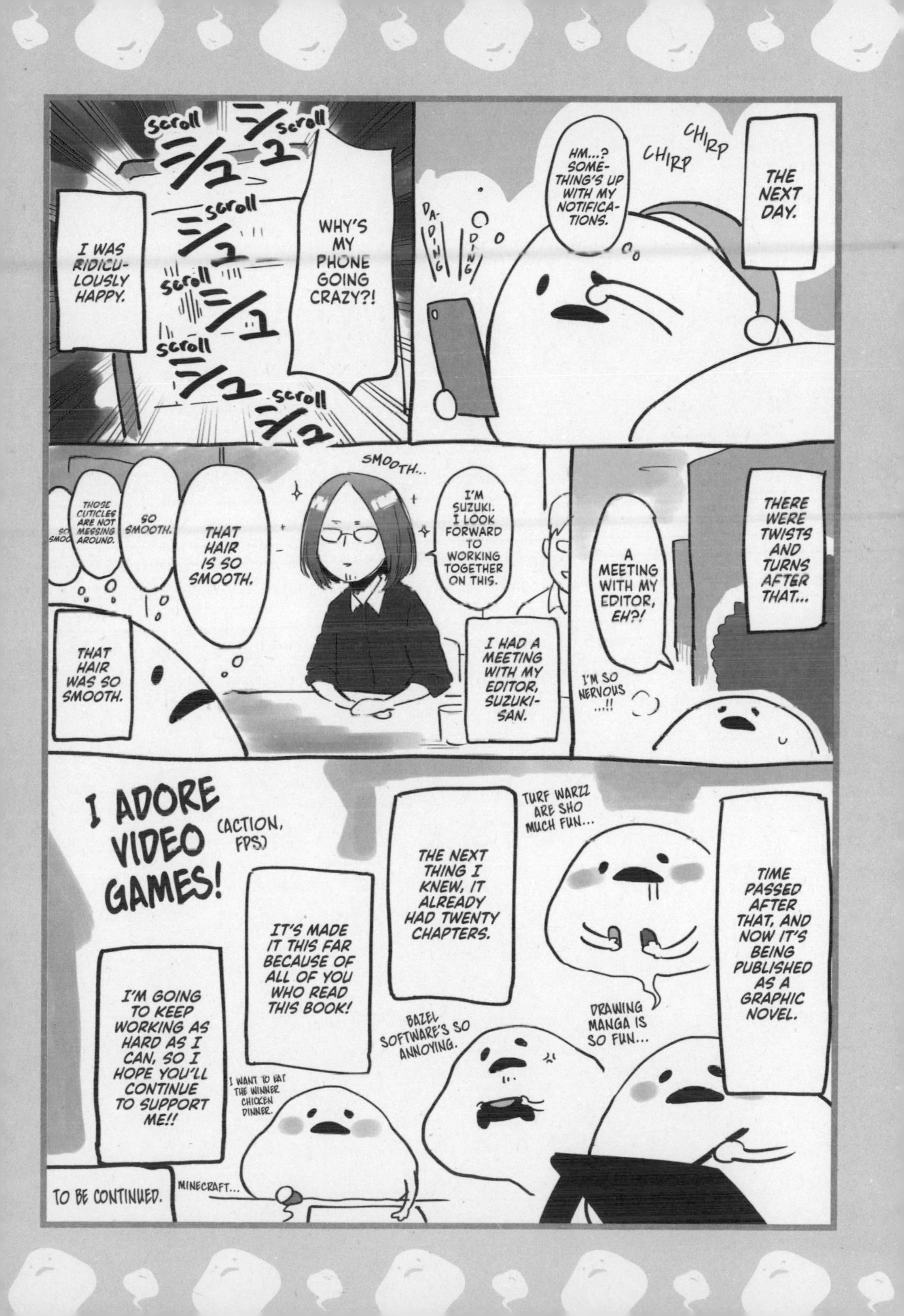

THE NEXT DAY.
CHIRP CHIRP
HM...? SOMETHING'S UP WITH MY NOTIFICATIONS.
DA-DING DING
WHY'S MY PHONE GOING CRAZY?!
scroll シュ scroll シュ
scroll シュ
scroll シュ
scroll シュ
scroll シュ
I WAS RIDICULOUSLY HAPPY.
THERE WERE TWISTS AND TURNS AFTER THAT...
A MEETING WITH MY EDITOR, EH?!
I'M SO NERVOUS ...!!
I'M SUZUKI. I LOOK FORWARD TO WORKING TOGETHER ON THIS.
SMOOTH...
I HAD A MEETING WITH MY EDITOR, SUZUKI-SAN.
THAT HAIR IS SO SMOOTH.
SO SMOOTH.
THOSE CUTICLES ARE NOT MESSING AROUND.
SO SMOO
THAT HAIR WAS SO SMOOTH.
TIME PASSED AFTER THAT, AND NOW IT'S BEING PUBLISHED AS A GRAPHIC NOVEL.
TURF WARZZ ARE SHO MUCH FUN...
THE NEXT THING I KNEW, IT ALREADY HAD TWENTY CHAPTERS.
DRAWING MANGA IS SO FUN...
I ADORE VIDEO GAMES!
(ACTION, FPS)
IT'S MADE IT THIS FAR BECAUSE OF ALL OF YOU WHO READ THIS BOOK!
BAZEL SOFTWARE'S SO ANNOYING.
I'M GOING TO KEEP WORKING AS HARD AS I CAN, SO I HOPE YOU'LL CONTINUE TO SUPPORT ME!!
I WANT TO EAT THE WINNER CHICKEN DINNER.
MINECRAFT...
TO BE CONTINUED.

しろまんた

SHIROMANTA

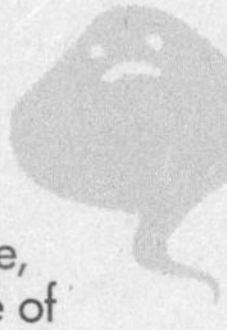

With the support of a lot of people, I somehow managed to make one of my dreams come true. I can't thank you all enough. Thanks to the one-person kotatsu I recently purchased, I think I can live the rest of my life without ever leaving my house. And if I die, I'll never be truly dead.

My Senpai is Annoying

先輩がうざい後輩の話

1

Senpai ga uzai
kouhai no hanashi
Written by
SHIROMANTA

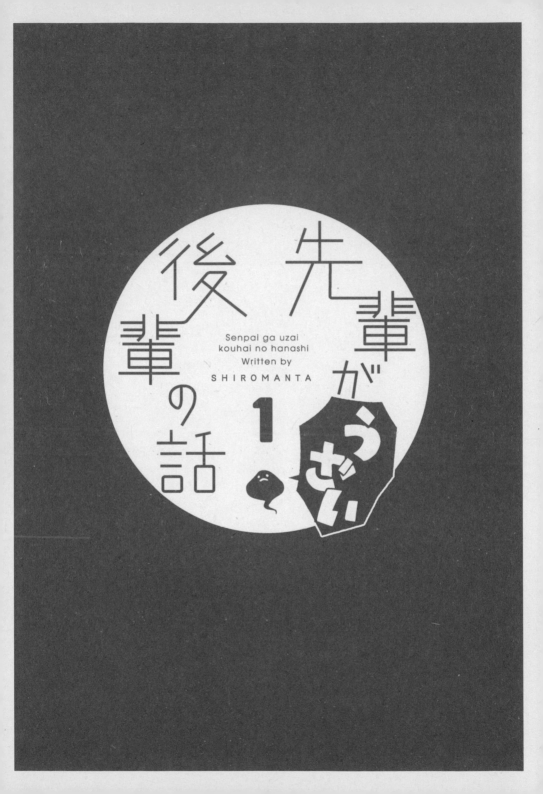

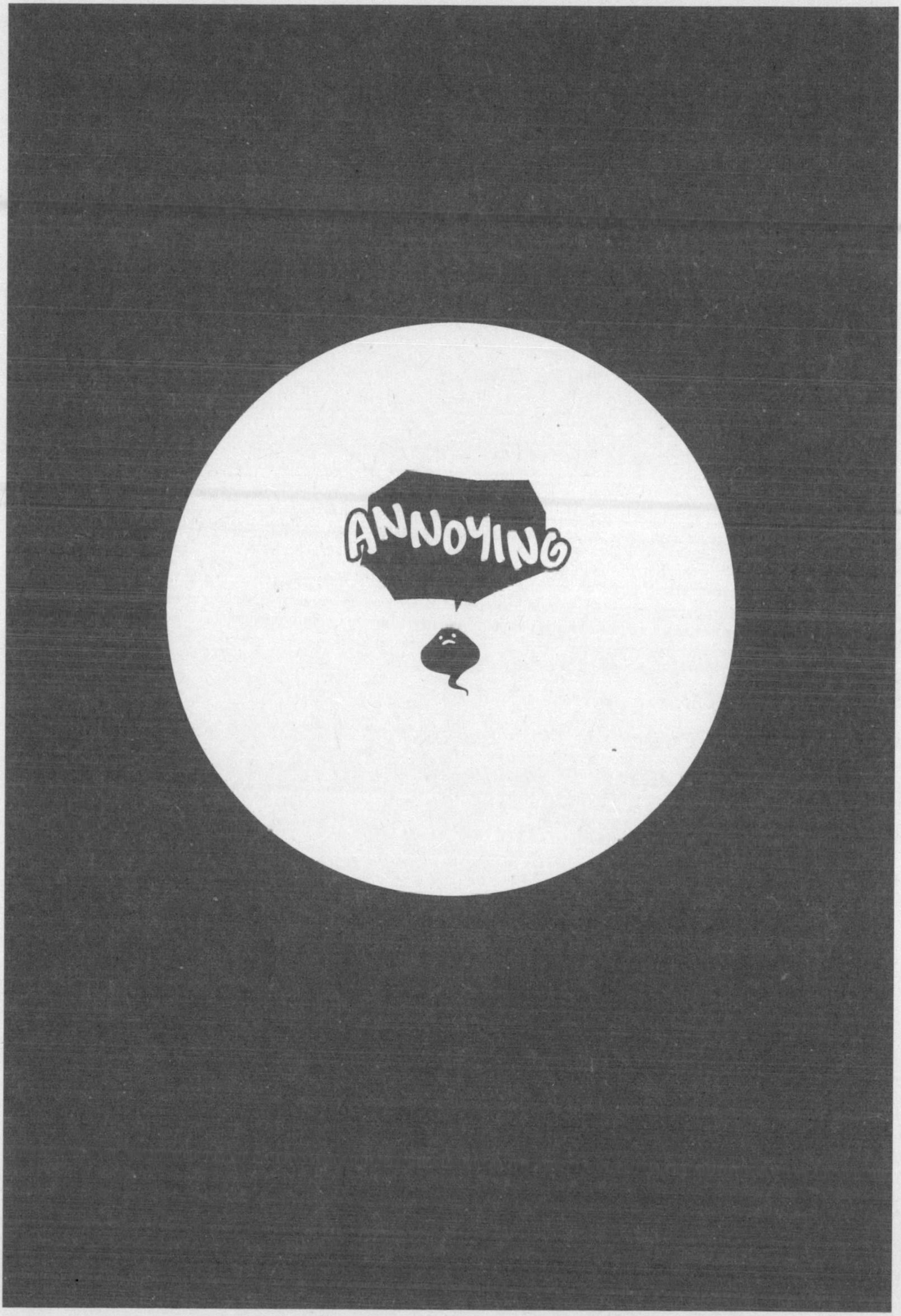
ANNOYING

ANNOYING

My Senpai is Annoying

SEVEN SEAS ENTERTAINMENT PRESENTS

My Senpai is Annoying

story & art by SHIROMANTA

VOLUME 1

TRANSLATION
Alethea & Athena Nibley

LETTERING AND RETOUCH
Lys Blakeslee

COVER DESIGN
KC Fabellon

PROOFREADER
Stephanie Cohen

EDITOR
Shanti Whitesides

PREPRESS TECHNICIAN
Rhiannon Rasmussen-Silverstein

PRODUCTION MANAGER
Lissa Pattillo

MANAGING EDITOR
Julie Davis

ASSOCIATE PUBLISHER
Adam Arnold

PUBLISHER
Jason DeAngelis

Seven Seas press and purchase enquiries can be sent to Marketing Manager Lianne Sentar at press@gomanga.com. Information regarding the distribution and purchase of digital editions is available from Digital Manager CK Russell at digital@gomanga.com.

ISBN: 978-1-64505-531-0

Printed in Canada

First Printing: May 2020

10 9 8 7 6 5 4 3 2 1

FOLLOW US ONLINE: *www.sevenseasentertainment.com*

READING DIRECTIONS

This book reads from ***right to left***, Japanese style. If this is your first time reading manga, you start reading from the top right panel on each page and take it from there. If you get lost, just follow the numbered diagram here. It may seem backwards at first, but you'll get the hang of it! Have fun!!

1
2
3
4
5
6
7
8
9

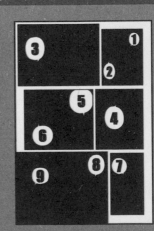